A YEAR IN THE MERDE

Coulis to Be Kind, or She Loves Jus:
Why Brits Need Help Translating Menus in London These Days
(internal report on British eating habits)

Starbucks Elbow: How Soon Will Brits Get into
the Habit of Carrying Huge Lattes Around in the Street?
(internal report on British coffee-drinking habits)

Giving Good Head:
An Analysis of the Expectations of Real-Ale Drinkers
(internal report on British beer-drinking habits)

A YEAR IN THE
MERDE

STEPHEN CLARKE

BLOOMSBURY

Published by Bloomsbury Publishing, New York and London
Distributed to the trade by Holtzbrinck Publishers

All papers used by Bloomsbury Publishing are natural, recyclable products made from wood grown in well-managed forests. The manufacturing processes conform to the environmental regulations of the country of origin.

Library of Congress Cataloging-in-Publication Data

Clarke, Stephen, 1958–
A year in the merde / by Stephen Clarke.
p. cm.
ISBN-10 1-58234-591-0 (hardcover)
ISBN-13: 978-1-58234-591-8 (hardcover)
1. British—France—Fiction. 2. Paris (France)—Fiction. 3. Tearooms—Fiction.
I. Title.

PR6103.L3748Y43 2005
823'.92—dc22
2005000978

First U.S. Edition 2005

1 3 5 7 9 10 8 6 4 2

Typeset by Hewer Text Ltd, Edinburgh
Printed in the United States of America
by Quebecor World Fairfield

CONTENTS

The author would like to thank the French government for introducing the thirty-five-hour week and giving him time to do more interesting things on a Friday afternoon than work. *Merci*.

The chief beauty of this book lies not so much in its literary style or in the extent and usefulness of the information it conveys, as in its simple truthfulness. Its pages form the record of events that really happened. All that has been done is to colour them.

—Jerome K. Jerome, preface to *Three Men in a Boat*

SEPTEMBRE

Never the Deux Shall Meet

THE YEAR DOES not begin in January. Every French person knows that. Only awkward English-speakers think it starts in January.

The year really begins on the first Monday of September.

This is when Parisians get back to their desks after their month-long holiday and begin working out where they'll go for the midterm break in November.

It's also when every French project, from a new hairdo to a nuclear power station, gets under way, which is why, at 9:00 a.m. on the first Monday of September, I was standing a hundred yards from the Champs-Élysées, watching people kissing.

My good friend Chris told me not to come to France. Great lifestyle, he said, great food, and totally un–politically correct women with great underwear.

But, he warned me, the French are hell to live with. He worked in the London office of a French bank for three years.

"They made all us Brits redundant the day after the French football team got knocked out of the World Cup. No way was that a coincidence," he told me.

His theory was that the French are like the woman scorned. Back in 1940, they tried to tell us they loved us, but we just laughed at their accents and their big-nosed General de Gaulle, and ever since we've done nothing but poison them with our disgusting food and try to wipe the French language off the face of the earth. That's why they built refugee camps yards from the Eurotunnel entrance and refuse to eat our beef years after it was declared safe. It's permanent payback time, he said. Don't go there.

Sorry, I told him, I've got to go and check out that underwear.

Normally, I suppose you would be heading for disaster if the main motivation for your job mobility was the local lingerie, but my one-year contract started very promisingly.

I found my new employer's offices—a grand-looking nineteenth-century building sculpted out of milky-gold stone—and walked straight into an orgy.

There were people kissing while waiting for the lift. People kissing in front of a drinks machine. Even the receptionist was leaning across her counter to smooch with someone—a woman, too—who'd entered the building just ahead of me.

Wow, I thought, if there's ever a serious epidemic of facial herpes, they'll have to get condoms for their heads.

Of course, I knew the French went in for cheek kissing, but not on this scale. I wondered if it wasn't company policy to get a neckload of Ecstasy before coming into work.

I edged closer to the reception desk, where the two women had stopped kissing and were now exchanging news. The company obviously didn't believe in glamorous front-office girls, because the receptionist had a masculine face that seemed much more suited to scowling than smiling. She was complaining about something I didn't understand.

I beamed my keenest new-boy smile at her. No acknowledgment. I stood in the "Yes, I'm here and I wouldn't mind being asked the purpose of my visit" zone for a full minute. Zilch. So I stepped forward and spouted out the password I'd memorized: "Bonjour, je suis Paul West. Je viens voir Monsieur Martin."

The two women gabbled on about having *déjeuner*, which I knew was lunch, and they made at least half a dozen "I'll phone you" gestures before the receptionist finally turned to me.

"Monsieur?" No apology. They might kiss each other, but I could kiss off.

I repeated my password. Or tried to.

"Bonjour, je . . ." No, my head was full of suppressed anger and linguistic spaghetti. "Paul West," I said. "Monsieur Martin." Who needs verbs? I managed another willing smile.

The receptionist—name badge Marianne; personality Hannibal Lecter—tutted in reply.

I could almost hear her thinking, Can't speak any French. Probably thinks de Gaulle had a big nose. Bastard.

"I'll call his assistant," she said, probably. She picked up the phone and punched in a number, all the while giving me a top-to-toe inspection as if she didn't think I was of the required standard to meet the boss.

Do I really look that bad? I wondered. I'd made an effort to be as chic as a Brit in Paris should be. My best gray black Paul Smith suit (my only Paul Smith suit). A shirt so white that it looked as if it'd been made from silkworms fed on bleach, and an electrically zingy Hermès tie that could have powered the whole Paris metro if I'd plugged it in. I'd even worn my black silk boxers to give my self-esteem an invisible boost. Frenchwomen aren't the only ones who can do underwear.

No way did I deserve such a withering look, especially not in comparison with most of the people I'd seen entering the building—guys looking like Dilbert, women in drab catalog skirts, lots of excessively comfortable shoes.

"Christine? J'ai un Monsieur . . . ?" Marianne the receptionist squinted over at me.

This was my cue to do something, but what?

"Votre nom?" Marianne asked, rolling her eyes upward and turning the last word into a huff of despair at my sluglike stupidity.

"Paul West."

"Pol Wess," Marianne said, "a visitor for Monsieur Martin." She hung up. "Sit over there," she said in slow, talking-to-Alzheimer-sufferer French.

The boss evidently kept the glamorous ones in his office, because Christine, the assistant who took me up to the fifth floor, was a tall brunette with poise and a dark-lipped smile that would have melted a man's trousers at twenty paces. I was standing mere inches away from her in the elevator, looking deep down into her eyes, breathing in her perfume. Slightly cinnamon. She smelled edible.

It was one of those occasions when you think, Come on, elevator, conk out now. Get jammed between two floors. I've had a pee, I can take the wait. Just give me an hour or two to work my charm with a captive audience.

Trouble is, I would have had to teach her English first. When I tried to chat her up, she just smiled stunningly and apologized in French for not understanding a bloody word. Still, here at least was one Parisienne who didn't seem to hate me.

We emerged in a corridor that was like a collision between a gothic mansion and a double-glazing truck. A long Oriental-looking carpet covered all but the narrow margins of creaky, polished floorboards. The ceiling and walls of the corridor were decorated with great swirls of antique molded plasterwork, but the original doors had been ripped off their hinges and replaced with 1970s-style tinted glass. As if to cover up the clash of styles, the corridor was lined with enough green-leaved plants to host a jungle war.

Christine knocked on a glass door and a male voice called "*Entrez!*"

I went in and there he was, set against a background of the Eiffel Tower poking its finger into the cloudy sky. My new boss stood up and walked around his desk to greet me.

"Monsieur Martin," I said, holding out a hand for him to shake. "Pleased to see you again."

"You must call me Jean-Marie," he replied in his slightly accented but excellent English. He took my hand and used it to pull me so close that I thought we were about to do the cheek-rubbing thing. But no, he only wanted to pat my shoulder. "Welcome to France," he said.

Bloody hell, I thought. Now two of them like me.

Jean-Marie looked pretty cool for a company chairman. He was fifty or so, but his dark eyes shone with youth, his hair was receding but slicked back and cut short so that it didn't matter, and his royal blue shirt and golden tie were effortlessly chic. He had an open, friendly face.

He asked for some coffee and I noticed that he called Christine *tu*, whereas she called him *vous*. I'd never managed to work that one out.

"Sit down, Paul," Jean-Marie said, switching back to English. "Is everything okay? Your voyage, the hotel?"

"Oh, yes, fine, thanks . . ." A bit basic, but it had cable.

"Good, good." When he looked at you, you felt as if making you happy was the only thing that mattered on the entire planet.

Sod global warming, does Paul like his hotel room? That's the important issue of the day.

"Everyone seems to be very happy here, kissing each other," I said.

"Ah, yes." He looked out into the corridor, apparently checking for passersby to French-kiss. "It is the rentrée, you know, the reentry. Like we are returning home from space. To us Parisians anything more than ten kilometers from the Galeries Lafayette is a different planet. We have not seen our colleagues for a month, and we are happy to meet them again." He snorted as if at a private joke. "Well, not always very happy, but we cannot refuse to kiss them."

"Even the men?"

Jean-Marie laughed. "You think French men are effeminate?"

"No, no, of course not." I thought I'd hit a nerve.

"Good."

I got the feeling that if Christine had been in the room, he'd have whipped down his trousers and proved his manhood on her.

He clapped as if to clear the air of testosterone. "Your office will be next to mine. We have the same view. What a view, eh?" He held out an arm toward the window to introduce his guest star. It was quite a star, too. "If you work in Paris, you don't always get a view of the Eiffel Tower," he said proudly.

"Great," I said.

"Yes, great. We want you to be happy with us," Jean-Marie said. At the time, he probably meant it.

When I first met him in London, he made his company, VianDiffusion, sound like a family, with him as the favorite uncle rather than the godfather or big brother. He'd taken over the meat-processing business about ten years earlier from his dad, the founder, who'd started out as a humble butcher. They now had four "factories" (basically, giant food mixers—mooing animals in one end, mincemeat out the other) plus their head office. Turnover was massive thanks to the limitless French appetite for hamburgers, or *steaks hâchés*, as they patriotically call them. It seemed to me when Jean-Marie recruited me that he was looking to lift the company out of the offal. My new "English" project was designed to make people forget his bloody beginnings. Perhaps that was why he greeted me so warmly.

Now to see if the rest of my colleagues would love me as much as he did.

"One thing, Jean-Marie," I said as he ushered—almost carried—me along the corridor toward the meeting room. "Do I call everyone *tu* or *vous*?" Not that I was capable of calling them either.

"Ah, it is quite simple. You, in your position, call everyone with whom you work *tu*. Except maybe anyone who looks old. And except if you have not been presented to them yet. Most people here will call you *tu* also. Some will call you *vous* if they are very less senior or if they think they don't know you. Okay?"

"Er, yes." Clear as onion soup.

"But in your team everyone will speak English."

"English? Shouldn't I try to integrate?"

Jean-Marie didn't answer. He gave a final tug on my elbow and we were inside the meeting room. It took up the full depth of the building, with windows at both ends. Eiffel Tower in one, courtyard and a modern glass office building in the other.

There were four other people in the room. A man and woman stood huddled near the courtyard window, and another man and woman sat silently at a long oval table.

"Everyone, this is Paul," Jean-Marie announced in English.

My new work chums turned to meet me. The two men were a

very tall, thickset blond, about forty, and a younger, skinny guy who was bald. The two women were a natural honey blonde, about thirty, with a tightly pulled-back ponytail and a jutting chin that just stopped her being beautiful, and a round-faced, kind-looking woman, thirty-five-ish, with large brown eyes and a dowdy pink blouse.

I shook all of their hands and instantly forgot their names.

We sat at the table, me and Jean-Marie on one side, my four new colleagues on the other.

"Okay, everyone. This is a very exciting moment," Jean-Marie declared. "We are, as the English say, branching away. Flying into new horizons. We know we can succeed in the restaurant business. The fast-food industry in France could not exist without our minced beef. Now we are going to take some more of the profit with our new English tea cafés. And we have someone here who knows this business." He gestured proudly toward me. "As you know, Paul was chief of marketing of the chain of French cafés in England, Voulez-Vous Café Avec Moi. How many cafés have you created, Paul?"

"There were thirty-five when I left the company. But that was two weeks ago, so who knows how many there are now."

I was joking, but everyone in the room gaped at me, believing totally in this Anglo-American dynamism.

"Yes," Jean-Marie said, bathing vicariously in my reputation. "I saw their success and I wanted their head of marketing, so I went to London and decapitated him. Decapitated?"

"Headhunted," I said.

"Yes, thank you. I am sure that Paul will bring to our new chain of English cafés in France the same success as he has known with the similar concept in England of French cafés in, er, England. Maybe you can continue to present yourself, Paul?" he said, apparently exhausted by his last sentence.

"Sure." I gazed along the line opposite with my best imitation of co-workerly love. "My name's Paul West," I told them. I saw them all practice saying my name. "I was in at the creation of Voulez-Vous Café Avec Moi. We launched in July last year—July the fourteenth, of course, Bastille Day—with five cafés in London and the southeast, and then launched the others in the major British cities and shopping malls in three waves of ten. I've brought a report with me so that you can read the full story. Before that I worked for a small brewery—beer company," I added, seeing their frowns, "and that's about it."

"You rilly yong," said the skinny bloke. Not accusingly, but annoyingly.

"Not really, I'm twenty-seven. If I was a rock star, I'd be dead."

The bloke made apologetic gestures. "No, no. Ah'm not criti-sahzing. Ah'm just . . . admirative." He had a weird accent. Not quite French. I couldn't place it.

"Ah, we are all admiring Paul, that's for sure." Jean-Marie again managed to make me feel like I was receiving a gay come-on. "Why don't everyone present himself?" he said. "Bernard, start please."

Bernard was the tall, stocky one, with a flat-top haircut and a neat blond mustache. He looked like a Swedish policeman who'd retired early because of bad feet. He was wearing a sickly blue shirt and a tie that just failed to be red enough. He could have had "dull" tattooed across his forehead, but that would have made him too exciting.

Bernard smiled nervously and began.

"Yam bare narr, yam responsa bull ov communika syon, er . . ."

Shit, I thought, didn't Jean-Marie say the meeting was going to be in English? How come some people were allowed to speak Hungarian?

Bernard of Budapest carried on in the same incomprehensible vein for a couple of minutes and then started to enunciate something that, to judge by the look of acute constipation on his face, was of great importance. "Alok for wah toowa king wizioo."

Hang on, I thought. I don't speak any central European languages, but I got that. He's looking forward to working with me. Holy Babel fish. It's English, Jim, but not as we know it.

"Thank you, Bernard," Jean-Marie said, smiling encouragingly. Had he chosen the crappest one to highlight his own excellent English? I hoped so. "Next, Marc."

Marc was the bald, skinny one. He was wearing a dark gray shirt, unbuttoned at the collar and unironed. Turned out he'd spent a few years in the southern United States, hence the weird accent, which made him sound like Scarlett O'Hara after too much Pernod.

"Ah'm ed of hah tee," he said.

"Ed of hah tee," I repeated approvingly, wondering what the hell this was. Something to do with tea, anyway. Relevant.

"Yah. Compoodah sis-temm," Marc confirmed.

"Oh, IT," I said. He glowered at me. "Your English is excellent," I added quickly. "How long did you spend in the U.S.A.?"

"Ah've done a yee-uh uv post-grad at Jo-ja State, then Ah've worked fahv yee-uhs inna inshance firm in Atlanna. In da hah tee departmon, a coss."

"A coss," I agreed.

"Okay, Marc. Stéphanie?" Jean-Marie the MC again.

Stéphanie was the blond woman with the jaw. Her accent was strong and French, her grammar terrifying, but my ear was getting tuned. Stéphanie was the "responsa bull ov poorshassing" (purchasing) for the main meat-processing part of the company and was now "vairy eppy" to be "ap-wanted responsa bull ov poorsha sing" for the proposed chain of "Eengleesh tea saloons."

It was obviously as exhausting for her to speak as she was to listen to, and at the end of her short speech she gave Jean-Marie a look that said "I've done my fifty press-ups and I hope you think it was worth it, you sadistic bastard."

"Thank you, Stéphanie. Nicole."

The other woman, the dark, short-haired one, had a soft voice, but she spoke very clearly. She was the financial controller on this project, as she was for the whole company.

"You've been to England, haven't you, Nicole," I said. "Quite often as well, to judge by your accent." Rule one of office life—always flatter your financial controller.

"Yes, my usband was Hinglish," she said, smiling wistfully. Oh dear, dead or divorced? I wondered. Not the time to ask.

"Do not be fooled by Nicole," Jean-Marie said. "She looks like she is very kind, but she has a heart of iron. She is the reason why our finances are so good. She is our real boss."

Nicole blushed. There was some unrequited stuff going on here, I decided. Jean-Marie praising her professional skills, Nicole wanting to rip open her bodice and have him praise her boobs. Or was I being stereotypical?

"Well, your English is so much better than my French," I told them, taking special care to look Stéphanie and Bernard, my fellow linguistic invalids, in the eye. "I've bought myself a teach-yourself French CD-ROM and I promise I'll start teaching myself *toot sweet*."

They were kind enough to laugh.

As we were all chums together now, I decided to throw in my little idea. Nothing controversial.

"I thought we could decide on a working name for the project," I suggested. "Just something temporary, you know, to give us an identity as a team. Something like Tea Time."

"Oh." It was Bernard, jerking himself upright. "No, we av nem. Ma Tea Eez Reesh."

I frowned, the others laughed. I turned to Jean-Marie for help. He was looking elsewhere.

"My Tea Is Rich? As a brand name for the tearooms? It's not really a name," I ventured. "It doesn't really *mean* anything."

"Uh . . ." Bernard was crap at English but clearly very good at monosyllables. "Ma Tea Eez Reesh eez funny nem. Eaties Ingleesh oomoor."

"English humor? But we don't say that."

"Oh." Bernard turned to Jean-Marie for support.

"Of course, it should be my *tailor*," Jean-Marie explained.

"Your tailor?" I felt as if I was in the middle of a surrealist film. In a minute Salvador Dalí was going to fly in through the window with a baguette sticking out of his trousers.

"My tailor is rich," Jean-Marie said.

"Is he?" Here comes Salvador, I thought, but all I could see out the window was the Eiffel Tower, as usual.

"'My tailor is rich' is a typical English expression."

"It's not."

"But French people think it is. It was in the old language books."

"Okay, okay, I think I'm with you," I said. The others were peering at me as if I was about to get the joke at last and laugh. "It's like my postilion has been struck by lightning."

"Uh . . . ?" Now it was the French team's turn to look lost.

"It's from *our* old language books," I said. "I get you now." I put on a Eureka smile. Everyone nodded. Misunderstanding cleared up. Problem solved. "But it's still an awful name." I mean, I had to tell them for their own good. For the good of the project.

"Oh!"

"You absolutely want Tea Time?" Jean-Marie was not looking keen. "This is a bit flat."

"No, not absolutely. Just as a provisional name. I suggest we get a market survey done before deciding on the definitive brand, but meanwhile let's choose a simple working title. If you don't like Tea Time, how about Tea for Two?"

"Oh no." This was Stéphanie. "Dis is flat also. We want fonny nem. Like Bare-narr say, Ingleesh oomoor."

"And, er, if we coll eet Tease Café?" Marc said.

"Tease Café?" I was lost again.

"Yuh. Tea, apostrof, s, café," Marc explained. Stéphanie nodded. Good idea.

"Tea's Café? But that's not English, either."

"Yes," Stéphanie retorted. "You av many nems with apostrof. Arry's Bar. Liberty's Statue."

"Brooklyn's Bridge," Marc said.

"Trafalgar's Square," Bernard added.

"No . . ."

"Roll's Royce," Bernard said, on a roll.

"No!" Where did they get this crap?

"In France this is considered very English." Jean-Marie was playing interpreter again. "There is an American café on the Champs-Élysées called Sandwich's Café."

"Yes." Stéphanie confirmed this with a prod of her finger onto the table.

"Okay, but it's not English," I had to insist. "It's like when you call a campsite *un camping* or a car park *un parking*. You may think it's English, but it's not."

"Oh." Stéphanie appealed to Jean-Marie, the referee. An attack on the French language? Yellow card, surely?

"Each country adapts the culture of the other country," Jean-Marie said. "When I was in England, all the restaurants had strawberry crème brûlée. But crème brûlée is crème brûlée. Why not have a strawberry baguette? Or a strawberry Camembert?"

The French team nodded their approval of Jean-Marie's firm but fair discipline.

"Yes, it is like you Ingleesh you put oronge joo-eece in shompagne," Stéphanie said. "Merde alors."

The others winced in sympathy at this desecration of their national treasure.

"But you put blackcurrant liqueur in champagne to make kir royal." I'd read this in my guidebook, and now wished I hadn't. French eyebrows knitted at my English know-it-all repartee.

Jean-Marie tried to pour some virgin olive oil on things. "We will make a market survey. We will test these names and others. We will make a list of our suggestions."

"Right." I nodded like a plastic Alsatian in the back of a car, eager to accept this brilliant idea coming from the French diplomat.

"Bernard can maybe organize it," Jean-Marie suggested.

Bernard smiled. He was the man for the job. From the dull twinkle in his eye, I could tell he was confident of persuading the pollsters to go with his idea.

"Okay, very constructive," Jean-Marie said. "This is a real Anglo-style meeting. Taking decisions."

Decisions? We can't agree, so we decide to pay a consultant who's going to be bribed into agreeing with the guy with the crappest ideas. Didn't seem very constructive to me. But then it was my first ever French meeting. I had a lot to learn.

*　　*　　*

Outside of the office, my entrée into Paris society was just as depressing.

Jean-Marie was paying for me to stay in a hotel about a kilometer west of the Arc de Triomphe, not actually in Paris at all. It was just off an eight-lane highway called, romantically, Big Army Avenue, which charged out from Paris proper toward the skyscrapers of La Défense business district.

The hotel was a nondescript modern building made of artificial stone the color of snow that's been peed in by a dog. My room was decorated in the same color. It was supposed to be a double, but the only way for two people to stand on the floor at the same time would have been to have intercourse. Which was perhaps the idea, though there wasn't much of that kind of action going on while I was in it.

Anyway, the hotel was in a posh suburb called Neuilly, pronounced Ner-yee, and not Newly as I called it the whole time I lived there. It was dull but had two or three shopping streets full of the kinds of small stores that you don't get in the United Kingdom anymore. Fishmongers, cheese shops, chocolate shops, raw-meat butchers, cooked-meat butchers, horsemeat butchers, there was even a shop selling only roast chickens.

So when the batteries in my mini hi-fi system went into their umpteenth coma, I thought I'd go to my friendly local electrician's shop to buy a mains adapter. I wandered out one Saturday and eventually found a little painted shopfront full of radios and flashlights and other small electronic gizmos.

Inside, there was a long, fingerprint-marked glass counter and a chaotic shelving system stacked with everything from tiny watch batteries to Hoovers and food mixers. Among all the boxes stood a middle-aged guy with a gray nylon jacket and an equally gray face. The Addams Family's Parisian cousin.

"Bonjour." I smiled as an advance apology for the bad French that was to come. He didn't smile back. He just stared at me from under his barbed-wire eyebrows, weighing me up and coming to unpleasant conclusions.

I should perhaps add that I wasn't wearing my Paul Smith suit at this point. I was in an orange floral shirt that I found in the Portobello Road. It had a kind of Hawaiian-paint-factory-explosion motif that I thought made me look laid-back and friendly, especially when accompanied by long surfer shorts and fire extinguisher–red trainers. I had noticed that not many other people in Neuilly were dressed like this, but it was a pleasantly warm autumn day, and I never dreamed that it could have any influence on my chances of buying electrical equipment.

"Je . . . ," I began, and then suddenly realized that I didn't know the French for hi-fi system, mains lead, plug, adapter, or, to be totally honest, electricity. I mean, in the United Kingdom, if you want to buy anything electrical, you just go to a superstore and help yourself. At the very worst, the most you have to do is point.

"J'ai un hi-fi," I ventured, giving the last word a French lilt— "ha-fa." The electrician didn't look perplexed, which was encouraging. Though he didn't look interested, either. I ventured further into the linguistic wilderness. "J'ai un ha-fa anglais." Big apologetic smile. Sorry, I'm doing my best. Please bear with me. "J'ai un ha-fa anglais, mais ici . . ." I tried to look suitably helpless, which wasn't difficult. The shop assistant still showed no signs of assisting. Bugger it, I decided, and activated the linguistic ejector seat. "I need an adapter to plug my British hi-fi into the electricity here," I explained in English, with perfect diction and copious amounts of mime.

I always thought the French were into mime, but this bloke wasn't a Marcel Marceau fan.

"Parle français," he said with a little "huh" at the end that seemed to be Neuilly slang for "you ignorant English twit."

"If I could I would, you obnoxious tit," I told him, feeling marginally better because of the insult he'd never understand.

But in reply he just gave a shrug that seemed to say, "Whatever your problem is, it's your problem, not mine, which is sad but rather amusing, because from the look of you, you're the type of idiot that makes a habit of getting into stupid, no-win situations like this. And by the way, that shirt is totally gross." All this in one shrug.

There was no way I was going to win a shrugging contest, or get my hands on an adapter, so I walked out.

I'd gone no more than a yard when my whole body froze in a paralyzed tai chi pose, both knees bent and one foot lifted to knee height.

There was a ginger brown pat of dog turd troweled onto the toe of my beautiful red trainer.

"Shit!"

Was it my imagination, or did I hear the electrician call out: "No, you mean *merde*, you ignorant foreigner."

Paris is, I was beginning to realize, a bit like an ocean. An ocean is a great place to live if you're a shark. There's loads of fresh seafood, and if anyone gives you shit, you just bite them in half. You might not be loved by everyone, but you'll be left in peace to enjoy yourself.

If you're human, though, you spend your time floating on the surface, buffeted by the waves, preyed on by the sharks.

So the thing to do is evolve into a shark as quickly as you can.

And the first item on your evolutionary agenda is to learn to speak fluent shark.

I had my DIY French CD, but I thought Jean-Marie's assistant, Christine, might like to give me a few private lessons. After all, you might as well get yourself a shark with cute fins.

Christine—what a bad idea that was.

I'm not the sort of guy who thinks that love is just a tennis score. But I haven't made a great success of relationships. That was one of my reasons for jumping at the offer to leave the United Kingdom. I was with a woman in London, Ruth, but it was a mutually self-destructive thing. We'd phone, arrange to meet, then wait and see which one of us would get in first with a good reason to cancel. Finally we'd meet up for a bitchy row and/or earth-trembling sex, then stay incommunicado for two weeks, then phone, etc., etc. We both agreed that my wanting to emigrate was a sign that maybe things between us weren't ideal.

It was almost two weeks since I'd done any earth trembling when I first got in that lift with Christine. But I didn't need the unused hormones washing about in my bloodstream to see that she was excruciatingly beautiful. Her hair was long, barely styled at all, the way lots of French girls wear their hair, and gave her the chance to make coyly seductive moves like pushing a loose lock behind an ear or sweeping it all back off her forehead. She was pretty skinny—again, the way lots of French girls are—but her slenderness didn't stop her having all the right curves and protuberances. And she had incredible eyes—almost golden colored—that seemed to be saying she thought I wasn't such a Quasimodo, either. She fluttered her enormous (real) eyelashes at me whenever I walked into her office, which I found myself doing more than was strictly necessary for the day-to-day business of starting up a couple of tearooms.

My abysmal French made her laugh. And making her laugh,

even if it meant humiliating myself, made me feel decidedly pleasant.

"Tu es professeur pour moi," I garbled one day in my first week.

She laughed. I pretended to be offended.

"Non. Je veux parler français," I told her.

She laughed again and replied something that I didn't understand.

"Tu apprendre anglais avec moi?" I suggested. "Nous, er . . ." and I did my best to mime an exchange of conversation lessons with a gesture that turned out a bit more gynecological than I'd intended.

Still, my cervical mime didn't put her off. We went for an after-work drink that evening at a viciously expensive underground cocktail bar just off the Champs-Élysées. The kind of place where everyone sits up very straight in their Philippe Starck armchairs so that they can be seen.

I leaned low toward Christine, and we talked about life in London and Paris in a sort of fun pidgin Franglais. And like a pigeon, I spent a lot of time cooing.

We were just getting cozy, at fingertip-brushing stage, when she suddenly did a Cinderella.

"Mon train," she said.

"Non, non, le métro est très brrmm brrmm," I objected, meaning that it would have her home long before she turned into a pumpkin.

She shook her head and showed me a little foldout map of the suburban trains. She lived miles out of town.

"Viens chez moi," I offered sportingly—one of the best phrases I'd found in my CD-ROM's vocab lists. Vee-en shay mwa. Sounded like a kiss.

She tutted, brushed her dark lips against my mouth, stroked my chin with a long finger, and left me nailed to the table by a hard-on that it would have taken a UN resolution to disarm.

I didn't get it. Most of the English women I'd taken out for after-work drinks in London would either have made it brutally clear I was not Mr. Sexy or had their calves clamped round my ears by now. But then maybe I'd been dating the ear-clamping type of gal.

First thing next morning, I brought her coffee in her office.

"Ce soir, tu veux . . . ?" I left her to fill in the gap with either a conversation class or something more physical.

"Boire un verre?" she decided. She mimed a drink. Okay for starters, at least.

"On se retrouve au bar à dix-neuf heures?" she articulated.

Meet up at the bar. Keeping it secret. Good, I thought. The previous day we'd left the office together, causing raised eyebrows in the corridor.

When we met up at 7:00 that evening, Christine didn't seem much into English conversation. She asked me in French if I was married and had kids back in London.

"Mais non!" I assured her.

"Pourquoi pas?"

"Pfff," I explained. My French didn't stretch to a more detailed description of my disastrous relationship with Ruth.

She did her eye-fluttering thing, and Cinderella'd off at 8:00 on the dot.

I really couldn't figure out French women. Were they fans of mental foreplay? Only into intellectual sex?

Or did they want to be jumped on? (I didn't think so—I've never met any woman of any nationality who appreciated the rugby-tackle approach to seduction.)

Or maybe this was a French woman's way of symbolizing the relationship between France and the Brits—she dangles her sexy image in front of me but keeps her distance to avoid catching mad cow disease.

I looked for an explanation in a report I'd commissioned on what the French really thought of us.

There was nothing specific in there about why Christine wouldn't sleep with me, but it still made interesting reading. Apart from mad cow disease and hooligans, the most common things that the French associated with the word *anglais* were the queen, Shakespeare, David Beckham, Mr. Bean, the Rolling Stones (all of which were positive concepts, amazingly), and, yes, tea, which was seen as a stylish, civilized drink. The French had obviously never had milky horse piss slopped into a polystyrene beaker by a sixteen-year-old work-experience trainee in an English beach café (I know all about milky horse piss—I *was* that work-experience trainee). In French cafés, the price of a cup of tea was on average double that of an espresso.

Holy tea cozies, I thought, why the hell hasn't this English tearoom thing been done before? And why hadn't I got a better team working on it?

The rest of the team was supposed to be reading this and other reports as well, but whenever I asked for an opinion, all I got was a "vairy an-tress-ting." They weren't reading the bloody things at all. As far as I could tell, they weren't contributing anything to the project. Autumn had hardly started and they were already dead wood.

Looked like I'd have to talk to Jean-Marie about getting Stéphanie, Bernard, and Marc transferred over to a project they actually gave a damn about. Away from my tearooms, anyway.

They were going to hate me, of course, but I had no choice.

I told Jean-Marie that there was a delicate subject I wanted to discuss, and he insisted we go out to lunch together that very *midi*. Very important day to go out to lunch, he said. He didn't elaborate.

We left the building at 12:30 with "Bon appétit" ringing in our ears. The people who saw us called it out the way you would say "Happy Christmas." Every lunchtime, it seemed, was a celebration. And why not.

The street was filling up with smart office people. This close to the Champs-Élysées, there was a lot of Chanel and Dior about. Sunglasses, bags, skirts. Among the middle-aged, anyway. There were also gaggles of young secretaries in designer jeans, their hair worn long and natural like Christine's, their tight tops attracting frank stares from the men in suits. Including Jean-Marie, whose eyes seemed to flicker constantly from bum to boob level as he walked.

Two posh women walked past in designer tweed. Paris clearly had its horsey set, though God knew where they kept their horses in this dense urban maze of streets—in an underground garage, maybe.

"What's so important about going out to lunch today?" I asked.

"You will see," he teased, grinning at a passing navel.

At the street corner there was a typical Parisian brasserie—six round marble-topped tables on the pavement, cane chairs, glass-fronted veranda jutting out from the building.

Jean-Marie grabbed a chair at the last free outdoor table, ignoring the huffy complaint of the man who thought he was about to sit there.

"We are lucky," Jean-Marie said. "In Paris, if it is sunny, all the outside tables are full. If it is a good café, of course."

Two plastic-covered menus arrived on the table. The waiter was a gray-haired, harassed-looking man in the typical waiter's uniform—white shirt, black trousers, and a black waistcoat with several bulging pockets full of small change. He paused just long enough to mumble something that I didn't get about his *plat du jour*. He poked his finger toward a blue Post-it note stuck on the menu and charged off toward another table. Whatever the *plat du jour* was, I couldn't read the scrawled handwriting. Unless it really did include *crétin dauphin* (cretinous dolphin?), which I doubted.

"What is this thing we must discuss?" Jean-Marie asked. He had glanced at the menu and put it aside.

"Er . . . ," I tried to read the menu and collect my thoughts.

Suddenly the waiter was there again, staring down at us. Jean-Marie smiled over at me, inviting me to order first.

"Er . . . ," I repeated.

The waiter huffed and was gone. He hated me already. Had my English "er" given me away?

"The reports are very . . ." Jean-Marie stopped and frowned. "How you say, *prometteur*? Prom . . . ?"

"Er . . ." We'd now been at the table for about thirty seconds.

"Promiseful?"

"Promising."

"The Marks and Spencer report was very promising. They were stupid to shut their stores in France. French people like English products."

"Yes. Er, what are you having?" I was lost.

"Chèvre chaud," he said.

"Chèvre?"

"It means the female . . . what is it, like a mutton but with—on its head—corns?"

"Corns on its head?"

"Horns?"

"Ah, goat."

"Yes, goat."

Hot goat?

The waiter was there again, hovering.

"Chèvre chaud," I said. If I got the horns, I'd give them to Jean-Marie.

"Deux," confirmed Jean-Marie.

"Et comme boisson?" the waiter asked. (Fish? You have to have fish with your goat?) This was why I usually lunched at the canteen. You just put what you wanted on your tray.

"Une Leffe," Jean-Marie said. "A sort of beer," he explained.

Of course, fish is *poisson*, *boisson* is drink.

"Okay. Deux," I said, getting into the swing of things.

The waiter grabbed the menus and left without taking any notes.

If the Parisians really did take two-hour lunch breaks, I thought, they still had one hour fifty-nine minutes free after ordering. Who said the Americans invented fast food?

"What is this thing we must discuss?" Jean-Marie asked.

"It's about your team," I began. In at the deep end. "My team . . ." I'd thought a lot about how to rephrase "I don't want them" and still hadn't come up with an answer.

"I don't need them," I said, which didn't sound at all as bad as not *wanting* them. Did it?

Jean-Marie gave a nervous laugh and reeled back in his chair. The waiter arrived with two sets of cutlery wrapped up in yellow paper napkins. The knives were serrated and pointed.

I hoped Jean-Marie wasn't going to get his out and use it on my jugular.

"You don't *need* them?"

"Not yet. I need someone to research locations. Someone to do a consumer survey based on the reports we're all *supposed* to be reading—what exactly do people expect from an English tearoom? What would they eat when? Someone to suggest names and logos. It's not something that Bernard, Stéphanie, and the others can do."

Jean-Marie was still reeling. He wasn't going for his blade, though. Not yet. He sighed.

"French companies don't function like English or American companies," he said.

The waiter came back with two large-stemmed glasses of frothy beer.

"Vous avez des frites?" Jean-Marie asked the waiter, who might or might not have heard. "You are right," he told me. "Except for Nicole, the finance director, who must survey all projects, and Marc, who will be very operative when we start to implement our stock systems and et cetera, I took Bernard and Stéphanie because I do not know what to do with them. They have work, but not enough. This is not to insult your project. On the contrary. I am depending more on you. I hope you can organize them, motivate them. Or if necessary, ignore them. They will occupy themselves."

"Occupy themselves? Are their salaries part of my budget?"

Jean-Marie laughed. "You are funny. A worker is going a bit slow, you fire him. Here it is not the same. They call the inspecteur du travail, the work inspector, they complain, and you pay damages or the union makes a strike and it is the merde générale. And Bernard and Stéphanie are working for us since at least ten years. You know how much that costs for compensation if I fire them? Even if there is no strike by the other workers? And if I do have a strike, beef does not smell so good when the workers turn off the refrigerators."

"I'm not suggesting you fire them. Just . . ." How should I express "make them disappear"?

The waiter returned with two plates piled high with glistening lettuce, topped with grilled pats of white cheese on small slices of toast. No horns. If he'd got the order wrong, I wasn't going to complain.

He put down the plates, wished us *bon appétit*, and turned away. Jean-Marie asked for his *frites*.

"Je n'ai que deux mains, monsieur," the waiter said. He only had two hands. If I understood correctly, the waiter had just told Jean-Marie, very politely, to bugger off.

"What about this waiter?" I asked when the man had scooted off again. "Wouldn't you fire him? He's totally obnoxious."

"Obnoxious?"

"Yes, you know, rude. A git."

"Ah, a git, yes, I know this word. Yoo stoopid French git." Jean-Marie smiled at some fond memory of being insulted by an Englishman. "Oh, the waiters are always hurried at lunchtime. They know if we are not happy, we won't leave a tip."

I'm not going to hire gits for my tearooms, I thought. Though I had to admit this guy was fast. A hypergit.

"And today, he is more hurried than usually," Jean-Marie said, smiling mysteriously. He started to unwrap his cutlery.

He really seemed to take the gittishness for granted, as he did the fact that we were about to eat in what felt like the middle of the road. There was barely a yard between us and the parked cars by the curb. Any passerby could have spat on our plates without turning his or her head. And if Jean-Marie made a sudden movement with his knife hand, he was going to perform a cesarean on an innocent pedestrian.

"Let us discuss the team later," Jean-Marie said. "Say, next month. Bon appétit."

"Bon appétit," I replied, even though he'd just ruined mine.

I took a tentative bite of my food and my appetite returned instantaneously. Now I understood—*chèvre* was goat's cheese, not dead goat. Very good, too. Warm and creamy on the brittle toast. And the lettuce was sprinkled with crunchy walnuts and quite simply drenched in vinaigrette.

A kind of warmth seeped into me with the salad dressing. Here I was, eating outside a street café in the autumn sun, oblivious to the passing cars and the people tutting because they couldn't get a table. The tall, imposing buildings, with carved gods, animals, and classical plinths holding up their stone balconies, didn't seem to look down on me anymore. The shop windows full of wildly expensive clothes, jereboams of champagne, or bank-breaking tubs of truffle pâté no longer seemed part of an alien universe. I felt, for a few wonderful seconds, what it was like to *belong* in Paris.

"Everything else at work is okay, I hope?" Jean-Marie asked. I could see that he really hoped it, too.

"Yes, fine. Well, there is a slight problem with my business card." I'd received a box of them that morning.

"Yes?"

I decided not to mention the fact that it introduced me as "Paul Vest." I stuck to the bigger picture: "Well, as we couldn't decide on a provisional name, I was given some with the main company logo on them, right? VianDiffusion."

"Yes?"

"Well, it might be okay in France, but a big red 'VD' suggests something not very appetizing to an Englishman. And as some of our suppliers are bound to be English . . ."

Jean-Marie looked anxious. "What does VD mean?"

I explained.

Jean-Marie's shocked laugh was choked off by a piece of toast lodging in his throat. He took a sip of beer and wiped a tear from his eye with the paper napkin. "When I went to visit your company in London, no one mentioned the problem of the name."

No, I thought, but we all had a giggle about it.

"It is lucky you tell me now," Jean-Marie said. "We have started to sell meat to other countries. I was going to change the logo to VD Exporters."

"Very lucky," I agreed. "So don't you think we need something genuinely English on the business cards? Like Tea Time or Tea for Two?"

"Hmm, or My Tea Is Rich?"

Now I was the one choking on my toast.

The waiter came back and tucked a bill under our little condiment set. He said something that I didn't understand and went away.

Jean-Marie grinned and wiped his mouth on his napkin. "This is it," he said.

"This is what?"

He explained that the waiter wanted to cash up now because, like all the other unionized waiters in Paris—that is, most of the blokes in black waistcoats, and they are, strangely enough, almost all male—he was going on strike as of now, "thirteen hours." The middle of lunchtime, just to be awkward. They were striking because, although French bills almost always included a 15 percent service charge, waiters also needed tips to make a decent wage, and since the arrival of the euro, tips had gone down. Before the euro, a standard lunchtime tip was a 10-franc piece, but many people were now leaving a 1-euro piece, which was worth only 6.5 francs. The fact that almost all café prices had been rounded up during the conversion into euros didn't seem to compensate.

The waiter came back, looking for his money.

"But we haven't finished," Jean-Marie complained, suddenly looking aggrieved. "We want a dessert and a coffee."

The waiter repeated something about being on strike, *en grève*.

Jean-Marie did the hugest shrug I'd ever seen, even outdoing the man in the electrical shop. His shoulders, arms, his whole rib cage, took off vertically in a gesture of infinite indifference.

"This is not our problem," Jean-Marie said, the Parisian mantra, and seemed to inquire why the waiter was on strike for serving but not when it came to collecting his cash.

The waiter wasn't into intellectual debate. He scowled as he weighed Jean-Marie up.

"Okay, what dessert do you want?" He listed them at Concorde speed. The only ones I recognized were *crème brûlée* and *mousse au chocolat*. I quickly chose the latter.

Jean-Marie opted for some kind of tart. The waiter eyed us malevolently and turned away.

"Et deux cafés," Jean-Marie called out to his back.

We got what we'd ordered, too, approximately twenty seconds later. And the waiter got his money and a tip. A 1-euro piece, of course. People at other table tried to get the same deal as Jean-Marie, but the waiter shouted them down or ignored them.

I saw that I was witnessing an important lesson in Parisian life: I mustn't try to make people *like* me. That's much too English. You've got to show them that you don't give a shit what they think. Only then will you get what you want. I'd been doing it all wrong, trying to win people over. If you smile too much, they think you're retarded.

So if I couldn't get rid of my team, I had to get tough.

The only difficulty with being tough on everyone was that they were all so damned polite, almost ritually so. Marc and Bernard always shook my hand the first time they saw me in the day. They all said "Bonjour" every morning and asked if "ça va," and when we parted, they wished me "Bonne journée"—Have a nice day—or if it was the afternoon, "Bonne après-midi," or if it was later on, "Bonne fin d'après-midi"—Have a nice rest of the afternoon. If we met for the first time after about 5:00 p.m., they said "Bonsoir" instead of "Bonjour." And if one or other of us was on our way home, we separated with "Bonne soirée"—Have a good evening. This was without all the "Bon weekend" stuff on Fridays, and Monday's "Bonne semaine"—Have a good week. It was Oriental in its complexity.

Once we'd greeted one another, there was hardly any time left in the day to broach the subject of why reports weren't being read and decisions not being made.

So I took an executive decision designed to show them that the laissez-faire days were over.

One morning I went down to see my human resources rep. This was apparently where I could sort out getting some new business cards with my name spelled as my father's forefathers had decided and with a "Tea Time" brand instead of the company's sexually transmitted logo.

Christine wasn't allowed to order cards, she told me. It was centralized at human resources.

I found the HR office and knocked on the door, its smoked glass made opaque by a blind that stretched down to knee level.

"Entrez," moaned a female voice.

Inside, I discovered Marianne, the bristly-haired receptionist, sitting behind a desk that was clear except for a computer and a small pot of what looked like deadly nightshade but was probably some kind of violet.

"Oh, vous êtes human resources aussi?" I said.

"Non, je suis receptionniste aussi." Marianne launched into a slow rant, something about how she was receptionist from nine till eleven in the morning and for part of the afternoon and, I think, how someone qualified in human resources shouldn't be forced to do reception work. After the first volley of grievances, my mind gave up bothering to translate. She complained that something or other was scandalous and intolerable, but it all turned into a general singsong whine, a sort of symphony in B moaner.

Why don't you just get a job with a company that needs a full-time whingeing cow? I wanted to ask, but I suspected that this wouldn't speed up the process of getting new cards.

I wrote down my name and "Tea Time" for her in crystal-clear capitals.

"You won't have them before the end of next week," Marianne said.

"Next *week*?" I groaned.

"The *end* of next week," she stressed.

"Okay, I come Friday."

"Oh, wait till the following Monday, just to be sure," Marianne said, almost gleeful about this inefficiency.

Partial success, though. In ten days, I'd have the cardboard proof that I was determined to win the logo war. We Brits were not to be trifled with.

*   *   *

Next on the list to experience my new "respect me" regime was Christine. The following morning, I was in early, as Christine always was. I marched into her office, put a coffee on her desk and a slobbery kiss on her lips. Not a rugby-tackle approach, more a little spot of compulsory mouth tango.

It was like waking Frankenstein's monster. Her tongue began probing my palate like a dentist's finger. This was a genuine French French kiss. Christine sighed hotly.

"Viens," she said, tugging me across the corridor and into the ladies' washroom.

She locked the door and we were suddenly rubbing our clothed bodies together and doing the full tonsil exploration thing.

I just had time to think, Damn, why don't you carry condoms in your jacket pocket, before she broke off the kiss and grabbed my face between her hands.

"Oh!" She kissed me again—hard—on the lips and took a step back, a look of deep regret on her lovely face. What are you regretting? I wondered. We haven't done anything silly yet.

"What's the problem?" I asked.

"We must stop."

"Why?"

"J'ai un petit ami," she said.

A small friend? What's that, I wondered, a euphemism for an undersized vagina?

She saw my confusion. "Un fiancé," she added.

"No problem," I wanted to say, "I'm not the jealous kind. Let's get on with it." But how did you say all that in French? Instead I just stepped toward her again.

"Non, ça ne va pas," she said, looking all regretful again, holding out her arms as if to push me away.

This was *folie*, she explained. She was twenty-five, she wanted to get married. She wanted kids. Her fiancé was a good man, and she didn't want to lose him because of an affair with an *anglais* who is only in Paris for a year.

"Mais . . ." I tried to think of arguments more convincing than "Surely un peu de sexe anglais wouldn't hurt your relationship" or "Don't worry, I won't tell him."

"Mais, pourquoi . . . ?" I finally asked, flailing my hands about in the general direction of my bruised lips.

She gave me one of her painfully kissable looks. "C'était une erreur," she said. A terrible *erreur*. She wanted me to pardon her. "Et merci," she added.

"Merci pourquoi?" Even I'm not vain enough to imagine that one lick of my tonsils is enough to provoke instant orgasm.

"Thank you for being so English. You are a gentleman. You let me kiss you without . . ."

No, I'm not a bloody English gentleman, I wanted to tell her. If she meant gentleman in the "not wanting to sleep with you immediately" sense of the word, the only English gentlemen I knew of were prepubescents who were just waiting until their pubic hair started to grow. Christine didn't know that we Brits had come a long way since Jane Austen's heroines could be sure that they wouldn't get a good rogering as soon as they said yes to a walk in the woods. Even Princess Di used to do it up against a tree with her riding instructor, didn't she? And now there was nothing at all gentlemanly going on in my brain or my boxer shorts.

"Pardonne-moi, mon Englishman," she said fondly, and left me standing there in the ladies, alone with yet another useless erection. Lucky hard-ons are biodegradable, I thought, because I was throwing a lot of them away unused.

"Fuck you, Mr. Darcy," I told the ceiling. "Fuck you, Hugh

Grant. How can you expect a Brit to get his end away if you go around being so bloody *polite* all the time?"

At least the waiters' strike made me feel a bit more popular.

After the first half day of chaos, when café owners were run off their feet and yelled at, the places where the waiters were on strike—virtually all the posher brasseries—began to take on temporary staff.

Suddenly the clients were being served by horrendously inefficient but cute students, who traded in their smelly, underpaid jobs at fast-food counters for the joys of earning tips and not having to wear a baseball cap.

Instead of cowering before a caffeined-up grump in a black waistcoat, suddenly you were being smiled at by an Amélie Poulain or an apprentice Latin lover.

They didn't know the ingredients of anything, they dropped plates, they got bills mixed up. It was just like being in England, where we think that waiting is a temporary job ideally suited to the totally unqualified.

But at the same time it was bliss, like discovering after a lifetime of watching only Ingmar Bergman films that there is such a thing as Monty Python.

Lots of these new young waiters and waitresses were only too happy to speak English as soon as they heard how badly I mangled French. Even if it was no good for my education, I was delighted to find that they *liked* talking to me. I even got a couple of phone numbers. Female, of course.

After a week of watching the young part-timers take their tips, the waiters started to realize that they might have screwed up, and suddenly the waistcoats were back at their regular jobs, their Post-it notes less legible than ever, their hover-by-the-table times cut to new world-record levels of brevity. Life returned instantly to normal, as it always seemed to do in Paris.

Nothing, not even a strike at the heart of the country's key industry—food—could push the city's daily rush off trajectory for long.

I had to get used to being hated again.

The final straw was the cards.

In the last week of September, several days late, grumpy Marianne brought my business cards.

I looked through the transparent plastic of the box. My name had been corrected. Good.

And in place of "VD" there was a new logo—My Tea Is Rich.

My Tea Is Rich? The bastards.

Marianne hovered, no doubt waiting for a chance to gossip about my reaction.

"Merci," I said, as cool as an English officer whose sergeant has just handed him the revolver with which he is going to blow his brains out rather than face the shame of surrender.

I made sure Marianne was still watching me and dropped the whole bloody box unopened in the bin.

OCTOBRE

One Foot in the Merde

THE FRENCH, AS we all know, love snails. Escargots.
One of their favorite ways of cooking snails is to put them
straight on the barbecue, alive. Before being cooked, the escargots
are covered in salt, the equivalent of giving them an acid bath, and
they get rid of all their slime trying to protect themselves.
Basically, people make the creature shit itself to purge its insides
of impurities. Even the French don't eat snailshit.

Given this extreme cruelty, it might seem strange to say that the
French love the humble snail. But what few people (and even
fewer snails) realize is that France has paid these sacrificial
mollusks the ultimate tribute—its capital city is, in fact, a giant
escargot.

I didn't realize this myself until the first Saturday in October.

It was a gray morning, a "first pullover of the season" morning,
when Parisians suddenly started to walk even faster than usual, as
if they were all scared to death the department stores would run
out of stock before they got there. I was sitting outside a café,
ogling.

Not women, though the selection walking past was of its usual
Olympic standard.

I was ogling the autumnal explosion opposite. It was a fruit-

and-veg stall like I'd never seen before. Not a square millimeter of cling film in sight, and everything seasonal. Great bunches of radishes with their leaves still on. It occurred to me that I'd never knowingly seen a radish leaf before. There were piles of things I didn't even recognize. Big white bulbs—*fenouil*, the notice said. I looked it up in my pocket dictionary—fennel. Yes, I'd had it before, but only in little grilled slices in a fish restaurant. These things were as big as hard white human hearts, with severed green arteries poking out the top. Next to them was a huge basket of red-and-white-speckled peapod things. *Ecosser*, the label said. "Scotsmen" was the nearest my dictionary came. No. A Scotsman often goes red and speckly when he becomes a football manager, but these looked more like some kind of bean. There were spectacular heaps of fresh purple figs and cascades of small, juicy-looking grapes that looked real and mud splashed, as though they'd actually been on a vine out in the fresh air at some point, as opposed to the polished clone grapes we see in English supermarkets.

As I sat there slavering, one of the fruit-and-veg sellers leaned over the display and started dunking his hands into a mound of wild mushrooms, scooping up whole fistfuls of gnarled, chocolate brown cèpes that still had their muddy roots attached. It was almost erotic. If you were a wild-mushroom kind of guy, that is.

I tore my eyes away from the food and focused on the map of Paris in my guidebook. The map gave each of the city's twenty arrondissements a different color. They were, I noticed for the first time, arranged in a spiral pattern, starting with a small rectangle, the First Arrondissement, in the center. The Second was a larger rectangle just above the First. Then across to the right was the Third. Below that was the Fourth, then down a bit more and across the river on the left bank was the Fifth, and so on, a spiral of numbers that took you up to the Twentieth on the far northeastern rim of the circular city.

The city's districts quite definitely formed a snail's shell. The snail itself had presumably been eaten long ago.

I scanned the map for landmarks. The First Arrondissement had the Louvre. The Second? Apparently nothing. It had one gray blob that seemed to mark the location of something interesting. "Bourse," it said. I looked this up in my pocket dictionary— "purse; stock exchange; (informal) scrotum." Aha, Paris's famous scrotum quarter.

The Third had the Centre Pompidou. The Fourth, the Place des Vosges, which my guidebook described as "a droolingly chic 17th-century square, formerly the site of a royal jousting field, where the French King Henri II was accidentally skewered by a British knight, the Count of Montgomery." Another reason to hate us.

The Fifth Arrondissement had the Pantheon, "a huge classical mausoleum where the French bury their famous writers." A bit harsh on the writers, I thought, just for being too intellectual.

The snail went on, unwinding a list of must-see buildings I'd never been in.

So far, I'd been chronically lazy about exploring my new hometown. Well, I had done a dutiful tour of the main sights—the Louvre, of course, Notre Dame, the Centre Pompidou, all seen from outside—but I'd spent most of my first month either working or sitting around trying to fill my bloodstream with caffeine and alcohol.

If, like me, you're able to find temporary happiness in a pint of beer and live, wide-screen football coverage, then you can inject your evenings and weekends with bliss in any one of Paris's many "English" pubs. You order at the bar (no danger of being assaulted by someone in a waistcoat), in English (a brief respite from humiliation), and you can eat typically English pub grub like chicken tikka masala.

My only real excuse for this cultural isolationism was a disease. Throughout history there have been many diseases that have baffled the medical establishment. Some aren't even recognized as medical conditions for centuries. In medieval times, for example, the cure for an epileptic fit was to burn some lonely old widow who was unlucky enough to possess a warty nose and a black cat.

Since moving to Paris, I'd begun to suffer from symptoms that seemed to have gone totally undocumented in medical textbooks. I didn't know it, but I was just about to have an attack.

After my coffee, and a last wistful look at the radish leaves, I wandered through the pedestrian Montorgueil ("mon-torgoy") area in the Second Arrondissement, with its slippery white-paved roads, its cafés and erotic food stalls, and went to check out the Bourse, which was not pink and hairy but Greek temple shaped and stony. The old stock exchange, in fact, as my dictionary had hinted.

The streets around the Bourse were busy, full of darting scooters and impatient cars. In Paris, just because it's an office district doesn't mean that all two-legged life forms are sucked out of it after work on a Friday. I headed east with the flow of the rushing traffic, and at a crossroads, I suddenly came across the rue Saint-Denis, which was lined with the most brazen prostitutes I'd seen since running out of a bar in Bangkok because underage girls kept sitting on my knee and asking, "You want blow job, mister?"

These Parisian girls were all adults, though, more like ripe figs, bursting out of their hot pants and half-open blouses. Their eyebrows were savagely plucked, their mouths lipsticked to oblivion. There was something for all tastes—black, Asian, white, nineteen, thirty, gulp, fifty.

And everywhere there were men eyeing up the goods, asking the price, disappearing into doorways.

There was no plate glass here like there is in Amsterdam. This was quite literally in your face. Women standing there on the pavement trying to turn men on. If I hadn't been so terrified of AIDS, I could have let myself be sucked in on the tide of sex.

I turned off the main drag into a side street, relieved to have escaped temptation, and skidded on a gigantic dog turd that had been sitting in the middle of the white-paved street, shouting, "Here I am!" at my sex-numbed senses.

How could I have missed it?

I heard a laugh. A fifty-something prostitute, who looked like a Marilyn Monroe waxwork dummy after an overload in Madame Tussaud's heating system, was standing in a doorway a few yards farther along.

"La merde," she sang in a tobacco croak, "qu'on voit danser le long des golfes clairs."

I understood *la merde* and thought she was singing some typically French hymn to bodily functions. I didn't find out till months later that she was actually making quite a clever joke, adapting an old song called "La Mer." Only in France—an intellectual prostitute.

This, you see, was my disease—an uncanny ability on the part of my feet to home in on the nearest dog *merde*.

The more I tried to explore Paris, the more I messed up my shoes.

According to an article I found on the Internet, I wasn't alone—every year, 650 Parisians end up in the hospital after somersaulting over a sample of the fifteen tons of poop dumped on the city's streets by its two hundred thousand dogs. Two hundred thousand, I thought, that's more than Genghis Khan's army.

I began to bolster my defenses.

I went to a discount store and bought myself a stock of incredibly cheap North Korean canvas trainers for my weekend walks. I pooped them up for a day and chucked them in a bin outside the hotel. Not very ecological, but good for my hotel's carpets. And the receptionist kindly pretended not to notice me walking past in my socks all the time.

To get to work unsullied, I equipped myself with a bumper pack of string-tie bin bags that I slipped over my shoes as disposable galoshes. Okay, so people stared at me on the metro, and I had to make sure I took them off before I got within range of Marianne's gossiping eyes, but it was worth the bother.

This was just treating the symptom rather than trying to cure the disease, though, and I began to branch out from literal to metaphorical encounters of the turd kind.

At work, for example, when I went to confront Bernard about sabotaging my business cards. It was obviously Bernard, wasn't it? My Tea Is Rich was his baby, and I'd tried to abort it.

"Me? Me?" he replied, showing his usual talent for monosyllables and sounding like a French version of the roadrunner in the Wile E. Coyote cartoons. "No. Ah do not do dese cards, me."

His mustache danced about as he suppressed a victorious smile. He was looking very pleased to be able to shrug off my accusations. So pleased that he wasn't even hiding the sports magazine he'd been reading.

"If you're reading that, I hope that means you've had time to read my reports?" I asked pointedly.

"Zis? Oh, ah look at zis because eet as big publicity for us." He opened the magazine at a full-page ad for Jean-Marie's prime minced beef, with a famous puff-eared French rugby player looking orgasmic about biting into an undercooked hamburger.

"Good, uh? Zis rugbyman ee do dis for us because ee eez friend wiz me." Bernard was looking only slightly less orgasmic about the clumsiness with which I'd leapt with both feet into this diplomatic booby trap.

And outside work, too. I called up one of the waitresses from the strike days and arranged to go out for Sunday brunch. Before we met up, though, she sent me a terrifying e-mail with an attachment of "some lines that are very important to me."

I opened up the attachment, and from what I could gather, it was about some spirit visiting a woman and explaining that *tristesse* (sadness) was really *joie* (joy), and vice versa.

Oh God, said my head, get the hell away from that shit. No, no, said my groin, get in there.

She was a tall, studenty blonde who hid what promised to be a great body under baggy clothes. She had very fair skin, with a cute curved nose you just wanted to nibble and a tiny beauty spot on her left cheek that seemed to say, "Kiss here." Her face looked as if it had never seen a molecule of makeup in its life. She was the kind who doesn't seem to know she's beautiful. I love that. Alexa, her name was, she spoke great English, and she was doing a course in photography. What better excuse for a girl to ask you to get your clothes off?

So instead of deleting her and her e-mail, I replied with some bull about how it'd be all *joie* and no *tristesse* to see her (yes, groan—I'm sorry) and carried on fantasizing about the photo sessions to come.

At my request, we arranged to meet in Montmartre in the Eighteenth Arrondissement, at the place where Amélie Poulain's boyfriend looks down at her through the telescope.

I took the ultramodern funicular—a vertical metro—up to the

off white, wedding-cake Sacré Coeur. I was five minutes late, but luckily Alexa was over fifteen minutes late, as most Parisian women are.

We said hello with a chaste kiss on each cheek. She was brimming with understated sexuality in a battered old leather jacket, a baggy-necked sweater, and jeans with a hole in the knee. A fine-looking knee, too. She had a camera slung over her shoulder.

I was brimming with *underused* sexuality, and although it was a bit blowy up here on Paris's mountaintop, I'd left my shirt open enough to expose a manly hint of what I hoped was photogenic chest hair. I don't have much, but what I do have she was getting a good view of.

"Great to see you again," I told her.

"Yes," she agreed, apparently examining me for light sensitivity.

We then turned our backs to the Peruvian nose-flute band that was currently entertaining the hordes of tourists taking photos of one another and looked out over Paris's rooftops.

In Van Gogh's day, Montmartre was a hill in the countryside where artists came for inspiration, fresh air, and cheap booze. Now it had been well and truly sucked into the city, but it still felt somehow outside, mainly because of the altitude. You could look down over a chaotic jumble of gray zinc roofs that had probably changed little in a century. With the Eiffel Tower hidden away to our right by a stand of gold-leafed chestnut trees, there were very few intrusions into the low skyline until you got the tower blocks around the city's fringes. There was the blue-and-white piping of the Centre Pompidou and of course the Tour Montparnasse, jabbed like a black glass dagger into the heart of Paris. But apart from that, the city seemed to be a collection of a million romantic garrets for budding Baudelaires to scribble away in. I couldn't prevent myself from smiling.

"It is a real visual cliché," Alexa groaned.

What was this, I wondered, my *joie* equals her *tristesse*?

"It's not a cliché for me, it's the first time I've been here."

"Hm," she grunted.

I turned away from the clichéd view. Keep her talking, I urged myself. What *does* she like?

"What did you think of *Amélie*?" I made telescope-focusing motions down toward the street a hundred feet or so below.

"Oh." She shrugged. "Jeunet is an intelligent director. But I preferred *Delicatessen*. Have you seen that?"

"No. What's it about?"

"What's it *about*?" She winced. This was apparently a film that was too good to be *about* anything. Another gaffe. "There were so many *close-ups* in that movie." Alexa sounded outraged. "Half of the movie was just a poster of Audrey Tautou's eyes."

"Cute eyes, though," I tried to joke.

"Exactly," she huffed.

I suffered a moment of panic. Maybe, I thought, Alexa was under the impression I'd invited her out for a lesson in contemporary French aesthetics rather than a pre-bed snack.

But the conversation flowed a bit more smoothly as we wandered through a small art market selling paintings by all of the worst Renoir imitators in the world. We chatted about why I was in Paris, about her time in England (she'd spent a year in London as a photographer's assistant), and only a little bit more about where she thought contemporary French aesthetics were going (to Disney-style oblivion, apparently).

She wasn't aggressive, I discovered, just honest. She hid her physical beauty inside a baggy jacket and the softer side of her personality behind outspoken opinions that probably scared men off in droves, thank God.

Near the Moulin Rouge, I naturally managed to stumble into a dried-up dog deposit that was like some foul brand of poisonous cocoa powder. It had been lurking at the base of a tree and made me do my own version of can-can dancing as I kicked the tree trunk in an attempt to dislodge the cocoa from my shoe. Like a fool, I'd worn some smart, non-Korean trainers. Alexa coped very well with the situation. Better than me, in fact. She waited outside my swearing zone for the first couple of minutes, then guided me to a gutter where there was a small puddle of water to wash away the dirt. She didn't seem at all put out by this sudden crack in my veneer of cool. And in a way I was glad she'd seen me at my worst. It kind of cleared the air between us, if doggie-do can be said to clear the air.

Over freshly squeezed orange juice, fresh figs, and scrambled eggs salted with flakes of smoked salmon, she encouraged me to talk about my handicap, and I tried out my theory that it was a psychological condition that had been dormant until it was exposed to Paris's unique pavements.

"It's a sort of dyslexia. You know dyslexia?"

"Yes." Alexa nodded, peeling a ripe purple fig with painful symbolism.

"I'm in some way dyslexic. Or color-blind. Some people can't make out the meaning in words or the differences between colors—I can't make out dog turds. I'm shitlexic."

"You are a little obsessed, no?" Alexa folded back the fig's foreskin and bit into it with sharp-toothed relish.

"Obsessed? Maybe. I never see anyone else wiping their shoes. Do you ever see anyone else wiping their shoes?"

"Rarely." Alexa thought about this. She seemed to be taking me seriously, at least. If I'd tried out any of this DIY psychology on my English "girlfriend," Ruth, she'd have accused me of trying to bore her into dumping me. Apart from new agers, most of us Brits belong to the "for God's sake, stop moaning" school of psychotherapy.

"You are sure it is not because you English are so snobbish, you walk with your nose in the air?"

"Turning our noses up at all these foreigners, you mean? Yes, you might be on to something."

Alexa seemed pleased to have helped me toward awareness. She took another fig and treated it much more gently than the last one.

"It is a pity for you that you came to Paris at such a bad time," she said, a flash of humor at the corner of her eyes.

"Bad time?"

"Yes, because of the strike."

"The strike?"

"Yes, the . . . how do you say? The men who clean the roads."

"The street cleaners?"

"Yes. They will be on strike. It will start on Monday."

"Tomorrow?"

"Yes."

"No.

"Yes."

Alexa was examining me anxiously. How long had I been in catatonic shock? I wondered.

"Why are they going on strike?" I choked back the tears as best I could.

"It is their . . . you know . . ." She made sweeping gestures with her arms. "Brushes?"

"Brooms."

"Yes, they want more serious brooms."

It was true that the street cleaners' brooms looked a bit silly. They were modern versions of the witch's broom—a long aluminum pole with a sheaf of green plastic switches in place of the traditional birch twigs.

Alexa said that the street cleaners now wanted their trade-mark broom replaced by a less humiliating version, a shoulder-borne automatic contraption like a giant electric toothbrush. The city authorities had refused, the cleaners decided to strike, and while negotiations went on concerning the relative cost of plastic twigs and giant electric toothbrushes, the dirt was going to pile up.

Soon, I felt sure, it would be my turn to somersault into a French ambulance.

I looked up to see Alexa giggling madly.

"What is it?"

"You make laugh, Englishman. You are so . . . you know, like Hugh Grant."

"Hugh Grant?" The phantom of my lust for Christine sprang up before me, its face an amalgam of every English actor who's ever failed to get off with his costar.

"Yes, you know, his lost little boy thing. It is very . . . touching."

"Touching."

"Yes, like a . . . how do you call it? A puppy."

"Puppy." So now I'd morphed into some kind of stray dog. Best to take me away and give me the lethal injection right now, I thought.

"What are you doing for the rest of the day?" I asked Alexa when I'd paid the bill.

"Why?" There was that little twitch of humor in her eyes again. A bit of a tease, our Alexa.

"I thought we could maybe . . ." The time wasn't right to say "go to bed," even I knew that. I tried desperately to think of something nonthreatening and nonclichéd to do together.

"Look for some photos." I nodded toward her camera. "You know, walk about looking for photogenic things and people. It could be fun."

"I don't usually try to make photos happen. They happen."

"Ah." None had happened during our morning together.

"No, anyway I must visit my father."

"Oh, right." In a hit parade of crap excuses, I reckoned that was only just below "I have to stay in and pluck my nipple hairs."

"We can meet up again soon, can't we?"

"If you want."

"Great. Like, tonight? We can do something a bit livelier."

She laughed. "No, sorry. I can't tonight." And that was it.

A quick mutual cheek rub and "Ciao." I didn't even get an "*Au revoir*." I didn't blame her. How could a self-respecting Parisienne fancy someone whose only topic of conversation was the rear end of dogs?

Next morning I woke up at five, listening to the silence. Well, the relative silence. I could still hear the background rumble of traffic on the eight-lane highway at the end of the road. What I couldn't hear was the dawn chorus of swishing brooms and humming cleanup machines. Paris has a whole army of green machines— spray trucks, buggies with brooms or nozzles at the front, reservoirs on wheels with a power hose that could sweep away a riot in Tiananmen Square. And the broom men have a secret weapon, too, a key to open valves on street corners. These valves gush out water that flows along the gutters, carrying away the night's crop of beer cans, emptied café ashtrays, fast-food bags, and drunks toward the drain on the next corner of the street. At lots of street corners you see rolled-up lengths of carpet in the gutter. At first, I thought these were improvised pillows belonging to the tramps, but in fact they're an ingenious system dreamed up by the street cleaners to direct the flow of water. And now the carpets were going to dry up.

I left for work and ballet-danced my way down the street, my shoes wrapped in a double layer of black plastic bags.

It looked as if the dustmen had come out in sympathy with the cleaners. The pavements were jammed with overflowing bins that the concierges had optimistically put out for emptying. There were also various bits of rubbish I never normally saw. A three-legged chair in front of a restaurant, a small sheaf of stale baguettes outside a *boulangerie*.

I stopped off at the cash dispenser, and the machine spat my card out again as if it tasted of stale baguette. "Request rejected," the machine informed me. I asked for a balance and understood why. My salary hadn't been paid in.

Someone was trying to shit-stir, and if they wanted their shit stirred, then stirred their shit was jolly well going to be.

As soon as I got to the office, I challenged Marianne.

"Not paid?" she said. "Oh. Come and see me in my office at eleven o'clock."

She was on receptionist duty. Urgent things like not being paid apparently had to wait until she put on her HR cap.

"Is possible I see someone in . . . ?" I didn't know the French word for "accounts." I needed cash, not counseling.

"In . . . ?"

"Finance?"

"Come and see me in my office at eleven o'clock," she repeated in her special French-for-retards voice. "Bonne journée."

As in, Get lost.

She turned up at 11:15, a coffee in her hand. We went into her office, and as soon as she'd found a mat for her coffee cup, arranged her cardigan across the back of her chair, opened the window a notch to let in some air, and managed to remember how you turn on computers, she sat down and began clicking her mouse with a nail-bitten forefinger.

"Ah, I see." She smiled—or widened her mouth to show her gray teeth, anyway—at me. I was standing, threateningly, I hoped, over Marianne's poisonous-looking desk plant. "You don't have a carte de séjour," she said, and smiled again as if she expected me to be grateful to her for coming up with this annoyingly meaningless answer.

"Carte de séjour?"

"Yes."

"What is?" I asked, screwing up the grammar in this short question so badly that I saw Marianne consciously resist raising her eyes toward the ceiling.

"I don't know exactly. We never had a foreign worker before."

Carte, I knew, meant "card." "Is identity card?"

"I suppose so." Marianne gave a good impression of someone not giving a toss about the unfathomable mysteries of the universe.

"Where I, er, find a carte de séjour?"

"I don't know." Marianne performed a full-body shrug with, accompanying pout of indifference. "I only know that accounts couldn't pay you because you haven't got one."

"And you not say me?" The worst thing was, we were calling each other *tu*, as if we were best pals swapping makeup hints in the ladies' toilet.

"Didn't accounts tell you?" Marianne asked, outraged at such gross inefficiency on somebody's else's part.

"No, nobody say me. J'ai besoin argent," I said, ungrammatically but understandably. "Maintenant."

"Tu veux une avance?"

An advance? How could it be an advance if it was last month's salary? But this was no time for French-style logical debate.

"Oui, une avance," I said.

"I can arrange that now by phone." As she dialed, Marianne seemed to brighten with the sudden realization that the problem was going away. Even if it wasn't really her problem, it had been in her office and was therefore almost as annoying as if it was her problem, but now it was going to leave her in peace.

"They will bring the check to your office this morning," she said after a brief conversation with accounts. "Half a month's salary."

"Okay. Thanks."

Marianne was looking almost radiant.

"You will have to sign for the check," she said. "You have some identity? Your passport? A carte de . . ."

My mind was suddenly flooded with deliciously violent images of human resources people choking to death on soil and fragments of plant pot.

Christine phoned around to find out about getting me a *carte de séjour*.

I sat there happily in her office for half an hour, gradually becoming drunk on the aromatic scent of her hair as she waded through bureaucratic switchboards.

She explained the list of addresses and documents she'd written out.

It seemed that, as an EU citizen, I had to go to the *préfecture*—the central police station—which was next to the flower market on the Île de la Cité, just along the river from Notre Dame. Sounded very picturesque.

All I had to do was take my passport, work contract, three passport photos, a recent electricity bill, and the marriage certificates of any hamsters I'd owned since 1995, all photocopied onto medieval parchment. No *problème*.

The good news was, Christine told me, I was allowed to take a day off work to deal with this boring red tape. How civilized, I thought.

"Stop looking at me like that" (*comme ça*), Christine said, picking up the gratitude in my eyes and assuming it was lust. Which it partly was.

"Comme quoi?"

"Comme ça!" Christine laughed and shooshed me away.

"Va travailler!"

How was it that French women managed to shrug off sexual advances while still remaining flirtatious? God, even telling you to get lost they were sexy.

A new day, a new lesson in French life: The reason they give you a day off is that you need at least three.

I went down to the *préfecture* the next morning, picking my way through a drift of long, empty flower boxes that had spread across the square from the unswept market.

I and my bag were X-rayed, metal detected, and sent to wait our turn to be humiliated by a woman in a bombproof booth who, after half an hour of dealing with the line of people in front of me, sniffed at the documents I'd brought and explained to me that I ought to have photocopied more pages of my passport and that I shouldn't have smiled in my photos. Back to square one.

Second morning, she discovered that I didn't have an electricity bill as proof of address. That was because I was living in a hotel, I told her. Therefore I needed a letter from my employer explaining that I was living in a hotel. No, a fax sent through while I was in the waiting room wouldn't do. She needed the original, signed in ink, and anyway I wasn't allowed access to the waiting room without the necessary documents. Couldn't the woman possibly have mentioned this the day before? No, shrug, apparently not.

Finally, on the third morning, after mountaineering over an alpine heap of soggy flower boxes and crushed bulbs and tiptoeing round rolling drink cans and fluttering newspapers, I experienced a fierce glow of pride at being congratulated on the quality and quantity of my paperwork. I was allowed to pass through the forbidden door and entered a typically drab official waiting room with a kind of open snail pattern of low booths running around three walls.

Facing the curved line of booths were rows of chairs, about a quarter of which were taken by exhausted-looking *carte de séjour* candidates. Some of them looked just like me—suited up for the office. Others were versions of me with skirts. I wondered how much our collective days off were costing our employers.

There was also a group of no-hopers. They looked as if they were here to try to convince someone that the EU had already admitted fifteen new member countries. This sounds racist on my part, but judging by the argument coming from booth six, I wasn't far wrong.

"C'est l'Europe, non?" a black-mustached man shouted. "Je suis européen, moi!"

The eyes of the woman civil servant behind the reinforced glass glazed over. The women in booths five and seven broke off from processing the people in front of them and leaned round the partitions to back up their colleague. A flurry of monosyllables wafted through the glass.

"Eh oh!"

"Ho là. Eh!"

"Non, mais je suis européen, moi! Merde!"

The fateful word had a magically powerful effect.

"Oh!" The woman who'd been annoying him shoved his file back under the glass and told him to take it away.

The mustachioed man blathered on about human rights and other similarly irrelevant stuff, but his tormentor retained a stony indifference. The women from booths five and seven leaned round again and fired off some more monosyllables. The man said he refused to leave. Finally, a cop came in and gestured tiredly for the rejected candidate to go. The man looked around the room for support, but we all avoided eye contact. There's no room for human rights in a government waiting room.

A mere twenty-four hours or so later, it was my turn. Booth six, too. The booth of death. I said a cheery (but not too smiley) "Bonjour," tried my best to look European, and pushed my pile of papers forward with a silent prayer.

The woman ticked off each of my documents in a row of boxes on the inside of a pink file. Then she came to my sheet of photos and pursed her lips.

"You should have cut the photos," she told me.

"Ah," I said. (Thinking: Aaaaggghhh!) "I didn't know."

My voice suggested I'd be sickeningly grateful for the chance not only to cut my photos to regulation size, but also to massage her feet with the aromatherapy oil of her choice if only she'd allow me to kneel under the table for her.

"That's okay." She produced a pair of scissors and expertly

snipped the sheet of four into individual photos. She slid one back to me. "We need three, not four."

"Ah. *You* not want it?"

This was meant to be a tension-easing joke, but she froze and glared at me.

I could see the headlines: ENGLISHMAN DEPORTED FOR MILD SEXUAL HARASSMENT OF FRENCH CIVIL SERVANT. "Britain must leave the European Union," demands President Chirac. "We French are the ones who sexually harass people, not you."

As I looked into her eyes—dark and deadened by too many years dealing with people who despised her for making them waste their time—I knew that this was a key moment. The mustachioed bloke had got it wrong. I had to get it right.

I picked up the photo and said, "I am very triste" (sad). "This photo is not beautiful." I scowled at my mugshot and hid it away in my bag.

She nodded and almost, *almost* smiled.

"Smile is interdit in the photos," I said. "Dommage. Everyone can be less triste."

"Yes, it would be nice to see some smiles." She gave a microscopic laugh and brutally stapled one of my photos to a pink card. "This is your provisional carte de séjour. You will receive a letter telling you when you can get your definitive carte de séjour."

"Merci beaucoup."

"Bonne journée."

"Bonne journée."

I bounced out of there, kissing my pristine pink card. France 0, me 1. This morning, at least.

The afternoon scoreline was up to Alexa. Yes, Alexa. I'd phoned her up and we'd had a really good chat. She'd laughed at my red-tape stories and even let slip that Hugh Grant was actually "très sexy" in *Notting Hill*. I tried desperately to remember—does Hugh get Julia in the end or not? It didn't seem polite to ask Alexa over the phone, so I fixed up a lunch date and hoped for the best.

She surprised me. She wanted us to have lunch on a *bateau mouche*—one of the incredibly touristy boats that shuttle visitors up and down the Seine, from the Eiffel Tower to Notre Dame and back again. She was the one who'd gone on about visual clichés. Maybe this was some kind of concession. Or a sign that she thought clichés were all I was good for.

I got out of the metro at Pont de l'Alma, near the road tunnel where Princess Di was killed. A few tourists, most of them young twenty-somethings, were standing in the middle of the roundabout above the tunnel, gazing at the golden flame statue, a facsimile of the Statue of Liberty flame, which has been adopted as an unofficial symbol of the lost princess. Two white-clad nuns were crossing to the roundabout, dithering in the middle of the road and running the risk of dying a very similar death to Diana's.

The river was flowing deep and green, but the water was not even touching the toes on the statue of the old soldier carved into the Alma Bridge. During an especially rainy period, the water starts lapping round his boots. If it gets anywhere near his genitals, Parisians have to start filling sandbags.

There were two or three massive *bateaux mouches* moored here, like horizontal glass apartment buildings.

Alexa was sitting on a bench, squinting up into the pale sun. She had on her leather jacket, but this time she actually wore a skirt—a long denim thing that hid her knees but showed off a pair of smooth, creamy white calves. It seemed she was revealing her body inch by inch.

I bent down and gave her a kiss on the cheek.

"You are surprised by my choice?" she said.

I turned to look at the huge, ugly boat. "Yes."

"I chose it for you. There are no dogs in the middle of the river."

The glass-sided boat set off along the Seine. It didn't feel much like a boat. There was no rocking and rolling, even though the water was flowing fast, causing small eddies and whirlpools under the many bridges. The boat was so big that it felt like being on rails.

But sitting up on the roof in the autumn sun, with a slight breeze blowing between the high, built-up riverbanks, we got a view of the city undisturbed by the urban rush.

Alexa produced some foil-wrapped sandwiches and cracked open two small bottles of chilled beer as the recorded commentary began—first in French, then a different voice for English, German, Spanish, and finally what sounded like Russian and Japanese.

We headed toward the city center and Notre Dame.

"A votre droite," the (female) tape announced, "l'Hôtel des Invalides, la tombe de l'Empereur Napoléon Bonaparte."

"On your right," said a cheerful American male actor, "the Hôtel des Invalides, tomb of . . ."

You could tell what nationality people were by the moment they chose to turn and look right. Though Bulgarians were presumably going to spend the whole cruise staring straight ahead.

"What's in this?" I began to unravel the foil around a long, half-baguette sandwich.

"Normandy sausage—andouille de Vire."

The Japanese Invalides commentary had only just time to end before the French returned with a request to look to the left and an explanation of how the gold-tipped needle in the middle of the Place Concorde was a gift from an Egyptian viceroy . . .

The half-baguette was filled with slices of a suspicious-looking gray brown substance.

"Sausage?" I let the word float skeptically above the German announcement about "der Concorde-Platz."

"Yes."

I took one bite and spat it back in the foil.

"It tastes—it smells—of merde!"

Alexa thought this was hugely funny. "Oh, please. Not your favorite subject again. That is the typical andouille."

She explained how they made it. I took a swig of beer to clean my teeth. Apparently I'd just bitten into a pig's rectum.

"You could have chosen something a little less *typical*."

"Ah, you English. Your farms are just factories where food grows in sterilized test tubes. Try a different sandwich."

"What's in the others, then? Cowpat fumé?"

Alexa laughed. "You are scared of France, aren't you?"

"Scared, moi? Get that sandwich open right now."

Alexa began to unwrap another sandwich. It was filled with runny yellow cheese and reeked. I couldn't stop myself turning away. I joined a family of Asian tourists who were looking at a tree that the Japanese commentary seemed to be calling Concorde.

"It is Reblochon." She waved it under my nose. This had to be one of the unpasteurized cheeses that were banned in the United Kingdom, presumably because to judge by the pong, they were scraped up off the floor of the cowshed. "It's good. Try it."

"Okay, no problem." I tried my best to look more Bruce Willis than Hugh Grant. Alexa laughed all the same.

"Honestly. It is not too strong. You have not tasted Époisse or Munster. They are *smelly*. We love them."

"I really don't fit in in this country."

Alexa gave my hand a comforting rub and breathed cheese in my face. "You will adapt."

I sat back with my beer and wondered.

The boat had just gone past the Louvre and now came alongside a pair of sand barges that the American voice described as the "legendary home of the Mona Lisa." There were going to be some confused photo albums in Arkansas.

"For example," Alexa said, "you must learn to tolerate the taste if you kiss a girl who has just eaten some Reblochon."

"Can I hold my nose?"

She gave me a punch in the ribs but let me taste her lips. I enjoyed it so much, I went back for seconds. For some reason, the idea of being a Parisian cliché—kissing as we floated down the Seine, how tacky can you get?—did not bother me at all.

I put my arm round her, pulled her head onto my shoulder, and thought, You lucky bastard. I've been using the worst chat-up lines known to man and still she likes me.

We stayed like this as the boat sailed beneath the towering gothic buttresses of Notre Dame cathedral.

"What are you doing for the rest of the afternoon?" I asked.

"Oh, I must see my father."

"Your father? Again? I mean, what . . . ?"

"Yes. He has problems."

"What sort of problems?" Pretty damn major problems, I hoped. Bankruptcy or a dicky prostate, at the very least.

"Oh, problems of the heart. My parents are divorced, because he has discovered he is gay. And now his boyfriend has left him."

"And you have to go and console him?"

"Yes, it would not be very diplomatic if he asked my mother.

And anyway, she is in Moscow, making a documentary about the gangsters. Who knows when she will come back."

"Right." Sometimes, I thought, it felt quite pleasant to be a boring, middle-class Englishman.

We sailed past the modernistic, glass-fronted Arab art institute, which the Germans frowned at skeptically when it was referred to as a *gothische Kathedral.*

"But we can meet tomorrow evening," she said. "We will do something other than eat."

I dived in for some more secondhand cheese. We floated under a bridge, and a kid whistled down at us. He didn't think we were a cliché.

In the office, too, things began flowing more smoothly.

Until now, I'd found it totally infuriating that we never came to any decisions. Every week, the team had a "committee" (every meeting was called a committee), for which I wrote an agenda reminding people of what decisions needed to be taken. And every committee consisted of one of the others in the team talking about whatever idea they'd had in the bathroom before coming to the meeting. Why not dress all the waiters in kilts? Or: I went to an Irish pub and they had an old bicycle hanging from the wall—why don't we get some old bicycles?

At one committee, Marc suggested that the waiters should all wear bowler hats and carry umbrellas like "Monsieur Stid" in *Melon Hat and Boots of Laid Air. (Chapeau melon et bottes de cuir— Bowler Hat and Leather Boots*—was the French name for *The Avengers,* apparently.) Everyone went off on a long verbal tour of what to do with your umbrella while carrying a trayload of salmon sandwiches. Stéphanie even stood up and used a ruler to mime the opening credits to the TV series. She was wearing tight trousers that showed very un-Avenger-like bobbles of cellulite on the outer thighs.

In my early, heavy-footed days, I would have been tempted to fetch an umbrella and show them where I'd like to stick it, but now I felt able to sit back and let them have their fun.

Jean-Marie also seemed unconcerned about this time wasting. He even joined in when they lapsed into French and greeted the end of the conversation with an almost sexual sigh of satisfaction. Only the French, I thought, could attain orgasm by listening to themselves. It was self-inflicted oral sex. A DIY blow job.

"Bernard, when exactly will you get the results of your study about the brand name?" I asked genially.

"Oh. Ah." Bernard's blond mustache seemed to blush. He was definitely flustered.

"Which *cabinet d'études* did you consult?" I'd asked Christine how you said "market research company."

"Uh . . ." Bernard appealed to Jean-Marie for help.

"It is my fault," Jean-Marie said, now looking much less as if he had a vibrator stuffed up his backside. "I told Bernard not to continue with the study to find a new name. I'm sorry, Paul. I should have told you. But . . ."

"You thought I'd take it personally. Not at all. I'm English. We accept defeat with a stiff upper lip." This is a lie about the British that the French believe. Fortunately, they never see news film of English football fans weeping when their team gets relegated or CCTV footage of road-rage attacks caused by someone cutting in line for a supermarket parking space.

"So you ordered those My Tea Is Rich business cards yourself, did you, Jean-Marie?"

Everyone except me was looking uncomfortable. So they'd all been in on the deception.

"Yes. This is true," Jean-Marie confessed. "But you are advancing well with other matters, so I thought the name is a minor thing. You see, Paul, My Tea Is Rich was *my* idea. And it really is a good name for France. You don't think it is funny or English, but you are not French."

The team looked at me to see how I'd take this crushing blow. Not French? The ultimate insult.

I took it like a man. "Okay. Fine, Jean-Marie. You know France better than I do. And you're the boss. But if I may say so, coming from outside the company, it doesn't look very *professional* if the head of a team is not told about a *key decision* relating to his project. It's not the way an *efficient* team is run. I think I see trouble up ahead if we carry on like this."

I topped this off with a Parisian-style shrug. "If you make cock-ups, it's your lookout," my body language was telling them. "You're mistaking me for someone who gives a merde." And it worked. The five French faces in front of me were looking anything but triumphant about my supposed humiliation. They were staring blankly into the future, fearful of the traps that might lie ahead.

Applied to daily life, this is the key to keeping your shoes clean on the pavements of Paris. As you walk, your subconscious scans the pavement ahead. It learns to spot the tiniest bump on the horizon and prepares your feet to step instinctively around it. Ask Parisians how they manage, against all the odds, to keep their feet clean. They don't know. It's an instinct that is part of being Parisian. Those 650 people a year who go to the hospital after slipping on *merde*—I bet they're tourists, or provincials, or the old and infirm suffering from depleted instincts.

*   *   *

My instincts, meanwhile, were just starting to fire on all cylinders.

On the evening I was due to go out with Alexa, I stayed late in my office, reading the business profiles of France's most successful food brands. It must have been about 7:30 p.m. I'd been sitting there silently in my office, working with just a desk lamp, for maybe two hours.

There had, I was dimly aware, been voices coming from the office next door, Jean-Marie's. Nothing unusual in that. I'd taken no notice. The first *unusual* sound I heard was a gasp. Like someone who's just got the bill in a terrifyingly expensive restaurant. Or someone who is approaching the critical point in an office *oh-là-là* session.

I stared at the partition wall as if that might help me hear more clearly. Yes, there was a very faint, regular creaking. An office chair being bounced upon, maybe. Or a desk taking the strain.

There was that gasp again. And then a female voice urging Jean-Marie not to stop quite yet. Who was the mystery mistress? Not Christine, I hoped. And not Marc doing a falsetto, surely?

There was a bit more gasping, a grunt or two, and then the creaking stopped. It would all have been a major turn-on if I hadn't been battling against the idea of imagining Jean-Marie seminaked. I really did not want to go there.

The voices became louder. Buttoning and zipping-up time. They obviously thought they were alone on this floor, because one of them opened the door and the woman's voice suddenly became clearer. Bloody hell, it was Stéphanie. Doing a bit more meat procurement than was called for in her job description.

I couldn't understand everything she said, but she mentioned something about *vache folle*—mad cow disease. And *importer du boeuf anglais*—importing English beef, which was still illegal at this point. Jean-Marie seemed to poo-poo what she was saying with a remark about no one finding out. Then he shushed her and I heard the clang of his glass door being pushed shut. The voices got louder, though, so I could still hear. Jean-Marie growled something about "boo-jay"—budgets. Stéphanie said, "Merde, what about our public image?" Even with my limited French, I could tell that the conversation had turned from postcoital banter into a full-blown row between the head of "poor-chassing" and her boss about illegally buying cheap English meat.

On a scale of one to ten, this particular *merde* was an eleven. I didn't think Bernard's French rugby chum in the ad would look quite so orgasmic if he knew what he was biting into.

I left my desk lamp on and my door open and padded silently away to the stairs and my date with Alexa.

We were in the Eleventh Arrondissement, in the Oberkampf district, walking arm in arm up the street of the same name. It was past its best as the city's trendy bar district, Alexa said, but this made it more fun. The kind of person who only came to a place because it was fashionable had gone and left the neighborhood (her neighborhood) with a great selection of new places to spend an evening.

We went and sat in a bar with a South American jungle theme—an air-conditioned jungle, luckily—and ordered some outrageously expensive Mexican beers.

The place had long sofas, so we were able to snuggle up cozily, alternating talking, drinking, and other more intimate mouth activities.

"Please, one thing for this evening," Alexa said, waving away a tequila rep who was trying to get everyone in the bar to wear huge sombreros. "Don't talk about your favorite subject, okay, Mr. Obsessed Englishman?"

"Okay, but it's not really an English philosophy. I never used to think about it at all until I came here."

"You call an obsession with dogs' bottoms a *philosophy*?" Alexa giggled. She was now on her second beer, with nothing solid except tortilla chips to soak it up. She ducked out of the way of the tequila rep, who was holding a straw hat the size of Mexico just above her head.

"Well, yes, it kind of sums up the French philosophy of life. You only ever think about yourselves. So instead of getting together to stop dogs from pooping on pavements, you just learn how not to step in the merde." I accepted a sombrero just to get rid of the guy.

"Okay, okay, stop now, please. Ay ay ay!"

"*¡Ándale!*" The tequila rep joined in the Mexican sound charades and jammed a sombrero over Alexa's eyes.

Out in the street, we frisbeed our Mexican headgear onto a mound of rubbish and moved on to a moodily lit bar with a DJ playing moody lounge music and a moody waitress serving cocktails at prices that put you in the mood for a second mortgage. Then we walked a few doors down to a cheaper place that was jammed solid with people, disco music, and smoke.

I crawled over the mosh pit at the bar to get two beers and joined Alexa in a corner that was relatively quiet because it was over five feet from a loudspeaker and at least a yard from the nearest drunk dancer.

It was too smoky to breathe, too noisy to talk, so we drank, people-watched, danced, sweated, drank some more, kissed, and laughed, as everyone else seemed to be doing.

The dancing was weird. Everyone bopped about normally enough to the dance and disco records, but then the DJ put on some punk. I went out there ready to pogo and found myself in the middle of an Elvis movie. There was Joe Strummer spitting about a white riot, and all the Frenchies were *jiving*. Alexa swung me around at arm's length and told me they call it *le rock* and dance it to any fast record. I thought it wasn't such a bad idea. The only physical contact you get with your "partner" during a punk record in the United Kingdom is a punch in the kidneys.

At some point during the dancing, Alexa and I agreed to lay off alcohol before we got too drunk.

But this was like agreeing to bung up the hole in your *bateau mouche* when your passengers were already up to their necks in river water. I remember shouting in someone's ear—not Alexa's—about being "rollock titted," which didn't (I realized vaguely even after so much booze) actually mean anything to me and probably meant even less to the black French girl I'd shouted it at.

After that, I recall Alexa telling me to get down off the table and a shaven-headed barman gently but firmly—well, firmly, anyway—putting her suggestion into practice.

I have a faint memory of tasting salty blood in my mouth and of seeing a lot of feet with dancing legs sprouting upward out of them. And there my evening ended.

Next morning, my cell phone ring tone howled at me to wake up.

"Voulez-vous coucher avec moi," it shrieked, a hangover (and hangover was the operative word here) from my London days.

I opened my eyes to blinding white. White ceiling, white light, white noise. Either I'd been buried in a warm avalanche or I was in someone else's apartment. (My hotel room was a muddy sea of beige.)

Oh yeah, I remembered. We went back to her place. There she was beside me in her bed, hidden beneath her blinding white duvet, still covering up her beauty.

Brilliant. Apart from the headache and the scorched dryness of my palate, my main center of physical awareness was a distinct sogginess down at willy level. A result at last, even if I couldn't remember it.

The phone was still singing at me. I reached down to the floor and managed to tug the noisy lump of plastic out of my jacket pocket.

"Hi, it's Alexa."

I laughed painfully. "Very clever."

"What?"

I looked across at her and stroked the duvet where her head lump was.

"Your alarm call," I said to phone and duvet. "But if you wanted to wake me up, you should have just reached across and tickled me. It never fails."

"What did you say? *Tickled* you?"

"Yeah."

There was a groan from under the duvet and a hand emerged.

"Hang on," I said.

I pulled the duvet down a few inches.

My memories of the previous night were hazy, but I could have sworn that the last time I saw Alexa, her arm was quite definitely not black.

"Paul? Are you there? *Where* are you?" the phone asked.

Oh, *merde*.

NOVEMBRE

Make Yourself Chez Moi

W ASN'T IT EDITH Piaf who sang "Je Ne Regrette Rien"? Well, speak for yourself, you silly cow.

Here was someone I'd been able to communicate with, who was funny and intelligent, and on top of all that had really cute knees. And I'd screwed it up. *Je* regretted *beaucoup*.

I didn't want to stay round until the black girl woke up.

From what I could see of her as she lay crashed out, she looked much stronger than me. Real swimmer's shoulders.

Men's shoulders?

I had a quick peek under the duvet from the other end of the bed to make sure. He/she/it was facedown, but I couldn't see any dangly bits between its legs.

Phew.

I was also immensely relieved to discover that I'd played it safe. The long, pink, shriveled appendage hanging off my willy was not a grotesquely stretched foreskin—it was a used condom clinging on where one of us had rolled it a few hours before.

When I got outside two minutes later, I had to screw up my eyes against the unusually bright light. It took me a few moments to realize that summer hadn't barged in in front of winter and spring. The street was lit up by the reflection off the damp, gleaming pavements.

The mounds of paper had gone. The skyscrapers of stinking boxes had been cleared away. An armored division of green cleanup machines had raged through the streets as I slept and swept all resistance before them. The strike was over.

I wanted to share my joy with Alexa, but it was too late. I left at least ten of my most abject apologies ever on her answering machine, and they were all unanswered.

Finally, in a bid to save her phone from overloading, she deigned to send me an au revoir e-mail saying she thought I was a "sad" person and she didn't want the responsibility for my "fragile happiness." Yes, the old *joie-tristesse* crap had come home to roost.

To console myself, I decided to devote November to finding an apartment. Jean-Marie had offered to pay for a hotel for three months, so I needed to start thinking about making a break for freedom. And now that the strike was over, the time was right. Christine told me that the cleaners had given up their demands for mechanical brooms and had accepted a raise plus the promise that once a week they could all have a go at driving one of the green machines. In short, I'd be able to visit places without messing up my future landlord's carpets.

On the first Saturday of the month, I sat down at a café terrace (I now seemed to do all my thinking at café terraces) and consulted my guidebook about places to live.

"In Paris," it said, "it's best to live near a big metro junction."

It's the same in London. Though saying you want to live near the most reliable tube line in London is a bit like saying you want to marry the camel with the sweetest breath.

The guide went on: "The metro is not brilliant everywhere, but in general it's a dream compared to London. For a start, it's cheap—a *carte orange* gives you a full month's unlimited travel on all Parisian buses and underground lines for approximately the cost of a one-hour pass on the London tube. And—get this—if you work in Paris, your employer pays half of it."

What the guide should also have mentioned is that the metro stations are usually full of seminaked women. Take the station near my hotel, for example. First time I went down there, a girl with three-foot-wide breasts was advertising a bra. A girl in a torn T-shirt was advertising a film. Several girls wearing nothing but skimpy thongs were advertising—I don't know what. A drink? Perfume? Vacuum cleaners? Whatever. They had great breasts. The platform walls were covered with nudie posters. How to keep commuters happy when trains are late. Male and lesbian commuters, anyway.

Commuting, I found, was much less stressful than in London. For a start, at rush hours there was a train about every minute. And yes, French minutes have sixty seconds. If you missed one train, you just waited a few seconds for the next one. No sweat. And talking of sweat, contrary to popular belief, the French didn't smell as though they'd been rubbing their armpits with raw garlic. I detected only perfume and aftershave. People were a bit more blank-faced than London commuters, and almost none of them were reading newspapers, but apart from that, the only major difference with London was that if you had to stand, you could actually stand instead of being bent double the way you are on the tube. Why did those London engineers build such tiddly tunnels? Did they think that only hobbits would ride the tube?

In short, Paris has public transport that actually transports the public rather than trying to make them give up and travel by car.

*   *   *

"Whichever metro junction you choose to live near," the guide said, "you should know that Paris apartments are small and packed very densely together. This means that you'll have a *lot* of neighbors. They'll be all around you, above, below, and on each side, in your own building and the ones opposite. You might have ten or more sets of people who can see, broadcast noise, or send smells into your apartment."

Smells? Were they all going to be cooking pig's rectums and using unpasteurized cheese as wallpaper glue?

"The safest thing to do," the guide went on, "is visit an apartment at different times of the day. See what the area's nightlife is like (it can be lively or deadly). Try to get a look at the people upstairs in case it's a family of overweight flamenco-dancing basketballers. Look across the street to the windows opposite (called the *vis-à-vis*) and try to spot telltale binoculars or flashing genitalia.

"But then again, all these precautions are pretty pointless, because if you actually get to the stage where someone is willing to rent you their apartment, you'll weep in gratitude. To get ahead of the dozens of people applying for anywhere decent, you'll have to go to viewings armed with copies of your family's page in *Who's Who* and a guarantee from a Swiss bank that you're sitting on a hoard of Nazi gold. As few people can come up with these documents, you should prepare to start out living in a hovel."

"Pessimist," I said. "Merci."

This last word was said not to my guidebook, but to the waiter who'd brought me a coffee. Well, not so much a coffee as a punch bowl of off white stew. My *merci* turned sour as I said it.

I'd asked for a café au lait and been served the combined annual production of Colombia's coffee fields and the dairy herds of Normandy. I looked at the bill—wow, the price included first-class rail fare for the cows.

It was one of the last aftershocks of shitlexia. To celebrate the fact that I could walk about without getting pooped up, I'd strolled away from my hotel and was now about half a mile closer to the Arc de Triomphe, sitting outside a brasserie with a posh green-and-gold awning and a waiter in a ruthlessly starched apron. Ripoff territory. Should have seen it coming. Too late now.

I picked up my two sources of accommodation ads. The hotel receptionist had recommended the *Figaro* newspaper—a daily with lots of For Sale and To Rent ads—and *De Particulier à Particulier*, a thick weekly magazine full of housing ads for all over France.

Both were spilling over with attractive-looking offers.

If only I could understand them.

"11E Oberkampf," one ad in the *Figaro* said. Okay, so far—Eleventh Arrondissement, Oberkampf district. "2/3P 2è ét, séj av mezz, 1 ch, SdE, parquet." Help.

I got out my dictionary and looked up the one complete word. *Parquet* meant "floorboards." Great, so it had a floor. What the hell did the rest mean?

Another ad offered "11è proche Marais." The dictionary seemed to suggest that this place was situated near a bog. Judging by the rent, it was a very desirable bog. I read on: "3P RdC s/ cour, SdB/WC, dressing."

Cour was courtyard, *WC* was presumably WC, but *dressing*? This one came with vinaigrette on tap? Very gourmet.

No, the dictionary corrected me, a *dressing* was a walk-in closet.

Here was one at Bastille, which was presumably a safe area now that they'd stopped guillotining people. It was a *beau 2 pièces*—beautiful two-roomed apartment. It was *5è étage* (aha, fifth floor, I thought, the *ét* is explained), *ascenseur* (an elevator, thank God), *gde chambre* (big bedroom), *balcon* (a *balcon* of one's own, brilliant) and a *SàM avec cuis amér* (oh shit).

My dictionary told me that this probably meant it was suitable for sadomasochists with bitter (*amer*) thighs (*cuisses*). However, I suspected that this might not be an accurate translation. I was right—in fact, it meant dining room (*salle à manger*) with open-plan kitchen (*cuisine américaine*).

It was only natural to find it hard going, I told myself. After all, flat-share ads in the United Kingdom must be just as impossible to understand for foreigners. All those demands for "N/S only"—foreigners would think there was something very attractive about Nova Scotian roommates.

I picked up my coffee—almost spraining both wrists under the weight—and watched the waiter arrive with another order. It was for a guy a couple of tables along, and it looked like—yes, it was—a normal-size café au lait.

"Merci," the customer said in what even I could tell was a strong American accent. And, to add insult to wrist strain, he was reading the *Herald Tribune*.

"Excuse me," I said, leaning closer. The American looked up from his paper. "How did you do that?"

"Do what?" He frowned. He was thirty-something, with longish Kurt Cobain hair, and was wearing a worn black suit on top of a faded New York University sweatshirt. A ripe target for ripoffs, surely?

I managed to raise my lake-size coffee a little higher. "Get a normal-size coffee?"

The American laughed loudly, a raucous smoker's laugh. He picked up his coffee, bill, and paper and moved to my table.

"I'm Jake," he said, holding out his hand.

"Paul." We shook.

"You on a visit in Paris?" Jake asked, looking down in wonder at the sheer enormity of my coffee cup.

"No, I've been living here for two months. You?"

"Oh yeah, I live here." Jake laughed as if this was a huge joke.

"What, here?" I asked, waving my hand at the neighborhood around us, hoping that this was Jake's regular café—it would make getting ripped off just that little less painful.

"No, I just work round here sometimes. In that bank over there." Jake pointed his newspaper toward the noble-looking building that rounded off the street corner opposite with a sort of ship's prow of columns and curved windows. It didn't look like the kind of place that would employ unshaven grunge guitarists, except maybe in some nocturnal Hoover-pushing role.

"You work *there*?" I failed to keep the skepticism out of my voice.

"Well. I'm sent by my language school one time a week to give English courses."

"On a Saturday?"

"Yeah. Some French banks open on a Saturday."

"They don't make you dress a bit more, you know . . ."

"Nah. You work in a bank?" He jerked his newspaper accusingly at me.

"No, a food company."

Jake nodded meaningfully at my chic shirt and designer jeans. "You like putting on your thirty-ones even on weekends," he said.

"Doing what?"

"You know, dressing up chic. Don't we say that in English? Putting on your thirty-ones? Damn." He snorted in annoyance and asked me what I was doing in Paris. When I told him, his only comment was, "As if Paris needed another café." *Charmant*, I thought.

"You looking for a new apartment?" He flicked at my open *Figaro*. "Where you wanna live?"

"Uh, don't know. Where do you suggest?"

"I live in the Fifteenth."

"What's that like?" I tried to picture it on the snail's shell. Bottom left, I thought.

"Bourgeois as hell," Jake snarled. "You can't advance along the sidewalk without kicking over a baby buggy. It's full of rich white Catholics with 3.6 children."

"Ah."

"The Nineteenth is more abordable."

"More what?"

"Cheap, you know? Affordable." He tapped the tabletop as if to rememorize the word.

"Near the butt place?" Alexa had said the Nineteenth was becoming the new "in" place to live. There was a big urban park with an artificial mountain in the middle and a name that began with "butt."

"Butte de Chaumont? You can't live there. Miles from the metro. And it's a real *balade de dimanche* spot, too."

I looked suitably confused.

"You know, Sunday strollers," he explained. "The hordes lining up to watch their kids have a go on some measly carousel."

"Ah. Not good?"

"Nah." Jake thought for a moment. "For good transport connections, there's Montparnasse, but since you're not a lord, you won't be able to pay yourself the best quartiers. And it's a bit rang-gar."

"It's what?" Jake spoke a very weird kind of English. I was beginning to wonder if he wasn't Cajun or something, his American English mixed with swamp-alligator French.

"Ringard, you know, tacky. Touristy."

"Oh. What about Chatelet?" That was a huge metro junction slap bang in the center of the city.

"Chatelet?" Jake nearly choked on the word. "*Forget* it, man. Too near Les Halles, which could have been the Greenwich Village of Paris, but some so-called architects turned it into a seventies-vintage drug dealers' toilet."

Wow, this bloke was depressing.

"You don't seem to like Paris much, Jake. Why do you stay here?"

"I got stuff to do." He swiveled his cup thoughtfully on its saucer and did a Parisian middle-distance stare. "Damn." He focused back on me again. "Coffee break over. Got to go to my next lesson." He stuffed his folded newspaper into a jacket pocket. "See you around? I come here same time every week."

"Yeah. Sure." Next time I feel like getting suicidal.

Jake was about to leave when he had a thought. "You know the best way to find an apartment?"

"What?"

"Get yourself a Parisian girlfriend and move in."

"Right."

"I'm serious. Most guys do it."

"Yeah, yeah. I've already tried it. I found the right girl but moved into the wrong apartment."

Still, if I couldn't live with Alexa, maybe I could live next door?

I shied away from the certain humiliation of trying to answer one of the small ads by phone and got the metro as far as Oberkampf station. I took the escalator up to street level and did a 360-degree turn in search of an estate agent. It was about midday, and a crush of cars was edging its way up and down the wide boulevard.

I headed toward the rue Oberkampf itself and soon came across a bright yellow shopfront marked "Immoland." In the main window there were photos advertising apartments for sale, with the usual incomprehensible jargon—"triplex RdC s/cour," "SdB + SdE." And in a small section of window by the door, a list marked LOCATIONS. These were not, I knew, suggestions for outdoor filmmakers, but the agency's apartments to rent.

"Bonjour," I said to the guy sitting behind a computer.

"Yes, can I elp yew?" he asked in English. What gave me away, I wondered, the accent or the helpless look?

I explained what I wanted—an apartment to rent, at least till the end of the following August.

"Plizz. Seat down," the guy said, smiling. He was about thirty, with slicked-back blond hair, a Permatan, and a tight brown suit. He looked as if he should have been selling handbags rather than apartments, I thought. In an entirely nonhomophobic way, of course.

He asked me what "surface" I was looking for, which, after a few misunderstandings, turned out not to mean whether I wanted wallpaper or paint on my walls, but how many square meters I wanted.

Unfortunately, understanding the question didn't really help, because I wouldn't have known a square meter if it had slapped me in the face. I mean, I knew what a meter was, but how big was a thirty- or forty-square-meter apartment?

"One bedroom?" I hazarded.

"Separate living?" the agent asked.

"Yes, I'm living alone at the moment." Though I didn't see what business it was of his. I could tell from the way the agent closed one eye and jabbed his pen in his ear that we were in noncommunication mode again.

"Er, separate salon?" the guy asked.

Now he thinks I'm one of a couple of gay hairdressers, I thought. This wasn't going well at all.

"You want one bedroom and one separate uzzer room," the agent tried again. "*Salon* is living, you know? Living room?"

"Ah! Yes. Right. A bedroom and a living room." I nodded encouragingly.

"Okay. I av."

The agent picked up a folder and flicked through its plastic pages. He flopped it open to show me the plan of an apartment with a *chambre*, *séjour*, *cuisine*, and *SdB*, which turned out to be *salle de bains*—bathroom. *SdE*, he explained, was *salle d'eau*—shower room.

"Where is it?" I asked.

"Rue O'bare komf," the agent said.

"Perfect."

"You know zis street?"

"Oh yes." I mimed drinking beer and falling off a table.

"Okay. You want veezit now?"

"I want."

"You ave letters of garron tee?"

"No."

"Uh." (A look of pain.) "Ah." (Thinking hard.) "Oh." (Resignation.) "Ease no problem."

Six hours later, I was still trying to erase the humiliation from my mind.

First, there was the romantic garret with what the agent described as a "super view of roof." It was true—I could see lots of roof. And lots of holes in the roof.

"Is repair very quickly," the agent said.

Was it my imagination, or did the headline on the tattered newspaper blocking one of the holes read: NAPOLÉON EST MORT?

I conceded that the apartment was very conveniently situated for the bars—it was in the same building as a bar that was sending techno beats bouncing up the water pipes.

Another slight problem was that the apartment shared a *squattez-vous* hole-in-the-floor toilet on the landing with eight other romantic garrets, one of which was apparently inhabited by a blind man with dysentery.

"Ze concierge, she don't clean yet today," the agent said.

This might have been true, but even without the techno beats and the disgusting toilet, it could never have been my dream home for one simple reason—the flat was almost literally flat. I couldn't stand up in it. Well, not exactly true. I could stand in the doorway, but if I took a step forward, I hit my forehead on the ceiling that sloped down to floor level about three yards away. It was a triangular wedge in which you'd have to walk at forty-five degrees to avoid a fractured skull.

"It is not expon-seeve," the agent said.

"It is not an apartment," I said. "It is a storage cupboard for Toblerone."

The second place was a cave. Strictly speaking, in French *cave* means "cellar." But this place really was a cave.

From the street, we went through an immense wooden door into a cobbled courtyard—very picturesque. The walls around us were high and crumbling and festooned with reddening ivy—very quaint. In one corner of the courtyard there was an old wooden door, much less immense than the first one, into which the agent inserted a four-inch-long iron key—*très* exciting. The door creaked open and he reached inside for a light switch. I heard the click but didn't see the light.

"Is to be re-noved," the agent said, peering into the darkness. "Soon it will av more electricity."

"Yes, I think it needs a *lot* more."

We stepped inside onto an earth floor in which you could have planted potatoes.

"Soon will have beautiful floor," the agent said. "Window, every-sing."

In the windowless gloom I could make out bare stone walls and a pile of packing cases that might well have been coffins. Had the last resident been a certain Monsieur Dracula? I wondered.

"You sign contract now and when you arrive it will have every-sing in it."

"I sign contract now and my brain has nothing in it."

The third apartment already had everything, the agent assured me. A floor, windows, electricity, a very big bathroom.

He wasn't lying. It did have a very big bathroom. It *was* a very big bathroom. Equipped with a bed and a gas stove, two wooden chairs stacked in a corner, and a short, wide plank. Not forgetting an immense, seven-foot-long enamel bathtub that took up almost half of the room. I tried not to laugh or cry.

"What's the plank for?" I asked.

The agent put the plank across the bathtub and placed a chair on either side of it in the bath, facing each other.

"Dinner table," he said.

I exhaled slowly and deeply.

"You see this?" I said, pointing to the label on my shirt. "You see this?" I turned to show the agent the brand tag on my jeans. "You see—" I broke off from pointing at my feet when I remembered I'd put on one of my pairs of North Korean trainers, which were decorated with a distinctly Asian-looking Harry Potter.

"I don't have to live in caves or bathrooms," I told the agent. "I can afford an apartment. You said you were going to show me one with a bedroom, a living room, and a bathroom."

The agent did a guilt-free Parisian shrug. "But you tell me you av no letters of guarantee. Wizout, you must live in a bathroom. You want zis or not?"

Not. *Merci* all the same.

First thing on Monday, I went to see Jean-Marie, who'd said he might be able to help me out if I was looking for an apartment.

He wasn't coming in this morning, Christine told me. He was seeing the *ministre de l'agriculture*.

"Why?" No doubt to get a spanking about importing *le boeuf anglais*.

"He will get a medal for supporting French agriculture."

Christine beamed as if it was her own dad getting the honor.

"A medal?" I had to work so hard to suppress my snort of disbelief that I could feel the irony dribbling out of my ears.

Jean-Marie came in that afternoon and showed us his medal. He opened up a blue leather presentation box stamped with a crest and "La République Française." Inside, on a bed of white silk, there was a round bronze medal, embossed with a collage of various types of livestock and food plants. A certificate in the lid of the box announced that Monsieur Jean-Marie Martin had been elected a *chevalier de la culture bovine*.

While Christine cooed over the medal, I asked Jean-Marie what *chevalier de la culture bovine* meant, exactly.

"Knight of beef culture."

"Beef culture?" So he'd been knighted for services to cow cinema?

"I see you are confused." He broke off from looking pleased with himself for a second. "This word *culture* has two senses. We say *la culture du thé*, tea growing. In French it can mean culture, like art and fiction, or agriculture."

Of course. Anyone who examines France's claims for European Union subsidies can see all too clearly the confusion in French minds between fiction and agriculture.

"Okay, I see. You've been made a sir for services to the French beef industry."

"Yes, I suppose I am now Sir Jean-Marie." He laughed and went back to looking pleased with himself.

The man was amazing. No blushes here, no hint of hypocrisy. I had to admit it was a class act.

When Christine had returned to her own office, I told Jean-Marie about my housing problem. He had no time to discuss it now, he said, but he wanted me to come over to his apartment for dinner the following Saturday.

"My wife said I am neglecting you. You are here more than a month and I didn't invite you to dinner? She is right. I am a bad host. I am sorry."

He put his hand on my shoulder and begged me to allow him to repair the damage.

I suppose it was logical, really. In France, treason is a far less heinous crime than a breach of dinner etiquette.

It was lucky for me that Jean-Marie had put me in a hotel so close to his apartment, because that Saturday, the Paris transport workers went on strike.

And what was this strike about? Job cuts? Safety standards? No.

The unions were furious that the government had been rumored to be thinking about considering the possibility of maybe looking into the purely theoretical concept that it might one day (not now, but in, say, eighty years' time) be less able to pay for transport workers to retire at fifty.

Wow, I told myself, let's go to the transport company HQ this very instant to get a job application form.

Dammit, though, I couldn't get there—there was a transport strike.

Anyway, on that Saturday night I wasn't too inconvenienced by the transport strike. It was a fifteen-minute stroll to Sir Jean-Marie's place. The only obstacle was Big Army Avenue.

Both the metro line and the parallel suburban line were closed, so the main road into Paris from the west was totally jammed.

Eight lanes of gridlocked cars—four in either direction. They were hooting plaintively, like whales in a pod calling out to reassure the others that they're not alone in this vast ocean of tarmac.

But as soon as I'd crossed the road and coughed the pollution out of my lungs, I was in a different world. Behind the row of cafés, shops, and offices that ran along the highway, there were silent, leafy streets that were almost totally free of traffic. In place of the uniform Parisian lines of six-floor apartment buildings, these streets were interspersed with large town houses and private gardens.

After about three hundred yards I came to a wide avenue, overlooked by a line of chic apartment buildings. Not all of them in great taste—there were some tacky 1970s constructions with long, colored balcony rails. But there were also the type of supersmart nineteenth-century blocks that you could imagine King Edward VII buying as a pied-à-terre for his racy racing weekends at the nearby Longchamps course.

I'd have to sell a few zillion cups of tea to be able to live here.

But burgers were obviously profitable enough, thank you. This was *chez* Jean-Marie.

His building was almost the exact opposite of the ones I had visited with the estate agent. There was no peeling plaster and rotting wood. It was probably cleaner and in better repair than the day it was finished. The cream stone looked as if the concierge scaled the walls every morning with a bucket of water strapped to her apron.

It overlooked the Bois de Boulogne, the immense wooded park where toffs go riding and Brazilians earn the cash for their sex-change operations. About as exclusive a Paris address as you can get.

There was a six-digit code to get into the entrance hall, which had a carpeted marble floor and spotless white walls with ornate plaster moldings running around the ceiling cornice. Everything smelled of money and wax polish. At the end of the entrance hall, there was a thick glass door with an entry phone. Only ten names—the apartments had to be enormous. Unless some of the residents were so exclusive that they didn't even want their names on the bell push.

I rang and announced my arrival to the videocamera above the glass door.

"Montez, c'est au cinquième," said a smooth female voice. Madame, presumably.

The lift's outer door was a heavy iron gate, the inner doors were varnished walnut, with engraved glass. The lift rose slowly, creakingly, up into the heart of the building. It felt like riding through an antique shop in a Louis XV wardrobe.

Jean-Marie was waiting to open the lift door, a huge welcoming grin on his face.

"Come in, come in," he gushed. "Ah, flowers! My wife will be instantly in love with you." He pointed to the tiny bouquet that I had bought for a small fortune at the florist's near my hotel. At that price I hoped they were an endangered species.

Jean-Marie showed me into a lounge the size of a football pitch. It was decorated with a mixture of antique exuberance and modern restraint. Gold-lacquered, embroidered armchairs alongside a black leather sofa. Black-and-gray abstract print next to a medieval-looking oil of a cow.

Set in the middle of this was a woman who epitomized the posh de la posh. Blond, shoulder-length hair, immense pearls, Dior-style cardigan over an impeccably simple linen dress, and a figure that had been bolstered against aging by the best surgeon in Europe. She walked to meet me, holding out her hand at what was almost certainly the Académie Française's prescribed wrist angle.

She shook (or rather pressed) hands, said she was *enchantée*, and accepted my micro-bouquet with almost no hint that she thought it a soupçon less than spectacular.

She begged me to sit on the sofa while she went to get a vase and ordered Jean-Marie to offer their guest a drink immediately.

Behind the socially charming exterior, you sensed the steeliness of a lady who would protect her public reputation with a Louis Vuitton baseball bat.

She returned with an art deco porcelain creation that would sell for the price of a car in the Portobello Road, and what I assumed were her two children.

The male was a student, that much was clear. Faded jeans, baggy but expensively logoed T-shirt, black hair trying to get up the courage to grow into dreadlocks, bare feet.

He shook my hand limply, and Jean-Marie introduced him as Benoît.

The girl he introduced as Élodie was altogether more interesting. Blond like her mum, but with none of the baseball bat. From the look of her clothes, she shared her mum's credit card but not her classic tastes. Élodie was all skintight designer labels and visible lingerie—intricately lacy black bra straps and, I later saw, proudly displayed thong waistband. The kind of woman my friend Chris had warned me about. Yum. She crushed my hand almost numb.

"Élodie is studying at Ashersay," Jean-Marie said. Sounded like some obscure English university, and when I didn't look sufficiently impressed, it was explained to me that this was HEC, France's most expensive business school. I raised the necessary eyebrow in Élodie's direction and was rewarded with a very pleasant smile.

"And Benoît is studying medicine." Jean-Marie made it sound like a punishment.

"Non, Papa." Benoît grinned and informed his dad that he'd just changed over to biology.

"Biology!"

This was something of a surprise to Jean-Marie, so, as we all sipped champagne and nibbled on petits fours, they had a family row about when the son (who was twenty-four, apparently) would get round to deciding what to do with his life, with Jean-Marie occasionally breaking off into English and asking me things like "What were you doing when you were twenty-four?" before returning to harangue his offspring again.

The daughter seemed to think this was all very humorous and kept giving me "Don't worry, it's like this all the time" smiles. She had a very cute way of eating petits fours, I noticed. Dainty but greedy.

I think I used all the right cutlery at dinner. Well, I didn't need any for the oysters. I just followed the others' example and squeezed some lemon juice into the open shells (the oysters were still alive and flinched) before tipping the contents down my throat.

It was not unpleasant. A bit like swallowing lemony, salty bronchial mucus.

I had a serrated knife for the almost raw beef—bought, the mum assured me, from her "divine" local butcher. I just hoped Jean-Marie wasn't his supplier.

When I'd finished this and wiped the blood off my lips, I was given vegetables. A *gratin dauphinois*—that is, potatoes cooked in a nutmeggy milk sauce under a cheese crust—and some green beans that were almost drowning in butter.

I avoided committing the social gaffe of cutting the points off the dribbling wedges of Camembert and Brie with my small rounded knife and went for a beautifully pungent cheese called Cantal. It tasted like a soft Cheddar, with just a hint of athlete's foot.

Finally, I used an expensive silver fork and spoon on my *gâteau mi-cuit au chocolat*—a chocolate sponge pudding that, like the beef, was uncooked in the middle. It was like oral sex with extra cocoa butter.

In between groans of pleasure, I fielded the usual questions about England.

"Does your mother really make your Christmas pudding six months in advance?" From Madame.

"Do all English pubs have strip-teasers?" From Benoît.

"Is it very easy for a young man to get a job in London if he is too lazy to finish a university diploma?" From the provocative Jean-Marie.

"Are Englishmen scared of women?" From the even more provocative Élodie.

*   *   *

We sat on the sofa and talked about my accommodation problems.

Élodie giggled at my adventures with the estate agent and immediately leapt in with a solution.

"He can sleep with me!"

I almost tipped my coffee over my groin. Madame looked tempted to empty her cup down there, too.

Élodie was just being provocative, of course. "I have a room in my apartment. Paul can have that." She spoke excellent English.

"But your apartment isn't at all expensive, you don't need anyone to help you pay for it," Madame objected in French. I was okay as a dinner guest, it seemed, but she didn't trust me to be satisfied with sharing just a fridge with her daughter.

"Yes, Maman, it costs almost nothing, so it will cost Paul only half of nothing."

"Is it your apartment?" I asked Jean-Marie, giving him the chance to veto the idea.

"No, it is Paris's apartment," Élodie interrupted. "I am a poor, underprivileged student, so I live in a poor, underprivileged apartment. It is like—what do they call them in the Bronx? You know, the projects."

Ah, the princess slumming it. I could picture the place—no roof, a smelly hole for a toilet, a mud floor. No thanks, I'd been there, done that.

"Well, I'm very grateful, Élodie, but—"

"I will take you there. When do you want to come? What's your phone number?" Élodie's business school seemed to give a lot of weight to assertiveness classes.

I refused her offer of a lift home. Call me old-fashioned, but I don't bed the boss's daughter on the first date. Not in the middle of a traffic jam, anyway.

But when she called me next morning, I agreed to come and visit her apartment as soon as the metro strike was over.

Meanwhile, it was a waste of time trying to get anywhere around the city center outside walking distance, unless you had the patience of a hunger striker or the aggression of an American football player who's just been called a pussy.

Driving—forget it. Jean-Marie offered to run me to the office, but he was leaving at six in the morning to beat the jams.

Biking and inline skating—not bad, as long as you stuck to the sidewalks and were willing to kill pedestrians.

Bus and metro—for gladiators only. This was the subtly sadistic thing about the strike. It wasn't a total lockdown. The members of some unions kept working, so you had a skeleton service on some routes, which attracted huge masses of desperate commuters and were very soon in real danger of being littered with skeletons.

Parisian commuters take their fast, efficient transport service for granted. So if the bus and metro go slower than usual, they get irritated. And if said bus or metro has to wait at every stop for ten minutes while people wanting to get off, get on, or stay on gouge one another's eyes out with briefcases, the atmosphere is a lot less sedate than usual.

So I made sure my Walkman had a fresh supply of batteries, picked a quiet route away from the pollution-spitting jams, and went for a long morning walk to work. As I strode briskly through the Bois de Boulogne, I even exchanged nods and hellos with my fellow foot sloggers, and they responded instead of staring at the middle distance. It was getting to be fun.

At which time, of course, the strike ended. The last thing the transport workers wanted was for people to start getting by without them.

So one morning we all turned back into mute commuters.

This was my cue to go and check out Élodie's place.

Her building was as much like social housing as Chanel No. 5 is like the emanations from a marathon runner's socks.

For a start, it was slap bang in the middle of the Marais, which was not the bog that my dictionary had told me about, but the hypertrendy medieval center of the city, awash with cafés, clothes shops, and stores selling décor accessories that only gay men understand what to do with. There was also one estate agent per square meter, all with slavering clients window-shopping. And here I was, waltzing in effortlessly.

The apartment building itself was fairly modern—1930s, I guessed, made of pale orange brick, in better repair than any brickwork I'd ever seen, with every bit of grunting or groping or whatever they do around bricks in perfect condition. The windows were tall, with glossily painted white metal shutters and small balconies. The art deco ironwork on the balcony railings was decorated with what looked like giant sperm but were probably meant to be flowers. Real red flowers were tumbling from window boxes in front of several of the windows.

"These can't really be social housing," I said.

"Oh, yes, they are." Élodie was enjoying my stupefaction (and relief) that she wasn't inviting me to doss down with a bunch of dealers and social outcasts. "They're ashlem," she announced.

"They're what?" It sounded like some sort of oriental commune. Oh no, I thought, not compulsory yoga at six every morning.

"H.L.M." She spelled it out in English. "It means habitation à loyer modéré or something like that. Low-cost apartments." She giggled. "Although all the residents are lawyers, doctors, etc. Or the sons and daughters and friends of politicians. Papa got me this apartment from a friend at the Hôtel de Ville. You know, the City Hall?"

"Cheap housing set aside for the chronically overprivileged?"

"If you prefer, you can live in that cave."

"No, no, my goal in life is to become chronically overprivileged."

We entered an astoundingly clean-smelling concrete courtyard and were promptly attacked by a dustbin.

A small, round, dark-haired woman emerged from behind the green wheelie bin and barked at Élodie in a language that sounded like Spanish being spoken by a Dutchman. She then sulked away through the lace-curtained door marked CONCIERGE.

"She wasn't telling you that you're not allowed to have male guests, was she?" I asked.

Élodie almost wet herself laughing at this suggestion. I took it as a no.

If the concierge did object to Élodie inviting men home, she probably had a very busy, and totally pointless, time of it, because no sooner had we stepped inside the apartment than Élodie was clamped to my mouth like some kind of oversize lip gloss.

She really had taken her M.B.A. course to heart. Sex for her was like a business model.

We did some swift, efficient asset stripping, carried out the required amount of research and development, and then I was invited to position my product in her niche market. I did my best to satisfy her high demand with as much supply as I could muster. After a period of violently fluctuating market penetration, the bubble finally burst and we sank back, our sales forces completely spent.

"I'll show you your room," she said about ten seconds after the market had collapsed.

How to take the shine off a guy's post-orgasmic glow. Mind you, I had to admit she was much more welcoming than the last estate agent I'd met.

So there I was, in clover. I had a cheap, sunlit room in the heart of the city. No housework, because part of Jean-Marie's deal with his daughter was that she got hot-and-cold-running cleaning lady. And I had a kitchen again, which would be fun—it'd been a long time since anyone had tasted my pasta surprise (surprise—I forgot to put salt in the water).

And on top of all this, whenever Élodie got bored with business theory, she invited me to her room to give her spreadsheets a going-over.

La belle vie à Paris or what?

Even the concierge was doing her bit to make my life easy. The language she had spat at Élodie was Portuguese. The old French concierges from Maigret stories are gone these days, replaced by cleaning subcontractors or Portuguese families with second jobs, working in France to finance the construction of big houses back home.

Madame Da Costa had given up on talking French to Élodie, because like all the other posh tenants in the building, Élodie never took any notice. Élodie's bad habit, it seemed, was to leave her rubbish bags out on the landing overnight. When they leaked, it was the concierge who had to clean up.

Madame Da Costa was a brutally efficient concierge—she got toxic chemicals free from her second job as an office cleaner, and every Sunday night she and her husband and son attacked the hallway and staircase, taking lumps out of the plaster with their broom and leaving the place smelling like a lemon juice factory.

However, this didn't stop her stinking everyone out most evenings with a glutinous cloud of frying-fish odor that crept under doors and through any chinks in the brickwork. You'd be sitting in your living room watching TV when suddenly you felt as if your head was being slowly jammed into a bucket of tepid cod-liver oil.

She took a shine to me because I said "*bonjour*" and meant it. Also because I, like her, was foreign. She was very careful to make sure that I got my foreign mail. Plus the foreign mail addressed to all the other residents of the building. If it had a foreign stamp or a foreign name on the envelope, it must be for me. Of course, I wasn't going to contradict her. I just used to creep out of the door at night and discreetly redistribute the mail that wasn't for me. It was worth the trouble to keep in her good books.

I wasn't the only guy getting samples of Élodie's merchandise, but that didn't bother me overmuch, even when my attempts at sleep were disturbed by her rhythmic yelping through the dividing wall.

And it was lucky I didn't have an exclusivity deal, because one Saturday morning, as I sat in the kitchen willing my espresso to hurry up and finish pouring itself, who should walk in but Jean-Marie.

I wasn't naked, but I'd only pulled on a pair of jeans, which were unbuttoned and showing hair.

I could see the question framing in Jean-Marie's mind: Where and with whom had I slept?

Then in came Élodie, wearing nothing but smeared lipstick and a man's shirt. Bad timing.

"Bonjour, Papa." She kissed him.

"Morning, Paul." She kissed me, which she didn't usually do in the mornings. Jean-Marie narrowed his eyes at me.

"Oh, Papa, Paul, this is Chico."

In wandered my salvation in the form of a towering angel. A seven-foot-tall Latino supermodel type, all hair gel and cheek-bones, totally naked, circumcised, and proud of it.

It was pretty clear who'd been shagging whom.

"Chico, chéri, this is my father. Why don't you go and put on some clothes?"

Chico made sure we'd seen his all-over suntan, then ambled out again. I could have sworn he had shaven buttocks.

"I hope Chico and I didn't keep you awake last night, Paul."

"Doing what?" I raised my eyes toward Jean-Marie, making it clear that I was suffering as much as he was. We're in this together, boss.

"Can I . . . ?" Jean-Marie's voice trailed off. He switched to French. "I have to speak to you, Élodie."

My ten-liter mug of espresso was ready now, so I sugared it up and sucked some life into my system while father and daughter went and had a hissing match in the corridor. Chico didn't return. Probably didn't know how to dress himself.

I tried to listen in on the row, expecting to pick up some new French words for paternal humiliation, but they seemed to be arguing about *le dressing*.

Was this a French euphemism? I wondered. You're letting too many boys into your walk-in closet?

She told him to keep out of her closet, that much I understood. She'd probably been punishing the credit card and he wanted to get a refund on one of her five new pairs of gold-soled Gaultier trainers.

"I have the key," he said. So maybe he just wanted permission to come over occasionally and try on some frocks.

In any case, after a swift exchange of threats and rebuttals, Jean-Marie left and Élodie came back in the kitchen, flushed and mumbling Gallic insults.

I had noticed her *dressing* before. I woke up in the middle of the night in her bed once, and there was a light glowing under the closet door. I went to switch it off, but the door was locked.

Weird, I thought. Did she think I was going to steal her underwear?

Still, I wasn't going to criticize my landlady. I'm sure I was getting a much better deal than most Parisian tenants.

I couldn't resist going to Jake's café and bragging about my success at finding a Paris apartment.

He was impressed. Not so much because I was moving in with a woman, but because I was subletting in an HLM, getting one over on the Parisian establishment.

Jake was finishing work early that Saturday morning and offered to take me to "the best store in Paris." Why not, I thought, envisaging maybe a cut-price record shop with free beer and topless counter assistants.

Turned out, though, to be a bloody secondhand bookshop.

It was cute enough, housed in a timber-framed medieval building just opposite Notre Dame. Inside, it was pleasantly stuffy and smelled mustily of the books that thrust themselves at you from all angles. They covered most of the floor, climbed up the walls, and hung from the ceiling like dead, dusty bats. All of them were in English.

Jake said hi to the dopey-looking young bloke sitting at the cash register and beckoned me through to the back of the shop.

We went up a narrow staircase, also carpeted and wallpapered with books that threatened to take your eye out if you didn't watch where you were going.

"Not many people come up here," Jake said. I could see why. Unless they were really determined to get their skull fractured by a dusty copy of *Beyond History: A Metaphilosophical View of American Empire Building*, volume 4.

We climbed to the second floor, still with no sign of the book infestation abating, and arrived in a low, beamed room where five people were squatting at window seats or on piles of encyclopedias.

This, Jake told me, was his writing group. Three Americans, a Brit, and an Australian were there today—two men and three women, a mix of arty Jake clones and preppier types, age range about twenty to thirty-five. I was the only one who didn't have a folder of writing with me. They all registered this fact as I was introduced.

I sat on *Beelzebub-Cretinism* and listened to a woman explaining her novel in progress. Something about two girls finding themselves through masturbation. I wouldn't have minded seeing the film, but the book was hard going. She read us a couple of pages that almost put me off sex for life. We all had to give a verdict, too.

"Great idea," I said when it was my turn. "Chick lit's all the rage, isn't it?"

The writer let her head slump in despair. "It's not chick lit, it's a women's novel. Chick lit is just a meaningless phrase dreamt up by marketing people." She pronounced "marketing" the way Saddam Hussein probably said "George W. Bush."

"Good move, though," I said. "Women read a lot more than men. Bigger market."

The room was filled with groaning and head slumping.

Next up, Jake got his folder out of his bag and read us some poems about vaginas he had known. They were all really into telling us about their sexual habits, these writers, who (in my humble opinion) were some of the least sexy people I'd seen in Paris outside of the lines for a bed at the Salvation Army night shelter.

Jake's writing project was a cycle of poems about shagging every nationality of woman living in Paris. His latest offering was a fifty-line ode to the difficulties of getting it on with an Albanian—all under the thumb of vicious pimps, it seemed.

"Why not just pay the poor girl and get it over with?" I pleaded.

"No, man, I never pay. Where's the poetry in that?"

"How about: It cost only a nickel, for slap and tickle?"

"Yeah. Right."

"Or: To pay for her tummy tuck, she charged me to—"

"You seem to be doing enough travel screwing yourself, Paul. I don't know why you're giving me this shit."

He explained my living circumstances to everyone. The rent, the location, the compulsory sex.

The masturbator woman was shocked. Or envious. "That's profiteering. You know who those apartments are supposed to be for?"

They all went into a frenzy of one-upmanship, comparing their leaky roofs, pissed-in staircases, cockroaches, burglaries, and shitty salaries, if they had any salary at all.

"I bet heating's included in the rent, isn't it," an Australian woman said.

"Dunno," I confessed with a Parisian shrug.

It was the shrug that got them. I knew as I did it that it was infinitely more annoying than my ham-fisted attempts at literary criticism.

I was politely asked to leave. Then told to fuck off.

I got down the stairs without fracturing my skull and almost body-charged Alexa out of the door.

"Alexa."

She was looking as secretly gorgeous as ever. She blushed and kissed me chastely on the cheek. "Paul. How are you?"

"What are you doing here?"

"I can read, you know."

I nodded. I didn't know what to say. Or rather I did but didn't dare say it.

We went to the café next door—a bit of a tourist ripoff place, but I didn't care for once—and talked.

She was well, she assured me each of the ten times I asked her. Her dad?

Her dad was still gay and heartbroken, thank you.

"Right. God, Alexa. That night—"

"It doesn't matter."

"It does to me. Look. I don't think 'I was drunk at the time' is ever a really convincing excuse. But how about 'I was comatose at the time'?" She accorded me a smile. "That woman must have carried me home under her arm. I don't know who she was. I haven't seen her since. I don't know what we did. I only know that I woke up with a condom hanging from the end of my—"

"A condom? So you . . .?"

"I suppose so. I have no idea. I went to a hypnotist, but he said there weren't even any subconscious memories to dredge up."

I earned another smile.

"It was a nonevent, Alexa. A horrific accident."

"Hmm." She changed the subject, asked where I was living these days. I explained my good fortune. Though I may have omitted to mention Élodie.

"You got an HLM from your corrupt boss?" She laughed wholeheartedly. "Since you stopped walking in merde, you have become a real Parisian."

The teasing look was back in her eyes.

One coffee and one taxi ride later, we were in her loft, which took up the whole top floor of a superb converted industrial building in a leafy courtyard.

The sunlight was streaming in through a wall of windows.

"My parents lived here before they divorced. It was my father's first photographic studio."

"Holy shit, what did he photograph in here—cruise ships?"

However, we didn't hang around to compare our apartments' surface areas. We climbed a metal spiral staircase up to her bedroom, and there I finally saw all of her. From every angle at once—the walls were covered with artistic nude self-portraits.

She undressed, and I saw the 3-D version, too. She was everything my imagination had promised me, but with smells and tastes and softness and—at last—a bit of emotion.

We got to know each other's every curve and blemish and spent as much time kissing as doing anything else, breathing our breathlessness into each other.

She was a girl who shared her body rather than insisting I give it an overhaul. She whispered to me in French, whereas Élodie barked orders in perfect English.

"Là, là, là." It was as if she was singing me toward her most sensitive spots.

"Aaaaaah," I sighed, auditioning for an ad for automatic foot massagers.

I usually feel the need to make a fond little joke after coming, but this time I couldn't utter a word.

We lay silently sweating on top of her duvet, which was not

blinding white but bright orange, and I felt as if I'd finally come home.

"Paul?" She broke the silence a full two or three minutes later. "What do you think . . . ?"

Yes. She was going to ask me to move in. I wouldn't hesitate for a second. I'd even agree to do some housework.

Hey, I thought, maybe I could sublet my room at Élodie's place? Turn it into a sublet sublet.

Wanted, one male lodger to share apartment and landlady's vagina. Centrally heated, great location. (Apartment's not bad, either. Ho ho ho.)

Now all I had to do was work out the French abbreviations for the ad.

DÉCEMBRE

God Save the Cuisine

IN FRENCH, THE word *self* means self-service restaurant. Ironic, really—the ego as cheap cafeteria, when France sees itself as one huge gourmet restaurant.

It's a pretty apt description, though, because contrary to what they'd like us to think, the French love fast food. They tell the world that they eat only foie gras and truffles, but a huge percentage of them spend their lunchtimes and weekends with their faces in a hamburger.

This is because fast-food restaurants do things to food that the French love. Staff in uniform, repeating little set phrases, arranging your napkin just so on your tray. It all appeals to the French sense of ceremony. Like it or not, a trip to a fast-food place is a culinary event.

This French love of food events is so great that it sends them completely insane when they go to the *boulangerie* to buy bread. The *boulangerie* is the only place in the world where the French will stand patiently in line. No, not true—they do it in the line to buy cigarettes at the *tabac*, but that's only out of fear of getting ripped to bits by someone on nicotine cold turkey.

A visit to my local *boulangerie* was a real event. There were usually three or four women serving, or rather jostling with one another behind the cramped counter. They would dash around putting together my order, then had to queue themselves to tell the one woman on the till, the owner, how much I owed. Whenever I bought a baguette, the person who served me, and the owner, too, had the right to squeeze it in the middle, as if they were addicted to the cracking sound the crust made. If I bought a cake, I could expect to wait a full five minutes while it was lovingly gift-wrapped and decorated with a ribbon. Occasionally, a floury baker would emerge to watch the proceedings and be shooed away by his wife in case he got flour in the till. Amid the chaos, the line shuffled forward respectfully, even though it often stretched for yards outside the shop. People seemed to respect the system here simply because it was part of a food ritual.

Apparently I wasn't showing enough respect for such rituals.

"You're not really interested in food, are you." As if to make sure I heard the question, a naked female breast was jabbed in my ear. "I am making a wonderful raclette and you are not interested."

This was Élodie, adding a whole new layer to the French taste for food ceremony by wandering around the kitchen wearing nothing but a thong and a smile. It was early December, but there was not a single goose bump visible on Élodie's skin, most of which was in fact visible. This was because heating was included in the rent for the HLM after all, and she kept it permanently turned up so high that nudity or seminudity was the only way of avoiding heat exhaustion.

I was sitting—modestly dressed in shorts and a T-shirt—over a chilled glass of Apremont, a crisp white wine from the mountainous Savoie region that goes very well with cheese dishes. It was my third glass, which probably explained why I was fumbling so uselessly as I tried to assemble the cooking implement that was going to enable us to eat this "wonderful raclette."

The *grand magasin* (department store) near Élodie's place had a huge selection of the most intricate cooking implements in the Western world. They had *éclade* sets, which allow you to arrange mussels on their ends (yes, their ends) and cook them dry in a traditional west coast fashion. There were mini-*raclette* sets—grills with small frying pans in which you melt thick slices of Raclette cheese that you then pour over boiled potatoes, and bigger *raclette* sets that melt one edge of a great chunk of cheese that you slice off with a sort of guillotine. It's no wonder that the French make such good engineers—you need a degree in industrial design just to cook dinner.

I was battling with a big *raclette* set, trying desperately to keep my fingers out of reach of the blade. Élodie had bought a slab of Raclette the size of half a Mini wheel.

"Would you prefer a peanut-butter sandwich, huh?"

If I didn't answer to defend my nation's honor, it was because I'd just impaled my hand on the teeth that were going to hold the cheese in place and was gazing at my fingers in horror, wondering which ones were about to drop off.

"Or salmon from a can?"

"No. Look, Élodie, I am passionately interested in what we're cooking here. But I don't think the recipe includes amputated finger or boiled tit. Why don't you assemble this bear trap and I'll see to the potatoes." Even worse than the pain now throbbing through my fingers was the idea of all that bare skin getting scalded by the jumble of potatoes dancing around in the pot. I was the one who'd have to rub cream into the blistered bits. And I knew where that would lead.

"Yes, that is one thing you English know how to do in the kitchen—you boil everything."

"That's not true. It's just an old cliché. British cuisine has come a long way since then."

"*Cuisine?* Huh! How has it come a long way?"

"We don't boil everything anymore. These days we microwave it."

We changed places. She sat at the kitchen table, I went and forked the potatoes to test how they were coming along.

It was undeniably pleasant cooking a meal with a beautiful young girl wearing only two square millimeters of clothing, but I would have preferred it to be another girl. A dressed girl, even. Trouble was, Alexa hadn't invited me to move in with her.

The question she was so keen to ask as we lay in her bed wasn't about us living together. She'd asked whether I thought two people who speak different languages can really communicate. I mean, intellectual or what?

My response—a shocked, disappointed silence—probably confirmed her doubts.

So now we were more or less officially a couple but living apart, with me doing my best to wriggle out of Élodie's invitations. I told Élodie that I had a girlfriend, but it amused her to carry on asking me to perform bedtime aerobics, and she hardly ever wore more around the apartment than she would have done in a lingerie shop changing room. She pretended to be in a huff about my resistance, but I don't think she really cared. There wasn't a drop of self-doubt in her blood. She regularly brought home blokes that *Vogue* readers would slaver over.

"Merde!" She was having just as much trouble with the *raclette* set as I'd had, with the difference that it was now a breast rather than a finger that was in danger of getting amputated.

"Why don't you go and get dressed and I'll finish that."

"Stupid, silly machine!" She threw the half-assembled contraption onto the table and drained my glass of wine. She showed no signs of going to get dressed, which was a shame because Alexa was due to arrive in five minutes and might be surprised to see that my landlady was actually a nubile nudist rather than the "boring business school student" I'd described.

"I'll go and get your clothes from the dressing, shall I? Just tell me what to bring."

"Uh? Oh. No, it's okay. I'll go and get dressed."

I checked over the other things on our menu. The lettuce—fresh, not from a bag—was washed and wrapped in a tea towel in the fridge, waiting to be torn—not sliced—into pieces that were just small enough to be picked up on a fork and eaten without cutting. In France, cutting your lettuce when it's on your plate is punishable by death.

I'd followed Élodie's recipe for the dressing—one tablespoon of vinegar, in which the salt had dissolved, a teaspoon or so of mustard mixed in, then three tablespoons of olive oil. I had no choice about following her recipe, because she'd resorted to physical assault when I threatened to digress.

"No, salt in the vinegar. Salt in the vinegar!" She pinched my arm viciously. "Wait until it dissolves. Wait!" She was as much a dominatrix in the kitchen as in the bed.

Two dozen microthin slices of raw ham were fanned out on a huge plate like the cards in a game of cholesterol poker. They were dark red, almost black in places. I was sure my local supermarket in the United Kingdom would have thrown them out for being in an advanced state of putrefaction, but Élodie said they were perfect, and I was too scared of her to say different. There was a cheese platter on the kitchen table that I'd inadvisably tried to stow in the fridge.

"In the fridge? You don't put cheese in the fridge! You'll kill it!" Élodie clearly thought that the bacteria had a right to live and breed.

My only real doubt was the dessert. This was my *typiquement anglais* contribution to the menu, and I was having second thoughts about it, even though I'd gone to a lot of trouble to get the ingredients.

It's true that if a black mound of Christmas pudding is not part of your family history, then Britain's main contribution to the festive season can look a bit like something that has leaked from an oil tanker.

But steaming and topped with a radish leaf? (I couldn't find any holly.)

"Come on, girls, you're overreacting."

Alexa and Élodie were recoiling in horror, as if the pudding was about to explode or talk to them in some alien language.

But this was true to form for the evening. Contrary to my fears, they'd bonded. Bonded against me and all things English, true, but bonded anyway.

"And what is *that*?" Alexa groaned when I poured my only slightly lumpy custard into a serving jug.

"It is Englishman's blood," Élodie pronounced. "Coagulated and without color."

"Just try some, you'll like it." I produced a half bottle of whiskey and a lighter so that I could douse the pudding with flaming alcohol.

"You are right. It is best to incinerate it before it does any damage," Alexa said.

They refused to even taste it, so I was forced by a mixture of male pride, patriotism, and genetic imbecility to consume the whole half-pound pudding and a pint of custard while the girls kept up their running commentary on English eating habits.

"I heard that basketballs are made out of English cheese."

"And English sausages are made out of old socks."

My only replies to this provocation were custardy globs.

"Fish and chips—why do you cook perfectly good fish inside a biscuit?"

"And what is this mint jelly you eat with meat? Shouldn't you eat it on toast for breakfast?"

"Ah no," I globbed, my digestive system now on the verge of erupting with pudding lava, "mint sauce with meat is one of the best combinations we ever invented." My praise of culinary refinement was spoiled by a loud and uncontrollable hiccup.

"I know it is traditional in England to be sick in the street, so please put your head out of the window if you are feeling nauseated," Élodie warned me.

Around 2:00 a.m., she decided that she'd go to bed—alone, thank God.

By this time, most of the Christmas pudding had dissolved away into my bloodstream and spinal fluid, so I was in a fit state to look forward to having Alexa stay over in my room.

"Don't worry, I won't listen through the wall," Élodie said, halfway out of the kitchen and already half-undressed.

Which naturally killed any chance of sex that night stone dead.

In light of the Christmas pudding incident, I thought it might be a good idea to give my tearoom team a lesson in authenticity.

"French people don't drink tea the English way," I told them.

There was a collective "oh" of disbelief around the table.

I'd assembled the team in a large brasserie. It had round marble-topped tables near the windows and orange leatherette booths at the back. Now, at 4:00 p.m., it was quiet in the lull between the midday rush and the apéritif crowd. There was a dusty-haired man in painter's overalls at the bar, drinking red wine. A bald traveling salesman type in a sharp gray suit was sitting alone by the window, reading the sports newspaper *L'Équipe* and pulling a pig's foot to pieces. He forked up a great chunk of sinewy pink meat and folded it into his mouth. Grease dripped down his chin and onto the newspaper.

My five usual suspects were crammed into a booth—men on one side, women on the other. It hadn't been planned like that—it had just happened. I sat with the women, rubbing thighs with Nicole, staring across at Marc, who looked as bored as a teenager at a meeting about how mobile phones destroy your brain, and Bernard, who seemed to be enjoying himself without really worrying about what he was supposed to be enjoying.

Jean-Marie was there, too, gazing with barely concealed irritation around the table. Only Stéphanie was looking grumpier, her eyes almost as coal black as her high-necked cashmere sweater.

"Look." I pointed to the incriminating evidence on the dark Formica table between them.

Everyone looked down.

On the table there were two beers, two cafés au lait, and two small, biscuit-colored teapots alongside two large white empty cups. There was a slice of lemon in one of the cups, a tiny jug of warm milk next to the other.

"Look what?" Stéphanie snapped.

"Okay. First, look where the teabags are."

All eyes focused on the teabags, which were lying on plates next to the teapots, with their little cardboard labels stapled at the end of a four-inch length of white cotton.

"The hot water—boiling water—really ought to be poured directly onto the teabags in the pot. The cooler the water is, the less taste the tea will have."

Stéphanie and Nicole lifted the lids of their teapots, picked up their teabags by the labels, and dropped them into the water.

They floated on top, and a faint brown stain began to leak out of them.

"Right. Next, look at where the teapots are."

I saw Marc and Stéphanie exchange a look. The *anglais* is crazy.

"So where are they, Marc?"

"Duh." This was a word he'd picked up in Georgia. "On ze table, yeah?"

Stéphanie and Bernard snorted a laugh. Stéphanie's was aimed squarely at me.

"As you so rightly say, Marc. Duh." These programmer types seemed to be all the same—thinking everyone else in the world was a dickhead and that wearing your company badge hitched to the belt of your too tight jeans was cool.

"The women," Nicole said.

"Ah, yes." Jean-Marie seemed to have snapped out of his mood. "Only the women took tea. Very good, Nicole." He gave her a beaming smile. Stéphanie gave her a murderous glare.

I had told everyone to order what they wanted. It was my treat. ("Trit?" Bernard had asked.) Marc and Bernard had ordered beer, Jean-Marie and me the coffee. QED.

"In the U.K., *everyone* drinks tea," I said. "Well, except for the London latte set. No British building would get built if the bricklayers didn't have tea. We only won the Second World War because our troops got copious supplies of tea."

"Ayund some elp by Americons," Marc said.

"Ah, yes, but you'll notice that before invading the Normandy beaches, all the Americans stopped off in England for a cup of tea."

"Yes, I see," Jean-Marie said. "It is all this." He flicked his fingers across the table toward the women. "The tea sachet, the plate, the teapot, the lemon. It is very feminine. But it justifies the price."

"Right, the price." I picked up the bill, which was sitting in a little plastic dish at the end of the table. "The tea is the most expensive thing on the bill. In England, it'd be the cheapest."

"But this is excellent, what you call it, valeur ajoutée, more value," Jean-Marie said.

"A good markup, yes. But when you buy these teabags, which are very low quality tea, you're paying more for the little label, the staple they use to attach the label, and the little envelope that each individual teabag comes in than you are for the tea."

"But it is lak dat dat tea is sell in Fronce," Stéphanie said.

"Maybe, but the teabag itself is *pleated*, for God's sake. How much does that cost?"

"Plitted?" Stéphanie asked.

I opened my teapot and lifted the bedraggled bag out by its label. The water was still only lager colored. I pointed to the pleats up each side of the little dripping rectangle. It was a very complex piece of engineering compared with your average flat British teabag.

"In the U.K., you can buy five teabags for the price of this one, and better quality, too. You can reduce the price of your tea, up the quality, and still make more profit."

"Excellent!" Jean-Marie was getting cheerier by the minute.

"But it is very chic, the labelle," Stéphanie objected.

"You want chic, you order a set of teapots with your chic logo on them."

This earned me a collective "ah." Collective except for Stéphanie, who felt that her purchasing territory was being invaded Normandy style.

"Ah, yes. The My Tea Is Rich logo, Bernard?" Jean-Marie asked. "You promised rapid action?"

Bernard blushed. "Yes, ze test for a logo is er, vairy soon finish."

Vairy soon started, I thought. Honestly, the guy was just a walrus with a day job.

"So what do you suggest to change this feminine image of tea?" Jean-Marie asked.

"I'm not sure we want to," I said, and the others started to grumble and shrug—why the hell had they all been dragged out here if there was no need to change anything?

"Not entirely, anyway," I went on. "This kind of complicated ritual when serving tea will be good for our image. For specialty teas, anyway—Darjeeling, Lapsang souchong, that sort of thing. We'll have to put some more male-oriented things on the menu. A large mug of extra-strong English tea, something like that. We'll keep the image of tea as a luxury product, but buy it cheaply. Which is why Stéphanie's going to have to get some quotes from Indian producers."

"Quartz?" Stéphanie wrinkled her nose at me.

"Quotes, prices. I know you prefer to buy everything from French suppliers"—she looked away, Jean-Marie stared ahead innocently—"but it'll be much cheaper to buy direct. I think you're going to have to go to London to meet them."

"Lonn-donn?" I could almost smell Stéphanie's terror at being forced to speak English for more than an hour.

"Excellent idea. I will accompany Stéphanie." Jean-Marie, meanwhile, seemed to be imagining all the cheap British beef he could stash in his suitcase.

Even Stéphanie brightened up when the boss invited himself along. She probably never saw him outside the office.

"Yes, maybe an-tress-ting," she said.

"Great," I said. "I'll give you a shopping list of English food to bring back. We'll have a tasting. You can all try some authentic British cuisine."

There was a pause while everyone finished translating this in their heads. Then eyebrows began to rise and jaws began to drop. "Oh!"

With Stéphanie and Jean-Marie away in "Lonn-donn," I was able to do some late night snooping. Stéphanie didn't lock her office door, and the security guard didn't do his first round till 8:00 p.m., so from about 7:00 the building was practically empty and I had undisturbed access to Stéphanie's computer.

Her office was large, with an orderly desk, a round meeting table, and a six-foot bookcase full of neatly labeled box files.

The whole of the wall above the meeting table was covered with framed photos. One was of Stéphanie and Bernard gazing up at Bernard's mammoth rugby player chum, apparently during the photo shoot for the ad. All the others were of a smiling Stéphanie standing beside immense, rosette-wearing cows. Some of these cows had the company's red "VD" logo stuck on their backsides, as if warning horny farmworkers that they'd catch something nasty if they tried a spot of *boeuf* boffing.

It took me about fifteen seconds to get into her mailbox—password "stephanie," the silly girl. She'd put dozens of messages into her wastebasket, or *corbeille*, as our system called it, without deleting them totally. Among these were several with the subject heading "BAng," which even an ignorant foreigner like myself could work out as *boeuf anglais*.

So, watched over by Stéphanie's cows and her rugby player, I read the semicryptic argument she'd had with Jean-Marie.

First there'd been a complaint from an annoyed French supplier of prime Limousin cattle that his orders were going down while VianDiffusion's production was reported to be soaring. Then there was a request from Jean-Marie to issue a purchase order to an abattoir just over the Belgian border. And finally a flurry of panic messages from Stéphanie about buying English animals that had been exported across the Channel and given the chop in Belgium before being sold at rock-bottom prices.

I printed them all out for future use.

No sooner was Jean-Marie back in town than this English beef business exploded in his face, almost literally. I turned up to work one morning and noticed something vaguely different about the building. Ah yes, that was it, there wasn't usually half a ton of cow dung blocking the main door. And I couldn't remember seeing tractors in this chic part of Paris before, with their angry-looking blue-overalled drivers yelling something about *boeuf anglais*.

Unfortunately for the company, half of Paris's radio and TV stations had their offices within a kilometer, so the street was also crawling with cameramen and microphone-touting journalists. They were interviewing farmers and filming a couple of beautiful, golden-colored French cows that had also come along, presumably to protest that English animals were robbing them of their chance to get minced up by Jean-Marie.

Not knowing what to do, I hovered on the pavement opposite with a crowd of passersby and colleagues. It was still way before 9:00, so none of my team were there.

This being Paris, the demonstration had been joined by drivers who were hooting at the pile of dung to get out of the way. The dung did not, of course, react, and the normally calm street was turned into a cathedral of hooting, chanting, and mooing.

Suddenly I was grabbed from behind and dragged into a doorway.

"It's me," Jean-Marie hissed. He was looking a lot less calm than usual, almost ruffled. His remaining hair was slightly out of place, his sea blue silk tie had drooped a millimeter away from his pink shirt collar. "Come, we must give interviews." Before I could ask what I was supposed to say, he put on a fixed smile and pulled me toward the nearest TV camera.

A peeling blue sticker told us that it belonged to a cable news channel. A young girl in a thick black overcoat was standing by a tractor wheel and talking to the camera.

Jean-Marie waited until she'd finished and then, still hanging on to my elbow, went and introduced himself. The girl, sensing an exclusive, pulled him in front of the camera and told her cameraman to start filming.

The cameraman, whose broad shoulders and battered sheepskin jacket looked as if they'd been carrying filming equipment for quite a few years, told her to change the shot. They had a quick squabble, during which he threatened to leave if she didn't do what he told her, and then Jean-Marie and the girl, with me being tugged along as a sort of afterthought, were set up so that the shot would include the company building and the pile of cow poop.

The girl started to ask questions. As she had almost no idea what was going on, her questions were mainly along the lines of "Tell me what's going on," so Jean-Marie was able to do his smoothie act and give an unchallenged view of things.

Not surprisingly, this was a pack of lies. *Boeuf anglais?* Ho ho, whatever gave them that idea? He'd just got a medal from the Ministry of Agriculture, did the farmers think that the ministry would give a medal to someone who'd been buying *boeuf anglais?* How *ridicule!*

He then launched into an impassioned bout of self-defense, which was just as two-faced as what had gone before but now gave him the chance to look hurt and self-righteous, too. This was where I came in.

I was introduced as the friendly face of England, come to open tearooms that would provide jobs for hundreds of French people. Hundreds? I thought. Was I going to employ one washer-up for every cup?

The reporter pointed the microphone at me for comment.

"Oui," I commented sagely.

Jean-Marie confessed that he had just been in London negotiating a deal with an English food company, but it was for tea, not beef. Wasn't that so, Paul?

"Oui," I confirmed.

It was all a sad misunderstanding, Jean-Marie said. He was proud to buy French beef, and only French beef, but he didn't see anything wrong with importing English tea. What's more, he invited all the farmers here to come and have a free cup of English tea as soon as his tearooms, called My Tea Is Rich, by the way, opened.

I could just imagine the farmers sitting there in their wellies wondering whether to order Earl Grey or orange pekoe.

"My Tea Is Rich? That's very funny," said the girl. Even the cameraman cracked a smile.

"Yes, we think it's a very good name, don't we, Paul?"

"Oui." What difference did one more lie make?

We went and did more or less the same interview to as many cameras and radio mike as Jean-Marie could hijack, then he led me away from the demo to take refuge in a café on the Champs-Élysées till the trouble blew over.

"Why don't the police come and break it up?" I asked. "I mean, letting your dog foul the streets is illegal, so surely cows are way outside the law?"

"The police? Just when we need them to defend French cuisine, they are on strike," Jean-Marie huffed.

*   *   *

Personally, I'm not sure the police would have made much difference. The Paris police are the best in the world at one thing—sitting in buses.

You see them all over the city practicing their unique skill. You'll walk into a street and find it jammed solid with traffic because the police have decided to double-park two of their buses there. Inside, whole brigades of riot police will be sitting, apparently having got prior warning of a riot about to break out in that very street. They might spend a morning there, getting out occasionally to stretch their legs, nip off to the *boulangerie*, or compare body armor, and then when the riot doesn't materialize (of course not, too many police about), they go and sit in another street.

Apart from this, the only time I saw the police was when they wandered about in gangs of four or five chatting to one another or when they mountain-biked around the gay Marais, apparently just to show off their thighs and their cycling shorts.

But then I never saw any crime, either, so they had to be doing something right.

In fact, it turned out that the police were on strike because of events *outside* Paris, where things weren't so quiet. The city is almost surrounded by poor suburbs—basically it is hemmed in by a ring of young and furious unemployed kids. And out there, where Parisians never venture, there were no-go zones, firebomb attacks on police stations, kids getting shot for driving through roadblocks, and the policemen's union was suggesting that the politicians might be more in a hurry to improve the social situation if they were the ones taking the brunt of the fury. President Chirac was suing for peace in Iraq, but he was making his cops fight a guerrilla war. Well, now the police were refusing to fight.

*   *   *

If Jean-Marie was annoyed about the police strike, it was only natural that his daughter felt the complete opposite.

One evening I'd been due to stay over at Alexa's, and we'd gone out for dinner, then to a bar. Suddenly Alexa got into a mood about how much beer I was drinking.

"In England, you can't have a good night out if you don't *get pissed*. You just want to *get pissed*, then take a woman home and screw her before you fall asleep. This is so English!"

I thought it was only polite to drink beer when sitting in a bar—the owner might get annoyed if you sat there and chewed your nails for two hours. And Alexa herself had chosen this Irish pub, one of about five million Irish pubs in Paris, which seem to employ the entire male population of Ireland as their bar staff.

"That's not fair, Alexa. I'm not drunk. I thought we were having a pleasant night out."

"But you are drinking that beer as if it was water. You don't even taste it."

I was on my second pint of Guinness, which was positively teetotal compared with how much most of my compatriots would have downed by that time of night. And I had the distinct impression that I was enjoying the taste.

"You wouldn't say that if I'd had two glasses of wine."

"It is not the same thing."

"Isn't it? Beer is just as noble a drink as wine, you know. France's brewing tradition involves grapes, ours involves hops. Both have tastes. It's like saying you're a philistine because you eat goat's cheese instead of cow's cheese."

"There is farmer's cheese and there is industrial cheese."

"Yeah, well, when it comes to drinks, we know all about quality. And not just about beer, either. In one of my reports it said that Britain is the second-highest consumer of champagne in the world after France. And most of the best French wines are exported to the United Kingdom. The French are just miffed because we put wines from South Africa, Australia, and California on the same level as French wines. We're less snobbish, that's all. A good beer is as good as a good wine, from anywhere in the world."

"Yes, and you drink so much of it that you fall over. That's why Englishmen stand up in pubs. When they fall over they know it is time to go home."

"While the French just get politely tipsy, then drive off and kill someone. You have the highest drink-drive fatalities in Europe."

I drained off my Guinness triumphantly, and my stomach, maybe still suffering from an overdose of Christmas pudding, blew most of the gas back out of my nose.

Bad timing.

"If you think I am letting you in my bed tonight, you have another . . . what do you say?"

"Another think coming," said a helpful young Irish lad in a tight Guinness T-shirt who was clearing away empties.

"Thank you," Alexa said, smiling a tad too warmly at the muscular Irishman.

"Yeah, thanks a bunch," I told him.

When I got home, the apartment was empty. Élodie's door was open.

I stood on the threshold and looked into her bedroom. It was its usual self—a laptop open on an old Formica-covered desk, a black bra draped across the stereo, half a million CDs stacked or dumped on the bare floorboards, and an empty champagne bottle and two glasses standing like an altar at the foot of her enormous bed.

The floorboards creaked loudly as I headed for the *dressing*, but there was no one to wake up.

I bent down to look through the keyhole, and it felt as if I was getting a facial. The lock and handle were warm. I couldn't smell burning, but the whole door was as warm to the touch as a radiator. Perhaps, unlike Marilyn Monroe, Élodie liked to keep her undies at blood temperature? I couldn't see anything—the keyhole was blocked up on the other side.

I'd just got down onto my stomach to try to look under the door when I heard her voice out on the landing. A key scrabbled into the front door lock.

No time to get out of her room—I'd bump straight into her. And no point trying to crawl under the bed—it was barely two inches off the floor, so I'd have needed to iron myself flat first.

Should I bury myself in CDs and hope she didn't notice the strangely man-shaped heap?

No, only one thing for it. I undid my trousers and lay down on the bed.

"Paul." She strode in, a long black leather coat covering her from chin to knee. She looked confused more than anything. She gestured over her shoulder. "I think you know Marc."

Marc? My Marc from work? I grabbed at my fly buttons and tried to hide my boxers before total embarrassment walked into the room.

But no, the Marc who came in behind Élodie was short and punk-haired, dressed in a camouflage combat jacket and jeans twelve sizes too baggy for him. I'd never seen him before. His sunglasses were so black that I don't think he even saw me.

"Marc le Dark? He's a famous DJ," Élodie explained apologetically. "Why are you in my bed?"

"Ah, yes. I was hoping . . . but as you've already got . . . I'll go." I stood up, sportingly offering my place to the new pretender.

"Have you and Alexa, you know?" She made a tearing-paper motion with her hands.

"No, it's just that I was here alone, and feeling, you know, but no, you're right, I'll . . ."

Élodie was staring at me suspiciously, her gaze wandering from my half-buttoned jeans to her dressing room door. I hoped she wasn't going to go and brush the keyhole for eyeprints because I'd be caught red-eyebrowed.

"No, Paul, you can stay and help us."

"Help you?" I backed away from the bed.

"Not with sex. I haven't brought Marc home to fuck him. Come."

She opened her coat, took a key from the pocket of her jeans, and marched toward the dressing room door.

The warm wood swung open to reveal its secret, and I almost fell back on the bed.

"Holy shit."

She laughed at my openmouthed shock. Her friend Marc regained his vision and walked over, whistling in admiration at the small tropical garden growing alongside Élodie's clothes rack.

One wall of the closet was given over to clothes. The rest, about six feet by three, was filled from floor to ceiling with arc lamps and marijuana plants.

"Yes, you are right, Paul. Perfectly holy shit."

So this was what Jean-Marie had been so angry about. Not surprising. Even in France, where smoking is more or less ignored by the police, there was enough here to send her to prison.

"Is this your marketing project for business school?" I asked.

"No, I don't sell it. It is for my friends." She stopped looking amused and became businesslike. "Marc has his Jeep in the street, and you are going to help him carry all the plants to the car."

"What? No way."

"If you don't, I'll tell Alexa you were in my bed and my father that you fucked me."

How could an English gentleman refuse a mademoiselle in distress?

There were twenty pots in all, each weighing several metric tons. We couldn't use the lift in case it broke down and left us stranded with our booty till one of the other residents—a judge, maybe—let us out next morning. So that meant ten trips down four flights of stairs for Marc and me, with Élodie following to pick up any stray leaves that we knocked off against the walls or the stair rail.

Down in the street, Marc's triple-parked Jeep gradually filled up with illegal plants. It had tinted windows, of course, but you could see the characteristic leaves pretty clearly in silhouette.

"Is no problem," he reassured me. "No cops."

Of course, Élodie was taking advantage of the strike to get her dad off her back.

"You know the funny thing?" she asked me as I was sweating my way down the stairs for the last time.

"No." I didn't think multiple hernias were funny at all.

"In French we call grass *l'herbe* or *le thé*. Tea. Very appropriate, don't you think? You are going to open tearooms for my father. And now you are carrying tea for his daughter."

She laughed happily. I didn't. Now both father and daughter were using me as cover for their criminal doings.

A couple of days later, I got a call from Jake, the swamp poet. I must have given him my phone number at an unguarded moment.

"Hi, Paul, I'm, like, really sorry, for, you know . . ."

"Telling me to fuck off?"

"Yeah, well, I confess, but you can't, like, mock a guy's poetry, without . . ."

"Getting told to fuck off?"

"Like I said, I'm really desolated."

"Sorry, you mean."

"Hell, yeah. Sorry."

"Did you get an Albanian?"

"Yeah."

"Without paying?"

"Naturally. Well, almost. She was one of those beggars in the metro. You know, with all the skirts? Well, she said she was Albanian, but I think maybe she was Romanian."

"Screwed up your poem, then?"

"Well, yeah. I'm not sure what to write."

"There was a young girl from Romania, who said that she came from Albania?"

"Listen, okay, I'm not going to talk about poetry with you anymore, man. You don't peej."

"Peej?"

"Yeah, you know, understand. No, I only called because I wanted to excuse myself by proposing you some help."

"Help?"

"Yeah. Tell me—what do you say to the waiter when you order a coffee with milk?"

"*Un café au lait, s'il vous plaît.*"

"You need help, man. Meet me at the usual café tomorrow, eleven o'clock."

Against my better judgment, I went. When I got there at 11:15 (I was getting more into French-style punctuality by now), he was already sitting at a table by the window, scribbling in a notebook.

Same shiny suit, same shiny hair, but he'd exchanged his university sweatshirt for a more seasonal, though even less attractive, black roll-necked pullover that he'd presumably stolen off a giant squid, to judge by the way it had lost all semblance of shape.

A self-rolled cigarette was smoldering in an ashtray on his table, adding a few final milligrams of smoke to the blue haze in the busy café before it went out.

"Don't say a word," he said after shaking my hand. "Just watch and listen."

He raised his chin a few degrees, turned his head until he made eye contact with the waiter, and called out, "Un crème, s'il vous plaît."

"Un crème, un!" the waiter barked toward the bar.

Jake turned back to me, a smug look on his unshaven face.

"Crème—doesn't that mean cream?" I asked.

"Yeah, but it's the name the waiters use for a café au lait. You've got to use their language. Hasn't anyone told you this yet?"

"No."

"Merde. You are so going to get ripped off. An espresso is *un express*, okay? An espresso with a bit of milk in it is *une noisette*. A weak black coffee is *un allongé*. And so on. You use their words and they know you're not a tourist." He took an authoritative sip of his *crème*.

I got Jake to repeat the various coffee names and wrote them down on a page he'd torn out of his notebook.

"It's the same thing for beer," Jake said. "Haven't you seen these tourists sat outside cafés with, like, a two-liter flagon of beer?"

"Yeah," I confessed sheepishly. A few weeks earlier, I'd felt like a quick drink on the Champs-Élysées and ended up spending an hour emptying a glass the size of a skyscraper.

"It's because they've asked for *une bière*. You've got to order *un demi*. That means a normal, twenty-five-centiliter glass. Kind of like a half-pint. You say that and they know you're not a tourist."

"Right. Brilliant. Un demi." I wrote it down on my list.

"If you don't know this stuff, if you don't prove to them that you're chez toi here, they'll arnack you."

"They'll what?"

"Damn. What do you say? I just said it. Rip you off. It's like carafes."

"Ah, yeah, for water."

"Yeah. Every café and restaurant will give you a pitcher of tapwater if you want it. But you have to ask for *une carafe d'eau*. You just ask for *de l'eau* and they'll sell you mineral water. Carafe is a kind of password you need to stop you getting arnacked. Ripped off. Damn."

"Et voilà." With a spectacular sweep of his arm, the waiter delivered my normal-size coffee and a normal-size bill.

"Merci," I said. I stirred my two lumps of sugar into the frothy coffee and looked up at my reflection in the glass front of the café. Yes, I was looking almost as self-satisfied as a Parisian.

As Christmas approached, the food shops became even more ceremonial than usual. Some of them looked as if they'd been the scenes of ritual killings. Whole, unskinned hares hung upside down outside butchers' shops, looking as if they'd died from nosebleeds. One day I even saw a wild pig lying on the sidewalk, apparently enjoying a siesta. When I walked past the shop a couple of hours later, there were large furry hunks of the animal on display in the window, and its head was grinning down approvingly from the wall.

Supermarkets set up stands in the street, selling baskets of oysters, mounds of shrimps, and huge fillets of salmon, all arrayed on beds of crushed ice. The workers manning these seasonal stands shivered and swore as their hands froze in the chill wind.

There were similar scenes outside brasseries, many of which specialize in seafood. Even on the coldest winter evenings, I saw rubber-aproned men freezing their bollocks off outside seafood brasseries. Their job, apart from trying to lose all their fingers from frostbite, was to open oysters and disembowel crabs. Why they had to do this in the street rather than in the kitchen, I never understood. Maybe crabs taste better with a coating of car pollution, or perhaps the men wanted to give the live lobsters a sporting chance of escaping into the sewers and scuttling back to Brittany.

This winter feeding frenzy was exactly the right time for a food tasting. My chance to test what people thought of *real* British food. Except Christmas pudding, of course.

Jean-Marie and Stéphanie came back from London with everything I'd asked for apart from the tin of corned beef, which I'd ordered as provocation more than anything.

I bought various British kitchen implements on the Web, borrowed a microwave, and set up a buffet table one lunchtime in our meeting room. I tried to make it an event. The long meeting table was hidden beneath four paper Union Jack tablecloths. I'd hired some gleaming white china serving dishes from a caterer. The dishes were also decorated with little flags, and I'd bought a party pack of paper cups, plates, and napkins printed with typical London motifs—red double-deckers, black cabs, and the mythical smiling policeman.

No one was going to mistake this for a tasting of German food, put it that way.

As my French colleagues walked into the room, their nostrils twitched at the smell of grilling sausages. Or maybe it was the sight of my lady-in-underwear apron.

They were on their guard. Men had hands in pockets, women crossed arms. One or two had slightly fearful expressions, as if they were on their way to the dentist.

I'd invited all of my team, plus ten of the younger people in the company. The young office crowd was my main target audience.

They milled about in front of the table, wondering whether my display was to be eaten or simply observed, museum style. Jean-Marie was late, so the ice was not quite broken.

I welcomed them with a quick training session in filling out my scorecards and invited them to tuck in.

Christine and I had spent a whole morning typing out bilingual labels for the various dishes. It's not easy translating things like "jacket potato with a baked-bean and grated cheese filling." Before you get down to finding the appropriate French words, you've got to explain to the French person why one would actually *do* these things to food.

Nicole was the first to take the plunge.

"Mm, sausage rolls," she said, taking a bite. "I remember, mah usband used to—" She put an abrupt end to her Proustian moment by spitting the sausage roll into a napkin and spearing a chipolata with a cocktail stick.

"What in da hell is ze-uss?" Marc was sniffing at a steaming bowl of steak and kidney pudding that had made it through customs. He was playing up to a girl who was also in the IT department, to judge by her styleless hair and the hip position of her name badge.

He read the label in front of the bowl. "A pudding wiz stek? You ave sweet soce wiz yo meat and now meat wiz yo sweet? Oh!" He did a pantomime grimace at his groupie.

"When you were in the Deep South, I'm sure you explained to all your redneck friends why they should stop eating sweet potatoes with their meat, didn't you, Marc? Not to mention lecturing them on the gastronomic gaffe of drinking Coke at mealtimes?"

Marc grunted and wandered off to bitch farther along the table.

"Ah, Bernard, help yourself," I said, calling out to my blond walrus friend, who had shuffled up to the table.

"Plov man lernsh," he replied. This was not a walrus greeting, but his attempt to pronounce "plowman's lunch," that traditional excuse for English pubs to overcharge for a cheese sandwich by not bothering to put the cheese inside the bread. I'd laid out the ingredients for some more respectable plowmans (or plowmen?), offering a choice of cheeses (mature Cheddar or Stilton) and pickles and a green salad with proper dressing. I'd also managed to order some cottage rolls that looked like a small cowpat on top of a larger cowpat—I thought they would strike a subliminal chord with Parisians. The label explained that the plowman's was the traditional meal of *vieux fermiers anglais*. I could see Bernard wondering how they used to get the salads out into the field without spilling the vinaigrette.

"Taste some English Stilton cheese," I told him very slowly. "You'll like it—it tastes just like French Roquefort."

"Okay." He grabbed a half-pound slab of Stilton and wandered away before I could tell him that he was only supposed to cut off a slice for tasting.

The room was pretty full by now, with twenty or so people pressing against the table. Taller men were reaching over shoulders to get at the serving dishes. There was a gaggle rather than a queue around the tea urn, which amused people when they saw that it spouted brewed tea rather than hot water.

"Oh, garrot geck!" A young brunette from the sales department with a tight black T-shirt and even tighter trousers was bouncing around in ecstasy in front of the cubes of iced carrot cake. "I ev zis at con tear boory."

"Right, great." I didn't know what she was talking about, but she was my first satisfied customer.

"You know con tear boory?" She now had a mouthful of carrot cake, which didn't exactly help me decipher what she was trying to say.

"No, don't think so. What is it?"

"It is seaty. Next doovre?"

"Right. Yes. Pardon?"

"You know! Next ze tonnel. You go out ze tonnel, you go up. It ez catty drawl. Con tear boory!"

Something clicked. "Ah, Canterbury. The cathedral, right. You've been there?"

"Yes, we go wiz my class when ah was to school. We, comment dire? We steal lots CDs from shop. Was fun. I ev garrot geck in ze café. I love!" She was now on her third cube, and her T-shirt was flecked with golden crumbs.

"Great."

"Ah love ze English food. I go eat some creeps now."

The plates of crisps were labeled A, B, C, and so on, with a list of flavors to choose from. The game was to guess which was which and to check off your favorites. My colleagues were reading the translations and laughing at this overcomplex way of dressing up potatoes. Who on earth, I could see them asking, would want to eat crisps flavored with Worcester sauce, pickled onion, or hedgehog? Christine had explained in her translation that hedgehog was a joke and that those crisps contained an artificial meaty flavor, but this only confirmed French prejudices. Food is not a joke, after all.

Even so, they were tasting and enjoying. Soon, the pile of hedgehog had been flattened as if it had tried to cross the motorway.

"Zis is good," Stéphanie told me as I hovered near my small baked potatoes. I'd made up some miniature jacket spuds with various typical fillings. She'd taken cheese.

"You like it?"

"No." She pointed down at the grated cheese. "I mean zis cheese, it is fifty pourcent of hair."

"Hair?"

"Yes, foo foo." She made breathing-out motions.

"Oh, *air*. It just melts better when it's grated."

"Yes. Is good economy to sell hair, no?"

Ratbag. But the ratbag was right. Cheap grated cheese in a cheap microwaved potato was a very profitable thing to sell.

I spotted a riot at the other end of the table and excused myself. Christine was sending me help messages with her eyes as she grappled with what looked like a tribe of cannibals bustling around her, trying to tear off chunks of her flesh.

She was in charge of a sandwich-toasting machine that had turned into the biggest hit of the tasting. She was trying to slice toasted cheese sandwiches into bite-size pieces, but they were being stolen whole as soon as they came out of the machine.

"You seem a bit more enthusiastic about English food now, Marc?" I bravely placed my hand between a cheese-and-ham toastie and Marc's scrabbling fingers.

"English? Dis is French. Y'all nevuh erd of croque monsieur?"

For someone so disdainful of my cuisine, he was surprisingly brave about dodging Christine's knife and grabbing the whole toastie.

*   *   *

Afterward, Christine and I surveyed the leftovers, which any chef will tell you are more important than what's actually been eaten.

Steak and kidney pudding was a *non-non*. Virtually untouched. Well, it was English beef, after all. Pork pie? Few takers, and I could see why. From a French perspective, it was a crudely sliced, anemic imitation of French cold meats. The baked potatoes hadn't been very popular, but that might have been my fault—not a very practical dish at a finger buffet.

Still, the rows of empty plates and the much stained pile of scorecards seemed to prove that the tasting had been a success. They loved British cuisine despite themselves.

I gave Christine a hearty hug and a wet thank-you kiss on the cheek.

"Oh! You are becoming so French," she told me in French. "For you, food and sex are the same thing!"

It was probably the first time in human history that anyone had called hedgehog-flavored crisps sexy.

Jean-Marie didn't turn up for the tasting, but when I told him how well it had gone, he was enthusiastic, in a bored sort of way.

He scanned the approval ratings and my suggestions for making typically English food more acceptable for French consumers. He was looking even smarter than usual, if that was possible. Shimmering purple shirt with monogrammed gold cuff links, a suit so well cut that it was almost liquid. Sunlamp tan faultlessly even. He sat in his huge leather desk chair, his framed knighthood certificate apparently hovering by his shoulder, as if he was posing for a portrait.

"This is good." He put the list aside and smiled at me vacantly.

"Problems? Another demonstration?" I asked.

"Oh no. The farmers will not trouble us again."

"I expect they were convinced by your interviews on TV?"

"No, I gave them a list of fast-food restaurants that do not buy French beef from us. They are going to make sure that these people do not buy foreign beef." The noble old French tradition of collaborating with the enemy, it seemed. "And I will send Stéphanie to make some more photos with their French cows."

"That should make them happy."

"Uh?"

He seemed to be preoccupied. Though it sounded as if everything was under control. I wondered why the gloom.

"Anyway, Paul, you are going home for a family Christmas?"

"Yes, tonight." Now it was my turn to look gloomy. Five days sitting in my parents' overtidy living room, eating dry turkey and pretending to bond with my dad over satellite football matches. Alexa and I had planned to go away to her parents' holiday home in the Alps for a few days of log fires and snuggling up under the duvet, but she'd canceled at the last minute. Her dad had broken up with yet another boyfriend and didn't want to be alone at this family-oriented time of year. Her mum, meanwhile, was apparently shacking up with a Ukrainian DVD pirate.

"I've just sent you an e-mail giving you a rundown of progress on the project so far," I told Jean-Marie.

"Ah, yes, good."

"It's very short."

"Ah."

"I did warn you, Jean-Marie. My team is not exactly a working unit. More a weekly English conversation class. We're going to have to make radical changes after Christmas, don't you think?"

Before Jean-Marie could answer, Christine poked her head round the door and announced that *l'inspecteur* was down in reception.

"A policeman? So they're not on strike anymore?" I asked.

"No, no." The worried look had returned to Jean-Marie's eyes. "An inspector from the Ministry of Agriculture."

"Ah, yes? Come to congratulate you for . . ." I nodded toward the certificate. Jean-Marie's expression told me that the answer was no. I wondered if his hypocrisy might actually be coming back to haunt him like a half-digested bit of *boeuf anglais*.

He stood up and tightened his already tight tie. "Anyway, Paul, thank you. Do not worry about your progress. Why don't you go and get your train?"

He walked toward the door. I was being expelled.

"Okay, I'll see you after Christmas, Jean-Marie."

"Er, yes."

"Have a joyeux Noël. I'll bring you back some Christmas pudding."

"Yes. Thank you."

That *proved* he wasn't listening. He smiled wanly, shook my hand, and turned back toward his desk.

Was it wise, I wondered, to have booked a return ticket?

JANVIER

A Maison in the Country

NOT MANY PEOPLE outside France know the true story behind the creation of the European Union.

Apparently, Charles de Gaulle's family had a house in the country near a tiny farm that made the wrinkliest sausages in France. These were what the French call *saucissons secs*—long, thin, misshapen salamis that are hung to dry until they become as hard as a wine bottle. So hard that there are shops devoted entirely to selling the murderous clasp knives you need to cut the *saucisson* into edibly thin slices.

Anyway, de Gaulle was a big *saucisson* man. After World War II, things were relatively peaceful for France (apart from a few colonial wars), so the General managed to pop down into the country several times a year for weekends. Whenever he did so, he always insisted on having slices of this local delicacy with his apéritif.

But one Friday night when he arrived, *quelle horreur*, no sausage. "Pourquoi pas?" the General demanded, and he was told that the farm was in financial trouble and had stopped making sausages.

De Gaulle leapt into action. He proposed a bill in parliament to create a system of subsidies for small farmers. However, the industrial unions had the government under their thumb, and the bill didn't get through. So de Gaulle hit on a brilliant idea.

Why not, he thought, create a pan-European government to subsidize his sausages? He couldn't reveal his true motives, so he shopped around the vague concept of protecting European producers against global competition to the heads of state of Italy, Germany, and Spain (all renowned for their sausage, you'll notice)—and hey, presto, the Common Market was born. Pretty soon the General's local pig farm was swimming in euro-cash and producing so much sausage that half of it had to be fed back to the pigs.

Well, that may not be *entirely* true, but it's the only way I can explain Britain's deep-seated antagonism to Europe—our sausages are pathetically pale and limp compared with salami, wurst, chorizo, and *saucisson sec*.

Today, of course, the EU is much more to France than a source of subsidies for pig farmers. These days, it's also a source of subsidies for French cattle farmers, fruit farmers, cheese makers, winegrowers, olive oil producers, and every type of peasant activity you can imagine.

I have no real argument with that. It's what makes the French countryside such a fantastic place to visit. Just a few kilometers outside Paris, you can find bits of real rural France, populated by tractor-driving folk who think that Dior is a word you use to shoo stray dogs out of your garden. *Allez! Dior!*

By the time January came around, I wanted to join the great Parisian tradition of buying myself a piece of this rural time capsule—a *maison* in the country. Mad, you might think, for someone on a one-year contract. But I was now receiving all my salary and paying almost zero rent, and you can buy a small château up in Normandy for about the price Londoners pay for a semidetached ants' nest.

My motives were basically the same as those of the native Parisians. For a start, I was getting a bit sick of the sheer urban density of the city. Compared with London, there's hardly a square inch of greenery in Paris, especially where I was living in the Marais.

I was also sick of my neighbors, as most Parisians are. I now knew every second of the morning routine of the family upstairs. At 7:00 a.m. alarm goes off, boom, Madame gets out of bed, puts on her deep-sea divers' boots, and stomps across my ceiling to megaphone the kids awake. The kids drop bags of cannonballs onto the floor, then, apparently dragging several sledgehammers each, stampede into the kitchen. They grab their chunks of baguette and go and sit in front of the TV, which is always showing a cartoon about people who do nothing but scream at each other and explode. Every minute, one of the kids cartwheels (while bouncing cannonballs) back into the kitchen for seconds, then returns (bringing with it a family of excitable kangaroos) to the TV. Meanwhile the toilet is flushed, on average, fifty times per drop of urine expelled. Finally, there is a ten-minute period of intensive yelling, and at 8:15 on the dot they all howl and crash their way out of the apartment to school.

You've just made yourself a soothing cup of tea when Madame returns and gets her team of trained hippos to clean up the mess, clomping their hooves or whatever hippos have, in time to the nasal howl of some terminally lovesick French crooner. I once dared to go up and ask whether the hippos really needed to wear high heels indoors all the time, and a snooty woman in pearls slammed the door in my face.

It wouldn't have been so bad, but the kids had school on Saturdays, too. So, to avoid letting your thoughts dwell too much on arson or ax attacks, you start looking for a weekend *maison*.

I wondered if this wasn't what made Parisians so manic. Indoors, they are permanently assaulted by the unwelcome sounds of their neighbors' routine lives. And when they get outdoors, the only place to walk is on hard tarmac. The constant pounding on their eardrums and their feet must cause their brains to bounce off center.

Don't get me wrong. I was glad to arrive back in Paris after Christmas. Just getting off the train and stepping into the rush for the metro, I felt reenergized. It's a city that pulls you along with it. I knew that I could now get served in cafés, barge my way to the front of lines, infuriate people just by shrugging. It was like being good at a particularly tough computer game.

When I went into the office on the first Monday of the new year, things seemed to be running normally. No heaps of cow dung in reception. No police officers opening our bags to check for illegal meat. Like everyone else, I now felt entirely comfortable spending the first morning kissing colleagues, drinking coffee, and wondering where to go for my next holiday.

A large part of the afternoon was taken up with a tea party in Jean-Marie's office in honor of *la galette*. This was a seasonal ceremony centered on eating a sort of flat, round croissant stuffed with marzipan. Stéphanie cut the *galette* into slices, then Christine, as the youngest, had to get under the table and say who should get which slice. Once this was done, everyone tucked in gingerly, waiting to see who would break a tooth on the porcelain favor hidden in the pastry. It was Jean-Marie who eventually pulled a marzipan-smeared cow out of his mouth. I would have said it was a fix except that he was now forced to look stupid in a paper crown for the rest of the party.

Beneath his veneer of new year goodwill, Jean-Marie seemed

tense, but by no means out of his mind with worry. His medal was still on the wall, so presumably the ministry inspector had come over just for a chat about mincer blades. And when I mentioned the idea of getting a house in the country, in Normandy, maybe, Jean-Marie immediately offered to drive me out to "the most beautiful country town in France" the following weekend.

Alexa didn't want to come—her dad had just come off Prozac and was feeling "fragilized"—so at 9:00 on Saturday morning, I met Jean-Marie in the company's underground garage, where he'd left his plush silver Renault to be washed, and we set off for the country.

"There is no time to lose," he said as he sliced through the traffic, hooted pedestrians out of the way, and swung out into the mad rush of the Champs-Élysées. "All Paris will be on the road."

In fact, all Paris seemed to have gathered to drive around the Arc de Triomphe.

It was easy to see why. The Arc is much more impressive in real life than on postcards, a towering, 160-foot-high double building rather than a humble arch. Napoleon commissioned it to celebrate his victory over the Russians and the Austrians at the Battle of Austerlitz in 1805 (so my guidebook says, and I have no reason to disbelieve it), and today it stands majestically astride a small island in the middle of one of Europe's largest roundabouts, which is known as l'Étoile, or "the Star." The roundabout has twelve exits and is a massive quarter of a mile in diameter, which gives cars plenty of room to dash in at least twelve different directions at once. As a star, l'Étoile is part black hole, part supernova. Cars are sucked in, bounced crazily around, then expelled along one of the exits.

Jean-Marie accelerated into the throng of vehicles, hardly blinking as his flash new car was almost cut in two by a kamikaze

Kawasaki. He then hit the hooter as if this would stop us plowing into the side of a tiny Smart car that had appeared from nowhere a foot from his speeding hood. He seemed to have forgotten that his car had brakes. He slewed on through four or five near misses, and I wondered how many seconds it would be before his apparently God-given luck ran out and I was chewing air bag.

Though I must admit I was enjoying myself in a suicidal sort of way. I was in awe of the evasion tactics on display here and getting an adrenaline buzz from the sheer nerve of these drivers who had to swerve directly in front of oncoming cars to make their exit, sometimes stopping dead in the traffic even though Jean-Marie's executive assault vehicle was charging at their flank.

"Insurance companies never investigate accidents at l'Étoile," Jean-Marie explained. "It would be like asking how a boxer broke his nose." He laughed and closed his eyes for at least three seconds.

"Great," I said. I closed mine and waited for the inevitable.

Miraculously, the inevitable proved to be evitable after all, and we escaped from the gravitational pull of the Étoile. Now Jean-Marie's madness was limited to talking on his mobile phone, zigzagging from lane to lane to gain precious yards in the traffic, and speeding through red lights.

"Red lights are like queues," he said scornfully. "They are for people who have time to waste."

We came to a junction marked "North," and he turned west.

"Isn't Normandy in the north?" I asked.

"No, it's in the northwest," he said, turning again, southwest this time. "But we are not going toward the coast. It is too full of Parisians. They call it the Twenty-first Arrondissement. It is too expensive for you." So that was decided.

We headed away from the sun at approximately double the legal speed limit. He was driving so fast that it seemed highly probable he would leave the sun behind and take us back into night. He wasn't the only one. We were in fourth or fifth place in a column of large cars charging along the autoroute at the same speed, using their combined power to scare slower cars out of the fast lane. In fact, it felt marginally safer this way, because you floated past the chaos happening on your right, where people were suddenly shooting out unannounced from behind trucks, overtaking on the inside, or driving just inches from the rear bumper of the car in front. It was easy to see why France has the worst accident statistics in Europe. One breath of fog, one drop of rain, and this behavior becomes literally murderous.

Today was dry but slightly frosty. A small patch of black ice would have sent us skidding all the way to the Atlantic, but Jean-Marie was willing to take the chance. As he propelled us toward the country, he kept his eyes riveted to the car in front, looking for the slightest sign of failing speed so that he'd be able to overtake. Meanwhile, he ranted on about the ungrateful farmers. The ministry had received a tip-off about him, it seemed, and he'd had to provide proof to the inspector that all his beef came from legal sources.

"Which was no problem, of course."

"Of course."

And today he had to go and see someone "with influence over the farmers," he said, "and kiss their feet like a slave in front of the caïd."

I didn't know exactly what a *caïd* was, but from Jean-Marie's expression, they probably didn't wash between their toes.

We turned off the autoroute before Chartres and headed into a hilly, wooded area dotted with small farms and four-house hamlets.

We emerged from the hills into a wide, sunlit plain, and Jean-Marie lowered his window to take in a deep lungful of chilly country air.

"We are here," he said as we rolled into the central square of a quaintly crumbling country town called Trou-sur-Mayenne.

It was market day. There were white vans parked higgledy-piggledy everywhere. People were wandering around with shopping bags that looked as if they were about to burst and cover the road with lettuce and crusty loaves. There were groups of old men in blue dungarees, caps on heads, chatting against the wall of the market hall through little fogs of cigarette smoke. They were farmers, no doubt getting updates about new subsidies for painting their pigs with the EU flag.

The market hall was basically just a high, tiled roof on thick stone legs. The roof was held aloft by a crisscross pattern of massive, roughly hewn beams and metal ceiling joists that had lost most of their paint. Inside, there were rows of stalls staffed by red-fingered people wearing several coats who were keeping themselves warm by barking at the milling shoppers to buy their share of the typical French opulence. There were stalls selling only potatoes and green vegetables, stalls selling only apples and pears, a busy butcher's van, another butcher's van with zero customers, and a blue-awninged fish stall with a huge decapitated tuna head attracting gawping children. I could also see a long rotisserie of suckling pigs next to an enormous cauldron of sautéing potatoes—a snack bar for ogres.

"Much more typical than Normandy," Jean-Marie told me. "But much cheaper houses. You go over there."

He pointed across the market square to a stone house with a name that I couldn't read painted in gold above a small, curtained shop window.

"It is a notary," Jean-Marie said. "His name is Lassay."

"Lassay," I repeated, trying not to imagine a collie dog.

"He is a lawyer but also sells houses. He is waiting for you."

"You're not coming?"

"No, I have business. He will drive you to the houses, and take you to Chartres, where you can get the train to Paris. Put your train ticket on expenses."

Next minute I was out of the car and Jean-Marie had driven off into the market crowd. So much for helping me. He takes me where I don't want to go and dumps me. What if this Lassay fella had gone away for the weekend? Did they have taxis round these parts? Or would I have to hitch a ride on the back of a fish truck?

But Lassay was there, and he wasn't a very encouraging sight. He was warming his backside by a log fire in his small, overheated old shop. The only furniture in the low-ceilinged room was a heavy, leather-topped wooden desk, a modern swivel chair, and two dark red metal filing cabinets. A smoke-blackened photo of the market square in pre-car days hung above the marble fireplace as if Monsieur Lassay had jumped out of it into the here and now.

He was like a Dickens character who had gone to a modern clothes shop and not quite understood what some of the garments were for. His badly knotted tie covered one side of his shirt collar, his trousers were baggy and bunched at the waist by a slim leather belt, and he was wearing a thick woolen jacket that looked as if it had been made from old doormats. His thinning white hair was long and straggly, brushed back vigorously so as not to get in his face.

"You are Monsieur Lassay?" I asked in French.

"Oui." He shook my hand amicably.

"You have houses to sell?"

"Houses for sale? No."

"No?"

"Oh, there are lots for sale. It's a good time to buy a house, but I only have one. Mine. You can buy that if you want." He chuckled to himself.

"But Monsieur Martin, he say you have houses for sale."

"Monsieur Martin? You know him?"

"Yes."

"Yes, of course!"

I turned round. This last voice had come from some spiral stairs beside the door. A thirty-something man, dressed as a dapper country gent in khaki cord trousers, yellow waistcoat, and a brown velvet jacket, was smiling broadly and holding out his hand for me to shake.

"Guillaume Lassay," he said. "This is my father. Hasn't Maman finished the shopping yet?" he asked his dad. Dad garrumphed. Seems he was killing time while his wife went round the market.

I introduced myself to Guillaume and tried to repeat what Lassay senior had said about it being a good time to buy.

Lassay the younger got the message and laughed. "There are lots for sale, maybe. But they're not all like you want. They are not all country houses. I have one such house for sale. A cottage. Beautiful, and not expensive. We will go and see it now."

He leaned across his desk, opened the central drawer, and took out a large bunch of keys. He tore off the paper name tag on the key ring and put the keys in his jacket pocket, ushering me toward the door.

"We will visit the house, then I will take you to the best restaurant in the region."

"Oh, but . . ." Beware of estate agents bearing gifts, I told myself. It'd be like a serial killer offering you the chance to slip on a pair of handcuffs to see how they feel.

"Monsieur Martin wants to invite us, to apologize for abandoning you."

"He comes with us for lunch?"

"No, but he will pay."

"Ah, okay, good." I let myself be escorted out of the door to a deep blue Mercedes.

Driving out of the town, we passed several houses with À VENDRE signs hanging from their front gates.

"These people want to leave the town and live in the country. As you do, Monsieur Vest."

"But already, er, there is country here, now, already, no?"

What I meant was, almost all of these town houses had gardens that backed onto open farmland. Compared with Paris, this was virgin rain forest.

"Ah, but this is the town. Where we are going is the *real* country."

We stopped at at least fifty junctions, drove through cold, shady areas of woodland and up and down steep-sided little knolls, and after about twenty minutes we arrived in a half-mile-wide river valley with banks of tall, skeletal trees lining it on either side. I saw farm cottages at about hundred-meter intervals along the valley until the river meandered round a bend and cut off the view. "Voilà."

I got out of the car and was hit by the deafening silence. You could almost hear the smoke coming out of the chimney of the house two fields away. Little birds hopped about everywhere. A crow fluttered its wings in a treetop, and I stared up at it as if it had just fired a gun. Monsieur Lassay was right—this was the real country.

We were parked on a grass bank outside a veritable bijou of a cottage, a square one-story stone building with a mossy tiled roof and pale yellow window frames. It was surrounded by tufty lawns and bare fruit trees. Beside the house there was a large barn that had been converted into a garage and outhouse, with new double doors and a skylight in the old wood-slatted roof.

"You also have the fields as far as the trees," Monsieur Lassay said as if I'd already bought the place. He pointed up beyond the fruit trees to two sloping pastures, one of which had a tractor in it, the other sheep. The house seemed to come with its own hobby farm.

Lassay took out his keys and let me in. The interior had been very tastefully modernized. In the lounge there was a huge stone fireplace, almost as high as the house itself, and exposed beams threatened to knock your head off at every turn, but there was also a swish new fitted kitchen, modern bathroom, flush toilet, and mighty-looking electric boiler. The lounge and two bedrooms were furnished with the basics—tasteful modern reproductions of rustic furniture.

"Everything is included in the price," Monsieur Lassay told me, his first words since we'd come inside. No hard sell, he was just letting me appreciate how incredibly cheap this was.

It was already a fully functional holiday home but was selling at the price you'd expect to pay for a roofless ruin.

"Why it is very, er, not expensive?" I asked. A stupid question if you want to buy something, but it needed asking.

Monsieur Lassay shrugged, not in an annoying Parisian way, but just to express his ignorance. "That is the price here. It is a long way from Paris."

We went out to the barn, which was now 50 percent modern garage space and 50 percent primeval agricultural building. The garage half had a concrete floor and a little lockup area, for bikes, I guessed. The primeval half still had an earth floor and crumbling walls. It smelled of petrol and dry timber.

"Bonjour."

A small figure in a flat cap was standing in the doorway of my barn. A trespasser, already?

"Bonjour." Monsieur Lassay apparently knew him and went to shake his hand. It was a farmer, about sixty years old, a semi-midget with enormous hands and bright red cheeks.

They began talking about me in the local patois, a mixture of French and ancient Egyptian that I didn't quite catch.

Monsieur Lassay seemed to be confirming that I might buy the place. The farmer's expression suggested that he was surprised. Didn't I look the country gent type? I wondered. No, not really. Looking down, I noticed that my trainers were already caked in a kind of snowshoe of mud. The country, I realized, is even dirtier than a Parisian sidewalk, and my feet were a picture of impracticality.

The two men talked on, with the farmer waving his arm rather threateningly up toward the fields. Not being an expert on French rural life, I wondered if the farmer came with the farm and I was effectively buying him, too. Would I have to feed him when crops failed? Would I have to take him to the woods and shoot him when he got too old to work?

Monsieur Lassay made soothing gestures, and the farmer went away, not back to the road, but up through my orchard. The nerve of the man. Did he think he owned the place?

"That is Monsieur Augème. He lives on the next farm. He uses these fields and wants to be sure that the buyer will continue to let him use them."

"It depends, er, how, er, why, er, what," I said. I tried to think of the French for "no satanic rituals or dungheaps outside the kitchen, please."

"He pays to cultivate one field and put his sheep on the other."

"He pays?"

"Yes, a symbolic sum."

So I was even going to get an income from the place? And, I thought, if the old guy starts plowing at six in the morning, at least I, as the landlord, can make him shut up, unlike the Madame living upstairs in the HLM.

"You like it?"

"Yes," I said warily, a bit of common sense kicking in at last. Even if the asking price was ridiculously low, there was no harm in making it lower. "It is small. And . . ." What the hell else could I complain about? "And there is very much, er, green, to, er, brrmm." I mimed pushing a motor mower. Not that I had one.

Monsieur Lassay nodded sympathetically. "You can ask Monsieur Augème to cut the grass and let him keep it for his animals. Or he can let his sheep cut the lawn now and again."

"Hmm," I said as if I wasn't really sure I wanted a farmer or a bunch of ewes doing the boring, backbreaking work for me.

"Why don't you rent it, for next weekend, say, and see if you enjoy it?"

"It is rent for weekend, this house?" Strangers would be sleeping in my rustic bed before I'd even christened it with Alexa?

"No, no. But if you are seriously considering buying it, you can rent it for a small price and test it."

"With not guarantee for I buy it?"

"No, of course. Until you sign, there is no guarantee."

"Okay, excellent. Next weekend, okay?"

"Yes. Good. Here are the keys."

"Already now?"

"Oh, you were introduced to me by Monsieur Martin. He says you are an honest young man."

Coming from Jean-Marie, I wondered if it was meant as a compliment or a slur.

I couldn't really complain about Jean-Marie, though, because he was being very helpful. Élodie was away in the United States, spending a term at Harvard on an exchange scheme. Twice a year, it seemed, kids from the top French business schools had to go abroad for three months to spend some more of their parents' money. So Jean-Marie gave me the keys to her car and said I could use it if I wanted to drive up the country.

He also asked if I would mind paying all the rent on the flat while she was away, given that I now had exclusive use of the place. When I objected, or rather started to choke with disbelief, he capitulated instantly and said he'd pay me a bonus to cover the extra rent for three months. Wow, I thought, those business schools must be very expensive indeed.

I mentioned this financial fixing to Alexa and said he might be hoping I'd crash Élodie's car so that he could write it off and claim on the insurance, but she said I was being much too cynical about my friendly boss.

Alexa and I were getting on pretty well. With Élodie away, she could stay over at my place without being subjected to nude cookery displays or 3:00 a.m. yelping contests. We could spend an evening and then a night together quite spontaneously without it causing a philosophical debate on the true nature of mixed-race male-female relationships in a postfeminist world.

Her dad was back on an up after meeting a handsome Danish

cutlery designer, so the weekend after my fact-finding tour, we headed out west together in Élodie's Peugeot 206.

The weather was cloudier than the previous weekend, threatening to rain, and the other cars all seemed determined to stay ahead of the clouds or die in the process. It was like dodgem racing out there.

As I drove, or rather quaked with fear while holding a steering wheel, Alexa cleaned out the car. Not because she was a hygiene freak, but because she'd found a strange pill with a skull stamped on it in the glove compartment. Her theory was, if we were stopped because of my overcareful driving, we were going to get arrested for possession of a whole recipe book of illegal substances. So anything suspicious she threw out the window as we traveled: a small plastic bottle, a lump of dark vegetable matter, an empty plastic envelope. After we'd stopped for a pee and a coffee near Chartres, she even got in the back and rooted round under the seats. Every few minutes I felt a rush of air pressure and something else flew out the back window. If a policeman was unlucky enough to be walking a sniffer dog in the woods just outside Paris, the mutt was going to pick up our scent and not stop running for two hundred kilometers.

We'd almost arrived at the cottage when I heard Alexa swear.

"What is it? The armrest stuffed full of heroin?"

"You didn't hear on the radio?"

"No." There was a news report on, but it was just a meaningless babble to me.

"There is a strike by electricity workers."

"Oh. We'll stop and buy some candles. And I think it's a gas cooker at the cottage."

"Gas and electricity, it is the same workers."

"Ah."

We went to the market in Trou and stocked up on food for the weekend, as well as a selection of candles and a couple of flashlights. I even had the brilliant idea of buying some charcoal and firewood so that we'd be able to cook no matter what.

A candlelit, fireside weekend in the country with a sexy French girl? Who needed gas and electricity to enjoy themselves?

The rain began as we pulled up outside the cottage. The whole valley was filling up with clouds, and the trees seemed to be holding them back so that they could pour down on our weekend retreat. But even in the damp, powerless gloom, the cottage looked wonderful. Alexa purred with delight. I was more determined than ever to buy the place.

What I really wanted to do was throw her on the bed, but I summoned up enough self-control to make myself useful and get the barbecue going. This was a brick construction just outside the kitchen door. It was still clogged with ash, so I had to find a small shovel in the barn and scoop it out into a plastic shopping bag (and over my jeans) before I could start the fire. The rain was getting heavier, but at least that prevented me from inhaling more than a few lungfuls of ash.

There was a sort of roof arrangement over the barbecue, but the rain was inconsiderately falling at a slight angle and killing the fire before it could take, so I spread out my arms crucifix style and protected the flames with my anorak until they had got going. I was now inhaling plenty of smoke to go with the ash already lining my bronchial tubes.

I emerged from a bout of coughing to see the farmer, Monsieur Augème, staring over the wall at me from five yards away. His cigarette bobbed up and down in the corner of his mouth as he gabbled ancient Egyptian at me through the beating rain.

I could guess the basic thrust of his speech.

"Are you nuts, or what? Don't you city dwellers know that

you're not supposed to have barbecues in the middle of winter during a torrential downpour?"

I nodded gratefully for his advice and did my best to direct my coughing away from the flames, which were in danger of dying of cold. Next time I looked up he was gone.

Alexa and I had a modest meal of steak, salad, and fruit and decided that we'd finish cooking our steaks the next day. Even Alexa didn't like meat that was totally raw except for a one-millimeter layer of ash-covered charcoal.

We spent the afternoon in bed (what else was there to do in an unlit, unheated house?), then used our flashlights to get dressed again and go out into the darkness for dinner. It was still raining, as the French so picturesquely say, "like a pissing cow."

Instead of heading all the way back into Trou, we stopped off at Monsieur Augème's house and I dashed through the rain with a map to ask him whether there was a country auberge nearby.

He stood on his front doorstep and talked at me again for a bit before I finally got him to shut up and listen to what I needed to know. He looked at me as if I was in idiot but consented to recommend somewhere to eat. He wasn't too sure about auberges but finally prodded at a town a few kilometers west and said that we could get a meal at the casino there.

It sounded posher than I'd envisaged—I would have preferred a tiny country inn serving food cooked by the same family since the Romans came through here on their way to fight Astérix, where we would rediscover a divine sauce that food writers had been hunting for for years—but failing that, I guessed dinner in a smart casino was infinitely better than anything our barbecue was going to produce.

"What did he suggest?" Alexa asked when I got back in the car and began dripping all over her.

"You'll see. It'll be a surprise."

It was here, I think, that I learned my lesson about the nature of mixed-race male-female relations in a postfeminist world. It was this: Don't promise anything as a surprise unless you yourself are 100 percent sure that the surprise will be pleasant.

You see, Alexa, being French, would have known that almost all the casinos in France were located by the sea or in spa resorts. Don't ask me why—maybe dipping yourself in sea or spa water dulls the pain of losing all your money at roulette. But whatever the reason, Alexa would have known that we were almost certainly not headed for a casino. We were headed for a Casino. That is, a branch of the supermarket chain called Casino, which in its larger stores often has a cafeteria.

She would have told me that waiting in line to have a uniformed supermarket worker shovel *steak frites* on her plate was not a food ceremony that she considered particularly sexy, even if it is enjoyed by many French people.

When we pulled up in the car park, she refused to get out of the car. We could have driven on from the industrial estate into the town center, but the supermarket seemed to be the only place for miles with light. It probably had its own backup power supply to keep its freezers from defrosting.

The upside was that I persuaded Alexa to go inside, and we had a hot meal. The downside was that almost everyone else in town had had the same idea, and we had to sit at the same table as a family with one kid of food-throwing age, one of banging-cutlery-on-table (and food-throwing) age, and one sulking teenage blob who didn't know that it's impolite to jab its elbows into Englishmen's ribs every five seconds.

Even my pet theory about *le self* being a good description of the French character didn't lighten the mood. Quite the opposite, in fact.

Needless to say, we drove back to the house in silence, with me thinking it was lucky we'd gone to bed that afternoon. Nighttime snuggles were not going to be on the menu.

We sat up in bed, reading by separate flashlights. I was reading an English translation of Émile Zola's novel *Le Ventre de Paris* about life in the old food market at Les Halles. Alexa was reading a French translation of *Women Are from Venus, Men Are from Some Pigheaded Planet Where They're Told That Women Shouldn't Be Consulted About Where They're Going to Spend the Evening*.

Suddenly, a violent and incomprehensible sequence of events interrupted our bedtime reading. First, someone appeared to drive a motorbike into the barn. This somehow ended the electricity strike, and the bedroom light flashed on. A few seconds later, someone (the lost biker, presumably) started banging at our door.

I put on my jeans and a jacket and went to investigate. The unheated air in the cottage was freezing, but now all the lights between the bedroom and the front door switched on normally. The strike was definitely over, which was excellent news. However, I could still hear the roaring of a motorbike from the barn. I opened the door to ask the rider to take his Yamaha elsewhere.

But no, it was Monsieur Augème, wrapped up against the cold and ranting at me. I picked up one or two words. I was getting the hang of this ancient Egyptian. "Grange," he said.

Even in normal French, that meant "barn."

But before I could ask him why he had used my *grange* as his garage, he had barged past me and gone into my kitchen. I followed him and found him fiddling about under the sink.

This puzzled rather than annoyed me. There's not much

damage you can do under a sink without getting yourself wet and dirty, I figured, so why not let him get on with it.

He stood up, walked to the cooker, and set a gas ring blazing.

"What's going on?" Alexa had arrived in the kitchen, fully dressed, I'm glad to say.

By the time Monsieur Augème had finished his explanation, I'd understood two other key expressions to go with *grange*.

When I thought back, he had used these two terms earlier in the day, mixed in with his incomprehensible patois, while I'd been trying to light the barbecue and when I'd asked if there wasn't a place nearby to get a hot meal. They were "emergency generator" and "bottled gas."

"Okay, so I don't know much about life in the depths of rural France, but neither do you, you have to admit that."

There was a squirming movement under the bedclothes.

"I mean, we both should have spotted the obvious clues, shouldn't we? Like, when I went to ask Monsieur Augème for directions, how come we didn't start wondering why his house was lit up like a Bastille Day fireworks display? They've all got generators round here, haven't they?"

The squirming figure emerged, at least down to the nose, which was wrinkling cutely as Alexa giggled, able to enjoy the joke now that there was hot morning coffee on her bedside table and hot air lifting the dust off the top of the radiators.

Peace had broken out and, as it always does, breathed new life into the property market.

"You must buy this house," she said. "It is a perfect refuge from the world. What do you do to buy a house?"

She asked this as she sat up and gripped her steaming bowl of coffee in both hands. One of my shirts was covering her top half.

"I don't know. Get a survey done, I suppose."

"A survey? Like a market survey?"

"No, like a structural survey to find out if the house is going to fall down or sink into the mud."

"Oh." She shrugged. "It looks okay to me."

I laughed, but I quickly found out that Alexa's attitude was almost exactly that of everyone in the French property business.

Monsieur Lassay had told me I could call him up anytime during the weekend, so I did so that Sunday morning, from the bed.

"Is it possible we organize an inspection of the house for problems with the structure? If it falls, you know?"

"An inspection?" Monsieur Lassay sounded confused by my attempts at architectural French.

"Yes, of the structure. The walls, the roof, the floor—"

He interrupted my list of the bits of a house to tell me he got my drift.

"There is already a certificate to say that you have no termites and that there is no plumbing," he told me.

"No plumbing? One moment." I covered up the phone and asked Alexa if she thought it was usual for the sinks, bath, and toilet not to be included in the price. She took the phone out of my hands and had a quick, efficient chat with Monsieur Lassay, which I found slightly unsettling, given that she was naked from the waist down and really ought to have been talking to no one else but me or her gynecologist.

She covered up the mouthpiece and explained.

"It's not plumbing, you idiot," she told me. "You mean *plomberie*—all the bath and things. He means that there is no *plomb* in the paint."

"Plomb?"

"What do you call it that was in old paint? They make bullets from it."

"Lead?"

"Yes, when you sell a house you must have a certificate saying there is no lead in the paint. And no termites. And no amiante."

"Ants? I've seen lots of ants in the kitchen."

"No, amiante. The stuff that you can't burn."

"Lettuce?"

"No, idiot. They use it for ceilings."

"Yes, lettuce."

"Imbecile. You talk to him." She handed the phone back to me.

"You must sign a *promesse de vente*," Lassay told me. "That is a promise to buy at a certain price."

"I sign promise buy?"

"You have seven days to change your mind. I can bring the promesse de vente to you to look at now, if you want."

"Now? Oh, but . . ."

As if to pressure me into agreeing, a band of real estate guerrillas stationed around the house suddenly started firing artillery rounds into the garden.

Alexa squealed.

"Yes. Come now, please," I told Monsieur Lassay. "With police quickly. Someone attack with boom boom."

By the time we'd got up the courage to get dressed (who wants to be shot while half-naked?) and peep out the window, there was a lull in the firing. Out the bedroom window I could see a corner of the barn, most of the orchard, and the fields beyond, sloping up to the edge of the valley. The orchard seemed to have grown new trees with fluorescent orange trunks and rifle branches.

These, I gathered, were hunters. A group of six or seven men armed with pump-action shotguns were standing and listening to Monsieur Augème, who was waving his arms around and pointing down toward the house.

"Why are they wearing those orange waistcoats?" I'd always thought that hunters were supposed to hide from their prey, not announce to every living thing within a kilometer that there were killers on the loose.

"Because they shoot each other," Alexa explained. "They are known for shooting everything that moves. Cats, dogs, people who go for a walk, and other hunters. So now they wear orange. Also, it is easier to find them in the forest if they fall into an alcoholic coma."

"Come on, let's go and see what's happening," I said, rather courageously, I thought.

Alexa and I made lots of noise unlocking the back door and emerged talking loudly in an attempt to let the hunters know that we weren't rabbits.

I called out, "Bonjour," and we strolled slowly up toward the orchard.

Monsieur Augème was distributing cigarettes. When he saw us, he shooed the hunters away, and they began to walk back up toward the fields.

Augème came down to meet us, shook our hands, and said it was a fine morning, which it was—the sky was dull gray, the clouds low, but the air was fresh without being chilly. Now that the guns had stopped, birds were lifting their heads from their trenches and daring to sing again.

"What here, er, is happening why?" I asked the old farmer.

Alexa translated the reply. "The hunters thought the house was empty. Usually they never come down here. They were trying to protect us from rabbits."

"There are giant man-eating rabbits round here, then?" I asked her.

"Yes, they come and devour the sheep and any vegetables you plant."

"But we love the rabbit," I told Monsieur Augème sternly.

Monsieur Augème seemed to agree. Alexa translated again.

"He says he is happy to hear this and the hunters will give us two for lunch if they shoot enough."

"Tell him I never eat animals that I have to peel myself."

"We must not refuse. We will be his new neighbors."

I felt a little jolt of happiness. This was the first time I could remember Alexa referring to anything between us as "we." It was "my house" we were trying out, and if we went round to any of her friends, it was always that they wanted to meet me, not that they'd invited us over.

"Okay, I guess we can always bury the rabbits once it gets dark."

"No, I will cook them."

Alexa thanked Monsieur Augème for the offer, and he went off up the field after the hunters, who'd almost reached the tree line and were fanning out into hunting formation again, their fluorescent jackets bobbing about like floats on a sea of plowed mud. The sheep in the next field instinctively moved away en masse from the men with the guns. Who said sheep were stupid.

Monsieur Lassay came over an hour or so later, and we conducted our negotiations around the kitchen table. Today he was looking even more English than last time, with a waxed jacket and shiny elastic-sided brown boots.

He'd brought the *promesse de vente* with him, a multipaged booklet with large blanks for the description of the house, the land, the present and future owners. He'd filled in some of the answers in tidy blue ink and talked me through the various stages of buying. I had to sign the form and deposit a check for 10 percent of the price and would then have a seven-day cooling-off period during which I could retract my offer without losing my deposit. If I pulled out after that, though, the seller got the 10 percent. Meanwhile, the seller couldn't sell to anyone else, even if they made a better offer. The form gave a date, two months away, on which we would sign the final sale agreement, the *acte de vente*. It all seemed clear, except for one thing.

"You are lawyer or man who sells?" I asked.

He nodded—fair question. "In small towns, we are often both the lawyer and the agent. People ask us to sell their houses because they know we can do the legal work for them." He fluttered the termite, lead, and asbestos (*amiante*) certificates at me and a stapled wad of papers that listed the exact surface area of the property—each room, the barn, the garden, the orchard, the fields, everything measured down to the last square millimeter by a certified surveyor.

"I find lawyer also, me?"

"If you want. Or I can do the administration for you, too. There are not many lawyers here, and a Parisian will not do it for you." He snorted a laugh at the ridiculousness of this idea.

"What you must do for me, legal things?"

"Oh, I make sure that the commune, the local mayor's office, does not want to buy the house for municipal housing. But he won't—" He placed a reassuring hand on my arm. "I make sure that the railway company does not want to send a new railway line through this valley—which they won't. There is already the TGV line south of here. I prepare the final acte de vente."

"How much I pay you for this?"

He didn't look at all offended by the question. "Me personally, not very much. The state, a lot. You must pay five percent of the price in tax."

"Five percent?"

"Yes, and it was ten until recently."

Even with the extra 5 percent on top, the price was still irresistible. Monsieur Lassay unscrewed his chic black Mont Blanc fountain pen, and I signed two copies of the forms, one for the seller, one for myself. I wrote out a check and wafted it around my warm new kitchen to dry the ink. Alexa was smiling at me encouragingly. Monsieur Lassay was looking as content as a man who is about to receive a check usually does.

"Can we come here also next weekend?" I asked.

"Yes, I think that is no problem. After all, the house is almost yours. You will let Monsieur Augème continue to use the fields?"

"Why not?" I shrugged.

"Good. I will go to see him and reassure him. He wants to begin planting."

"What plant?"

"I don't know. But do not worry, these old farmers are all practically biological."

"Biological?"

"Organic," Alexa translated.

We all wished each other "Bon dimanche" and Monsieur Lassay dug his car keys out of his jacket pocket. "You are so lucky here with your generator," he said. "In the town we have no electricity. It is like medieval times. We cannot read after six in the evening."

Oh, how smug I felt.

The following weekend could have been programmed by a software company making an interactive film called *A Hundred Reasons Why You'd Be Stupid Not to Own a Slice of Rural France.*

They'd got the weather exactly right—crisp air that dried the mud and made you want to bound out along the winding country tracks. They'd zapped the hunters (who, Monsieur Augème said, weren't trying to kill rabbits after all—they came to this part of the valley only because a wild pig had been causing damage to some new tree plantations). The programmers had given Alexa an enhanced libido and a newfound desire to make huge meals out of all the local produce we bought at the market (which in turn had been re-created using picturesque rural images provided by the French Ministry of Food Clichés). And the software writers even managed to get mains electricity restored, by keying in some agreement from Electricité de France to reinstate its plans to sell nuclear power technology to third world countries and thereby guarantee jobs for life for its French workers.

I'd have been crazy to pull out of the deal. I was drinking white Loire Valley wine and wondering which part of Alexa to kiss next as my seven-day deadline tiptoed discreetly past the bedroom window on its way to Lassay's office.

Buying my own bit of France seemed to cause a subtle change in my mentality. I found that I understood a lot more about Parisians' attitude to work. Workdays became a mild irritant inserted between weekends. Friday afternoons were little more than a short period after lunch during which you checked the Internet for traffic jams on the routes out of town.

My tearoom project hibernated through January, but I didn't fret. I was much more interested in Monsieur Lassay's progress through the legal morass. Whenever I called up for news, he always took the basic Alexa line on house buying—everything seems okay.

*   *   *

One Saturday afternoon when Alexa and I were down at the *maison*, which I was renting every weekend, Jean-Marie popped his nose in the kitchen door while we were having coffee. He was in the region "to kiss the caïd again," he said.

"The caïd?" Alexa asked.

Jean-Marie was much too interested in Alexa's physical attributes to bother answering. He asked who the "beautiful young lady" was and held her hand for so long, I thought he was trying to engrave her fingerprints on his palm. He was standing over her like a heron waiting for the right moment to skewer a poor innocent carp.

And the worse thing was, Alexa was smiling into his eyes and loving every second of it.

"Do you want to look around the place?" I asked Jean-Marie. As far as I was concerned, he could start at the top end of the orchard and keep going till he got stuck in the mud.

"Or have some coffee?" Alexa offered.

"Oh no, I would love to, but I must go," he said, tearing himself away from Alexa with an almost audible ripping of flesh. "Le caïd a un caillou à la place du coeur."

She simpered admiringly at his bit of poetry, and he was gone, leaving a cloud of hot testosterone in his wake.

"What did that mean?" I asked.

"I don't know. The caïd has a heart of stone," Alexa said, gazing fondly at the door. "He is very friendly, your boss."

"Friendly? No, that was him in a bad mood. When he's feeling friendly, he bends straight down and gives you oral sex."

"Oh, you are jealous!" she said as if it was somehow perverse to object to his lusting after her.

"Yes, I am jealous. Who wouldn't be?"

I thought Alexa would be flattered to hear this, and I was right.

I was lying, though. I wasn't jealous, I was mad. What a bastard, coming on to my girlfriend like that, right in front of me. If I'd been out weeding the potatoes, he'd have invited her for a ride in his company shagmobile. Or at the very least charmed a phone number out of her.

A rapper would have called up his homies to organize a little drive-by. But I was a gentleman farmer (well, almost), so I decided to take less violent action.

I was pleased to find that Stéphanie hadn't changed her password and still had her cute habit of deleting messages but not emptying her trash. What's more, she didn't seem to realize that the "Messages Sent" folder was storing all her correspondence for snoopers to read. People like that really shouldn't be allowed to send e-mails about illegal food imports.

I stayed on late one evening to click back through her recent mail. It was a Wednesday, when the offices were emptier than normal because lots of mums took Wednesdays off when their kids didn't have school.

So there was a deathly silence on my floor as I whistled my way out of my office and into Stéphanie's.

The first signs of what I took to be the *caïd's* presence came about a month earlier, with an e-mail from Jean-Marie saying, "Je m'en occupe"—"I'll deal with it"—in reply to Stéphanie saying, "Il faut absolument calmer le jeu avec FN." ("Calm the game with FN"?)

I did a search for messages containing "FN," whoever he or she was. I found her warning Jean-Marie that together, FN and "chasse et pêche" could cause "graves ennuis" in Jean-Marie's "circonscription," as well as for the company. Could it be right that "hunt and peach" would cause "serious boredoms" concerning Jean-Marie's foreskin removal? I would have to ask Alexa to translate for me.

I printed off the message and went further back in time, to a mail sent just before the demos outside our office building. That was when I'd found out that Jean-Marie was importing British beef.

The message was long and carefully typed, with all the accents included, and seemed to be some kind of circular. Stéphanie had forwarded it to Jean-Marie, then "deleted" it. It was from a representative of the Front National, a name that even I recognized. FN, of course. This was the extreme right political party that had got to the last round of the presidential elections in 2002. The e-mail seemed to be written entirely in euphemisms, but I thought I got the message. This was a time for patriotism, not internationalism. Globalization was a cancer eating away at the French way of life. The FN would be reminding the people of this at the municipal elections in May, in partnership with its associates in Chasse et Pêche. All French companies, especially those with interests in the rural economy, should remember this.

This could have been a simple "buy French" message, if Stéphanie hadn't added a little note when she forwarded it to Jean-Marie—if I understood right, she was asking him if he intended to stand for reelection in May. Reelection? So Jean-Marie was a politician as well as a seller of minced beef and a future café owner?

I printed off the other e-mails that I wanted to reread and got out of there.

I was careful about how I tackled Alexa for the translations I couldn't find in my dictionary. I wasn't sure how long the effects of Jean-Marie's seduction-by-hypnosis technique would last.

We were sitting in the cinema, waiting for the start of a Franco-

German documentary about the working conditions of the Chinese girls who made a certain well-known brand of girls' dolls.

We'd just bought our overpriced ice creams from an underpaid usherette when I casually asked, à propos of nothing, who Chasse et Pêche were. It turned out that they were a rural political party, formed by hunters and fishermen to defend their right to ignore EU laws against the massacre of any endangered species unwise enough to migrate across France.

And they seemed to put human migrants in the same bag as feathered ones—they were all fair game.

I'd heard, I mentioned to Alexa as we watched an ad for a massive diesel-powered 4WD, that the Chasse et Pêche might form an alliance with the FN for the municipal elections in May.

This didn't surprise Alexa, who bit unconcernedly into her chocolate Cornetto.

Who exactly got elected in municipal elections? I asked.

"My horse," she said.

"Uh?"

"My horse of towns and villages and arrondissements." She was irritated that I didn't understand, although the music for this never-ending ad for the gas-guzzling monsters was making conversation, even for people who spoke the same language, almost impossible. "Les maires!" she yelled in my ear just after the music had stopped.

"Oh, mayors," I said, rubbing my numbed ear and wondering why I had a sinking feeling in the pit of my stomach.

I sat back and prepared to be convinced that I shouldn't buy myself any more Chinese-manufactured dolls.

As soon as I got home—alone, because Alexa didn't feel sexy after such a depressing film (why go and watch the damn thing with me, then? I didn't ask)—I went on to the French government Web site and found the proof I wanted.

The mayor of Trou was a certain Jean-Marie Martin, "local entrepreneur and landowner." He'd been elected as an independent candidate, but, clicking around on other election results in the region, I saw that he'd benefited from surprisingly low percentages for the FN and Chasse et Pêche, who usually got high scores in nearby rural constituencies.

Call me suspicious, but this set me wondering about "friendly" Jean-Marie. It was about 1:00 a.m. Madame Hippo was upstairs dreaming of stomping through reed beds in Central Africa. There were only a few isolated shouts and laughs from passing revelers outside and the distant thud of music from the gay bar on the corner of the street. The relative silence helped me piece together fragments of doubt that had been blowing around in my mind like scraps of torn-up newspaper.

What kind of man, I wondered, arranges for someone to get a bonus of a few hundred euros that are to be paid back to him as rent for his absent daughter's apartment? It ought to have been pigeon feed to a businessman as rich as Jean-Marie. Unless, of course, his whole life revolved around never losing out.

So, my thoughts ran on, what was I to think about the fact that it was Jean-Marie who had so kindly introduced me to Monsieur Lassay? And lent me a car—*free of charge*—to go and visit the place?

It was a thought that kept me awake for the rest of the night.

Next morning, I called Lassay "to see how things were progressing." As usual, "everything was in hand," "what was there to worry about?" and so on. What indeed. I made an appointment to meet him for a more detailed progress report on the following Sunday lunchtime.

I then took Nicole out to lunch to a restaurant that had just opened up near our office, where the service bordered on the slavish. It made a refreshing change to be treated with so much respect.

I hadn't seen much of Nicole recently, because she didn't come to many of our "committees." I'd assumed this was for two reasons—one, we weren't at a stage where we were spending the budgets she'd set aside for us; and two, she had real work to get on with.

As a slightly chubby young waiter handed us the menus, hand-chalked on small blackboards, Nicole explained that I was wrong on the first count. My Tea Is Rich was spending quite a lot. Creating our logo (which looked to me like "My Tea Is Rich" written in beige Times Roman italics) had cost a small fortune. And the mortgages on our future premises were expensive, given the neighborhoods they were in. Though this didn't matter too much, Nicole said, because the premises had been let out to a chain of discount shoe stores on short-term leases.

Premises? Mortgages? Short-term discount shoes? Jean-Marie had been much busier than I thought.

But I wasn't really shocked to learn all this. If she'd told me that Jean-Marie had bought up the state of Darjeeling and had every other tea plantation in Asia napalmed, I don't think I'd have done more than raise an eyebrow.

I ate oysters, which I could now slurp down without thinking of bronchitis, and an inch-thick fillet of smoked haddock in a mustard sauce, served with a *tian*—a sort of courgette flan. This, washed down with a light white Sancerre, cost about the price of a bad pub sandwich in London.

Nicole talked me through the *promesse de vente* that had been lying, almost forgotten, on the desk in my bedroom for the past few weeks.

Everything standard, she said, the two-month deadline for final completion was shorter than usual, but this was presumably because I didn't have to sell a house to finance the transaction, so things were less complicated.

Was there any way of pulling out of the deal if I wanted to? I asked.

Nicole finished swallowing a mouthful of her seared cod and considered this.

Frowning, concentrating hard on a problem, she was, I decided, attractive in a dowdy sort of way. She fiddled with a slender gold necklace, put a clear-varnished nail to lips that still bore traces of her faint pink lipstick even halfway through lunch. She was a woman who looked after herself, and a tactile person, even though you had to watch her closely to notice it. A flicker of humor creased the laugh (or care) lines at the corners of her subtly made-up eyes.

"You want to buy a country château, no?" she asked.

"I'm not sure anymore."

"In that case," she said, leaning closer as if the businesswoman at the next table might eavesdrop above the voice in her mobile phone, "the classic way to stop a transaction for a ouse is with your bank. If hit refuses to give you the credit."

"The loan?"

"Yes, the loan. If hit refuses to give you the loan, you can recuperate your ten percent."

"Ah." Even a swill of the fruity wine did nothing to raise my spirits. There was no chance of the bank turning me down. When the bank manager had seen my salary, my rent, and the price of the house, he not only gave me a mortgage, he'd also tried to sell me a car loan, asked why I didn't also buy myself a small apartment in Paris, and suggested I avail myself of the bank's instant "thousand euros cash for small emergencies" facility.

"Is that the only way I can pull out?" I pleaded with Nicole as the waiter refilled our glasses.

"Yes, if the ouse does not fall down." She giggled, looking shyly around the restaurant to make sure that her delicate laughter was not bothering the other customers.

"Right, so I have only one option. Go and buy some explosives."

From the way my half-full glass splashed its load across the table, I think the waiter must have understood English.

The following weekend, Alexa couldn't come with me because her dad had been dumped by his spoon stylist guy and was threatening to do something drastic to himself with a knife.

I went out to the *maison* anyway. I needed to be there, to get a real feel for the place again before taking any decisions.

I arrived pretty late, after Saturday lunchtime. Rural France was looking its usual charming self. A gentle sweep of valley, empty except for the bare trees, the dotted houses, and Monsieur Augème's red tractor, which was pulling a seeding machine up the plowed slope toward the tree line.

I parked the car outside the barn and started walking up toward him. There was still dew on the long grass in the orchard, and my Parisian trainers were soon soaked. As I got to the top edge of the orchard, Monsieur Augème began rolling back down toward me.

It was a large tractor for such a small farm, I thought. And quite new for such an old farmer. It had a cab big enough for two and back wheels as tall as the old man himself. It was trundling, steady as a rock, along the deep furrows, not diverting one centimeter left or right as it flicked out its seeds.

He'd got about twenty yards down the hill when he looked up and saw me emerging from the orchard. I wasn't exactly in camouflage gear—I was wearing a bright orange sweatshirt and a white woolen hat to keep the damp chill out of my sensitive urban ears.

As soon as he caught sight of me, he steered a course away to my left, toward the gate that led down to his own farmhouse. At the gateway, he stopped, climbed out of his cab, and grabbed up three or four white plastic sacks, which he stuffed any old how into the cab. He then jumped nimbly up into the driver's seat and chugged back to his own barn at top speed.

I didn't think this was because he'd forgotten to put on a clean vest that morning.

I looked across a low wire fence at the furrows he'd been planting. The earth had been turned over again to protect the seeds from the hungry crows, but I could see a few whitish spots in the mud where dried grains of maize had fallen outside the furrow.

Over to my right, in the other field, the sheep were standing in two huddles, perhaps wondering whether or not to be frightened of the figure in orange. Next to the electric fence keeping the sheep out of the plowed field, I saw that there were a couple of large white bags like the ones that Monsieur Augème had been so keen to hide.

I wandered up toward the discarded bags. The sheep decided I might be a hunter and scattered away across the pasture.

Lying crumpled in the mud were two seed bags bearing the name of the crop (*maïs*), a serial number, and the logo of one of the world's best-known agrochemical firms, which was famous outside the farming community for trying to persuade people that we would all be a lot better off if we just gave in and accepted that the future of agriculture lay in genetically modified crops.

So, not content with receiving EU subsidies, Augème was also getting paid to test GM crops? No wonder he could afford a new tractor.

I turned away from the skittish sheep and saw that the old farmer was standing on his back tractor wheel, watching me from the safety of his farmyard.

Next morning, I was awakened by what sounded like a firing squad. I already had a headache after getting through two bottles of wine the previous evening during my long, thoughtful dinner.

It was the hunters again, but much closer this time. Orange-jacketed figures were stalking about in front of the barn, in the orchard, even just outside the kitchen door, across what I'd hoped to turn into my fennel patch.

One of them, a red-faced fatso with a mustache the size of an adult rat, was standing, camouflaged legs apart, shotgun over one shoulder, like something on the cover of a Rambo fanzine. He was staring straight at my bedroom window.

Having neither bulletproof vest nor rocket launcher to hand, I thought it best not to oppose the assault. Instead I ducked down and called in reinforcements.

"What?" Monsieur Lassay said blearily. Like me, he'd been woken out of a deep sleep. "Hunters? They probably think the house is empty today."

"No, no. One man looks my window bedroom," I argued, switching over to emergency, grammar-free French.

"I will call Monsieur Augème, he will tell them to go," Lassay said with the calmness of someone who's not surrounded by armed thugs.

I risked a peep outside the window. Rambo was still staring in at me, though he'd now moved two paces nearer and had drawn a knife that would have been called a sword in most parts of the world. He didn't look as if he was going to be scared off by a little old farmer.

"I am not sure for that. Can you arrive quickly here, please?"

"I will come tout de suite." Lassay sounded pissed off, I was glad to hear.

I hung up, thinking as I did so that the hissing I could hear was probably one of Élodie's tires breathing its last sigh of life down the blade of a hunting knife.

I was, quite frankly, shit-scared by now. I crept round the house on all fours, bolting all the doors, although a determined hunter could have broken in just by tapping any window politely with the butt of his rifle.

Then I went and sat in the fireplace, which was deep and dark enough to hide me, even before I pulled an armchair across to block the view from the window.

Fortunately, I'd made a fire the previous evening, and the residual warmth from the dead-looking embers calmed my goose bumps a bit. I was wearing only a T-shirt and underpants.

Crouching in my hiding place, I could hear the triumphant laughing voices that Bosnian Muslims must have heard before the paramilitaries burst in and dragged their menfolk away.

There was a shot and a smashing window, another shot and what I took to be the splatter of lead pellets against the house.

At last there was a knock on the front door. Lassay.

I crept out of the fireplace, sprinted into the hall, and threw open the door.

I was met by a rat-size mustache and an alcoholic's red nose. Rambo.

It had never occurred to me that they'd knock at the front door. Rambo the psychologist.

My already shriveled balls shrank farther up into my underpants as the hunter and I examined each other at close range. He'd slung his rifle behind his back and sheathed his knife, but he still looked scary enough for me, especially with his gaggle of chums hanging about in the background.

"Bonjour," he said.

Not wishing to be impolite to such a well-armed group of gentlemen, I replied in kind.

"Ça va?" he asked.

"Oui, et vous?" It was just like greeting one of my co-workers in the lift. Apart from the weapons, of course.

"You intend to buy this house?" He called me *tu*, the word for friends, family, children, animals, and people belonging to races you don't respect.

"I don't know. Is it good idea for me?"

He laughed with a great puff of alcohol fumes. If I'd popped a lighted match in his mouth, he'd have gone into orbit.

"You know if you buy the house, we have legal access, we can hunt here when we want?" He was speaking slowly, with his patois twang under control so that I got the full implications of every word.

"Even in my bedroom?"

He laughed again and glanced pointedly down at my bare legs. "You are Martin's little friend?" This was a slur on my manhood, which there was no point reacting to.

"Jean-Marie Martin? He is my boss. Why?"

"If you buy the house, you will prolong all the same agreements as him?"

"Agreements? What?"

"With old Augème, for example."

"Ah. The maize?"

"For example." He nodded slowly, as if congratulating me for understanding some complex point. "There have been protesters who tried to stop this. They have pulled up plants and tried to cause us all sorts of merde. They are city people. We are just farmers trying to make a living. And the gendarmes know that it is best to support us." He grinned a warning. So all this was because I'd caught the old bastard planting GM crops?

"You say me the agreements are with Monsieur Martin. Why with Monsieur Martin?"

"It is his house, non?" From the look on Rambo's face, I was supposed to know this already. He was right. I really should have known. But on my *promesse de vente*, the seller was named as someone local.

"It is his house? Merde."

The hunter smiled and relaxed. He turned to wink at one of his co-Rambos. Saying *merde*, admitting publicly that you are in it, seemed to soften even the hardest French heart.

"If it is his house," I said, "no, I do not buy it."

It struck me that I ought to ask the guys to burn the place down so as to release me from my contract, but I didn't have time. Satisfied with the success of their scare tactics, the hunters were already wandering off.

Rambo turned back and smiled. "Bon dimanche," he wished me.

The old executioners probably used to say "Bonne guillotine" before they cut people's heads off.

"No, it is not Monsieur Martin's house," Lassay insisted half an hour later. I didn't believe him. "He made a donation of it to this seller, who is a cousin and who does not want to keep it."

"So Jean-Marie receive zero euro if I buy?"

Lassay hesitated a split second too long before saying no.

I sat back, fully dressed now, in the armchair that had hidden me from the hunters. There was a wood fire crackling where I'd crouched, and it filled the small sitting room with a thin haze of sweet-smelling smoke.

I looked Lassay in the eye and shook my head. It was unbelievable. Not so much that I could have been taken in. After all, Jean-Marie had fooled the whole Ministry of Agriculture. And he was a French politician, so he was used to playing in a world-class league of double-dealers. At that very moment, practically the whole of France was being taken in by their president's show of pacifism with regard to the looming Iraq war, even though informed voices were saying that he was motivated by the oil contracts that France had signed with Saddam.

I didn't feel ashamed at being taken for a sucker. And I didn't blame the French public for swallowing the line that the president was throwing them. There was no shame in being fooled by a master shyster—it happens to all of us.

No, what I found unbelievable was that Jean-Marie would do it to *me*. Why not just put the house on the open market? At such a low price, someone was bound to buy it eventually, weren't they?

Weren't they?

"Monsieur Lassay—I have a question very important."

He shifted slightly in his armchair, and I thought I detected a real physical effort to look honest. A widening of the eyes, a tilting of the head.

"This house has a problem?" I asked. "Secret problem and no one buy it normally?"

"Secret problem?" He tried a Parisian shrug, but he was too provincial to carry it off. A Parisian's shrug would have dismissed the idea as pathetic stupidity. His simply tried to deflect it.

"You are lawyer," I said. "I ask you legal question now. I find other lawyer if you do not answer. For a first thing, it is not normal you are one lawyer for two people in this transaction, no?"

He didn't shrug this time.

"Alors, Monsieur Lassay. Has Jean-Marie a secret problem with this house?"

His shoulders slumped. "Okay," he said. "But I am not confident that it is a legal reason to withdraw from the contract."

"What reason?"

"In France we take a different view of some things."

"What things?"

"For many people, it is an opportunity for employment, an attraction for new businesses."

"What is?"

"The new nuclear power station."

FÉVRIER

Make Amour, Not War

T HERE IS ONE thing about love that you can't fail to learn if you live in France. An essential thing. A thing that makes us English speakers sound laughably ignorant in the arts of seduction.

It is this: Lingerie isn't pronounced the way we think it is at all. It's not "lon-je-ree" or "lon-je-ray." It's "lan-jree."

The French don't understand our pronunciation of lingerie at all. You try telling a French woman that you want to buy her some "lon-je-ree" and she'll be at a loss. At best, she'll think you want to buy her something from the *boulangerie*. What would you like for Saint Valentine's Day, *chérie*? A loaf of bread?

Alexa wasn't a lingerie type of gal. She was more a nudity kind of gal, which suited me fine.

So as we entered February, the month of love, I wondered what I should get her as a Valentine's treat.

A romantic weekend in Venice, maybe?

Late one night, as we were snuggling up on my bed, listening to the sound of Élodie still not being there to make strange noises through the bedroom wall, I asked her if she'd ever been to Venice.

"No."

"Would you like to go?" I gave her the lightest of kisses on the temple to try to conjure up some Italian romanticism.

"I don't want to think of travel in this climate."

My kiss obviously hadn't been Venetian enough. It should have been wetter, maybe, more canal-like.

"Too cold, you mean?"

"No." She de-snuggled herself and sat up. "In this political climate, of course."

It was true that the world was marching steadily toward war.

Or that certain English-speaking parts of the world were trying to convince the UN to give everyone a ride in that direction.

"It will be too dangerous to travel," she said. "A war in Iraq will make the Muslims believe we hate them and cause terrorism everywhere."

"Right. Shame Chirac can't nip down to Baghdad and persuade Saddam to turn into a nicer kind of guy," I mused.

Alexa wriggled completely clear of my arm and turned to stare at me as I lay back on the pillow. "Was that supposed to be ironic?" she demanded.

"No."

She took that as an ironic yes.

"I do not understand you British!" she huffed. "Supporting the Americans when all they are doing is protecting their own interests."

I'd heard this old chestnut so often in the previous weeks that I couldn't stop myself.

"What, and Chirac isn't protecting French interests? The oil contracts between Elf and Saddam? The fact that Saddam owes France billions of dollars and that the Americans want to cancel the debt if his regime falls? And France is quick enough to send troops into African countries to protect its interests, isn't it? This sudden outbreak of pacificism sounds to me like wanting to have your croissant and eat it."

"Croissants? What has this got to do with croissants?"

I tried to explain my witticism, but she cut me off.

"In any case, you are just anti-French at heart."

"What?"

"Yes, like all the Anglo-Saxons."

"Why do French people call all us English speakers Anglo-Saxons? The Anglo-Saxons were a tribe of hairy blonds with horns on their helmets who invaded the British Isles in the Dark Ages. Do I have a helmet with horns on?"

"In spirit, yes. You are all Vikings. Invaders."

"Yeah? Unlike the French, who started off all this hatred between Muslims and the West by massacring I don't know how many Algerians in a colonial war. And who screwed up so badly trying to hang on to their colony in Vietnam that they provoked twenty years of napalm, civilian casualties, and some of the worst movies in Hollywood history? Some of the best, too, mind you. *Apocalypse Now, Born on the Fourth of*—"

But Alexa wasn't ready to end our political differences with a joke. She got off the bed, pulled on her jeans, slipped into her trainers, and walked out of the bedroom. I heard her grab her jacket from the hook, and then the door slammed.

There was a muffled protest through the ceiling from the snooty woman upstairs.

"Too much noise, is there?" I jumped up and stomped into the hall. "One tiny slam of a door and you're complaining?"

I took a broom out of the hall cupboard and walked around the apartment, banging on the ceiling as if I was hopscotching upside down in platform shoes.

"There, is that quiet enough for you?" I growled at the ceiling as I thumped. "Did that wake you up?" Bump, bump, bump. "You don't mind making noise, but you don't like getting it, do you?"

Thud, stomp, bang. "You want to have your croissant and eat it, too, don't you?"

Boom, bam, *BOOM*.

Petty, I know, but ecstatically soothing when your girlfriend has just walked out on you.

I stayed away from the kiddies' bedroom, of course. Even Anglo-Saxon invaders have hearts.

Lingerie isn't the only interesting bit of French love-speak.

The English word *rupture* is brutal but simple—it's a hernia, a painful splitting of the stomach wall that can be put right with a few surgical stitches. In French, though, it means, among other things, the splitting-up of a couple. There's no simple operation to cure that. And quite frankly, I didn't have the mental energy to attempt the kind of microsurgery that would have been necessary to get Alexa back. I called a few times and left conciliatory messages. I think I might even have admitted that the Brits and the Americans were behaving a bit like Vikings. But all the time I was thinking, Hell, what kind of relationship forces you to leave political messages like that? Then finally I got the good-bye text. "Do not call me," she texted. "You cannot persuede me."

"Persuede"? A new word meaning to wrap someone up in soft leather? No, I was never going to do that to her. It'd be too frivolously erotic. She was just too serious for me. She put political principles above the chance of a little human affection.

I'd never met anyone like that before. When I was at college, the only reason anyone joined political movements was to get laid.

I thought back to the first time Alexa and I had ruptured ourselves (in the French sense). She'd said that two people from different cultures could never stay together. It seemed she was right after all. Especially with the French and the British at that moment in history.

There was one way I'd have liked to worsen Franco-British relations even more, but sadly Jean-Marie wasn't around for me to kill. I don't know if he was just keeping out of my way, but he wasn't coming into the office at all.

"He is on visits to clients," was all Christine would say.

Meanwhile, of course, my *promesse de vente* was ticking away like a booby-trapped bottle in a crate of vintage Burgundy.

I took the contract to a lawyer Nicole had recommended. The office was in a chic building just on the other side of the Champs-Élysées. There was a golden shield fixed above the entrance, as if inside you'd find gladiators for hire.

I explained to the best of my ability what I wanted, and the secretary seemed very interested until she understood that I didn't want her boss to take on the sale. She told me to "attendez ici" and left me to admire the thickness of the carpet and the intricacy of the engraved views of eighteenth-century Paris hanging on the wood-paneled walls. Legal work obviously paid pretty well.

Two minutes later the secretary came trotting back, her high heels sinking soundlessly into the carpet.

"No, I'm sorry, Maître Rondecuir cannot accept this commission," she said, smiling regretfully. She stood there clasping her hands in front of her crisp white blouse until I'd accepted defeat and was heading for the door.

"Bonne journée," she wished me, which seemed kind of inappropriate seeing that she'd just screwed up my entire financial life.

There was only one solution to my legal troubles. The good old English solution to any dilemma that requires careful thought and planning—go and get pissed.

It was the Saturday before Valentine's Day. What better time to drive an alcoholic dagger through your own heart?

I went up to Oberkampf, where I'd arranged to hook up with three English guys. I'd first met them at an English pub near my office, and we'd bonded in misery as England struggled to yet another gutsy nil-nil draw against some team of Central Asian part-timers. The three guys were a bit more rugby club than my usual drinking buddies, louder and more boisterous, but at least they preferred sharing jokes and football talk to hassling people about their head of state's attitude to the Middle East crisis. They were over here working for a telecommunications company, developing something to do with billing that I didn't understand, even after several pints of bitter had loosened up my mind.

They were already well in the swing of things when I arrived at the bar in the rue Oberkampf, a fairly normal-looking café that for some reason had been adopted by a young crowd as the place to be. The trendily lit place next door was almost empty.

"Paul! Just in time for your round!"

Bob, the loudest of the loud, was yelling at me from approximately two meters away. He was a blond giant, even taller than me, with eyebrows that were nearly white. He and the others were standing by the nicotine-colored wall midway between the entrance and the bar.

I plowed into the smoky throng and reached for my wallet. "Sure. What are you having?"

I shook hands with Bob, Ian—a prematurely balding Yorkshireman—and Dave, a baby-faced Londoner with a permanent grin.

"Demis all round, and whatever the ladies are having," Bob hollered.

"Ladies?"

Bob moved aside to reveal three twenty-something girls, penned in against the wall by the three Englishmen.

"Ladies, Paul," Dave announced grandly. "Paul . . ."

He let the girls introduce themselves, no doubt because he'd forgotten their names.

"Florence." A small but curvy girl, half Indian, with long silky hair and an attractive navel.

"Viviane." A tall white girl with vaguely Asian features and smiling eyes the color of cognac.

"Marie." A dark-skinned black girl, quite heavily built but slim waisted. A typical Parisian mix of ethnic backgrounds. And like typical Parisian girls, they all leaned forward to receive two kisses on the cheek. Except Marie, who gave rather than received.

"Hey, girls, vous n'êtes pas interested in Paul," Dave said. He seemed to have his eye on Marie.

"No, he's gay, is Paul," Ian told the whole bar. "Lives in the Marais."

There was much chuckling among the British contingent, which was cut short by Marie.

"No, ee eez not gay, Pol. Ah av fock eem before." No one was more surprised than me.

Bob guffawed at my embarrassment. "Come on, Paul, tell us all," he demanded.

I held up my hands in ignorance. "I . . . uh . . ." That was as much as I knew.

"Wah you leave me zat morning, Paul? You not Eengleesh gentleman, uh?" Marie whispered something to her two girl-friends, who burst out laughing.

The penny dropped. I pointed openmouthed to her hair, which was now jet black rather than acid blond, as it had been when I'd woken up beside her in her bed all those months ago.

"Loved you and left you, did he?" Dave placed a protective hand on Marie's muscular forearm.

"Lov? Huh! Ten mee-noots, then he sleep."

I was now being laughed at by six bobbing faces and felt even more like getting drunk than before.

"Yeah, I'm sorry, Marie. It was . . . I was . . ."

"You was so queeck, you don't even recognahz me."

"Yeah, well, I never really got a good look at your face."

This provoked shocked gasps from the girls and raucous laughter from the boys.

"You know what I mean."

"Oh, yeah? Strictly trademen's entrance only, was it, Paul?" Bob hooted.

"Touch your toes and clench your teeth?" Dave added.

Time to get the drinks, I decided. I pushed my way to the bar, wondering what suicidal instinct had made me want to drown my sorrows so close to the scene of my previous cock-up with Alexa.

"All French men are a bit effeminate," Bob was bawling when I returned with a trayful of glasses—beers for the boys, wine for Florence, gin and tonic for Viviane, and—scarily—a double rum for Marie.

Bob was big enough not to care if any of the twenty or so Frenchmen in the bar understood him. A couple of them, in their designer gangsta rap outfits, looked the kind to take violent offense, but he blundered loudly on.

"Some of them even carry handbags."

"Des sacs à main?" Marie frowned. The girls conferred as to his meaning.

"Yeah, like tiny little briefcases, with a handle and a strap. Just big enough for their ID card, a Camembert, and a packet of Gauloises."

"That's mainly older guys," I pitched in. "Outside Paris. I've seen them out in the country."

"Ah, oui!" Florence got what we were talking about and described the purselike bags to her friends.

"Yes, zat eez old men," Marie said. "Eez not feminine, eez old. Old Engleeshmen have teets like me. But zey are not feminine lak me." She cupped her T-shirt and heaved her breasts in my direction. I looked away politely. I really was not interested in waking up in her bed again. I was happy to see Dave, who only came up to Marie's chest anyway, moving in for a direct eye-to-nipple view.

As soon as Bob had finished swallowing half of his beer, he climbed back onto his soapbox.

"What about their names, then? They have women's names like Michel and, and . . . what's your boss's name, Paul?"

"Jean-Marie."

"Yeah—a guy called Mary! Weird or what?"

"Yeah." Dave nodded. "You'd never get a British guy with half a girl's name. Like if Bob here was called Bobby Jane."

"Bobby Sue," Ian suggested, gurgling at the sheer ludicrousness of a creature so bulky and hairy sporting a woman's name. The girls, though, were getting a bit pissed off with hearing foreigners knocking the local competition.

"Nems? Huh! Lak Sean Connery? Connerie is bullsheet," Marie protested.

"And mah ex, ee was not feminine," Viviane said. "Zat was beeg problem. E ad two, sree girlfriend always."

"Yes, Frenchmen, zey see a woman, she smile at him, he want to fock you direct, allez hop!" Florence said resignedly.

"Yes, guys, surely the most important thing is that French women are so much more feminine than French men," I said, hinting that maybe it would be in the lads' interest to change the thrust of the conversation.

I aimed my compliment at Florence, but it was Marie who sighed. "Ah, enfin! One of you say somesing pleezant." She grabbed my arm and almost wrenched me off my feet into a congratulatory embrace. "Paul, ee knows, a leetle flattery, zat is ow to get French woman."

"Yeah, you say somesing nice, please." Florence looked teasingly at Ian.

"Right, yeah." Ian finally got the message. "It's true, French women are feminine without being too feminist. Like, at work, they seem to be able to get respect without accusing men of sexism, you know? We've got this woman in human resources . . ."

"What, Sandrine?" Bob asked.

"Oh!" Dave's groan of desire told us all we needed to know about Sandrine.

"Yeah, but she doesn't hide it," Ian went on. "And if you say how good she looks, she doesn't report you to an industrial tribunal for sexual harassment. She just thanks you and asks you if you're interested in a training day on time management."

"With her, I could manage it anytime." Bob got congratulatory high-fives from Dave and Ian, and I felt like the Rollerblade trainer who's just seen his pupils go nose-first into yet another lamppost. Bob really didn't see that he was doing exactly what it took to go home without a Parisian girl that night. His short-sleeved shirt riding up over a hairy navel, his loud, beery voice, his conversation devoid of any of the diplomatic niceties—feminine touches, he would have called them—that a Parisian girl likes. He was a good-looking enough guy, but just too oafishly English to bed any of the Parisiennes I'd met. Unless he was rich and famous, of course, then they'd all be after him.

This was too depressing.

"You know, I might leave you people to it," I announced.

Anyway, getting drunk had become too risky with Marie on the hunt. Best to go home while I could still see well enough to make sure I was alone.

"Oh, yes! We go to different bar. Wiz music, maybe, dance!" Marie's swinging hip almost hoisted me through the window.

"Yeah, shut up and drink up, Paul, I need you to translate my chat-up lines." Bob's arm clubbed me chummily back down to earth again. As we trooped out the door into the cold, refreshingly smoke-free air, Marie's hand clamped itself to my bum. I was beginning to know how the snail must feel just before it gets thrown on the barbecue.

So I was relieved, some nine or ten hours later, to be sitting up alone in my own bed, drinking strong coffee and enjoying my lack of headache. I did feel a little tender down below the sheets, but that was only normal after the drubbing my poor willy had got during the night. I had a look—yes, it was as wrinkly as one of de Gaulle's favorite sausages. Much floppier, though.

"Un toast ou deux?" a voice called from the kitchen.

"Deux!"

There was the scraping of butter on toast from the other side of the wall, and then a naked female body walked in, carrying a breakfast tray. There was something rather comical about the way the tray bisected the body—bare boobs above, trimmed pubic hair below—as if it was a completely unsuccessful attempt to hide her modesty.

"Toast, more café, un oeuf à la coque."

"Thanks, Marie."

Yes, I'd spent the night with Marie. I was the one who'd suggested it, too.

At the second bar she'd dragged us to, a dark, mock colonial clubby place, I'd felt it only fair to tell Marie that she was barking up the wrong tree with me and explained why—Alexa, Jean-Marie, the *maison*. And instead of carrying me onto the dance floor, she sat me down and listened to my troubles.

"Oh, eet eez no problem," she finally said when I got to the bit about the nuclear power station. "I work in bonk, you know."

"Bonk?"

"Yes. Crédit de France."

"Ah, bank, of course." I almost heard the pop as a light bulb went on in my head. "You work in a bank?" Suddenly my spirits were lifted by visions of an open safe spurting out enough cash to refund my 10 percent deposit on the house, fund a candidate to beat Jean-Marie in his local elections, *and* maybe have enough to build a pollution-free wind farm in Trou.

"Yes. I can geev you—what you say? Conseils?"

"Oh, advice." Not money, then. My hopes were deflated like a tire that's been knifed by a drunken hunter.

"Yes."

She talked me through her advice. And it sounded plausible, and I began to worship her.

There was only one more thing I needed to ask her: "Are you going on the big antiwar march tomorrow?"

"No. Why? You sink ze Americans and ze Breetish, they will stop because we march in Paree? Oh no, ze Parisiens do not want a war, we must stop!" She did an excellent impression of an American war strategist not giving a monkey's armpit about French public opinion on Iraq.

"But do you agree with your Mister Chirac or my Mister Blair?"

"Pff! Quelle différence? All ze politicians, zey are like different colors of merde. Pah!" She spat the bad taste out of her mouth.

I laughed and said that I knew it was still early—about 11:00—but did she fancy going back to my place for a spot of *amour?*

She did. So we did.

When we got back, she immediately undressed us both and insisted we take a shower together. We did all the usual soapy, sexy, lathery stuff in the cramped and creaking shower cubicle, and then, when we'd rinsed off, she showed me why she'd wanted us both to have all-over clean bodies. An imaginative girl, Marie, and not just where banking strategy was concerned.

I went to see my bank manager at the first available opportunity—8:45 a.m. on the following Tuesday. My bank, like many shops, was closed on Mondays.

As Marie had advised me, I simply explained why the *maison* wasn't such a good investment after all and that I wanted him to refuse my application for a mortgage. He warned me that I'd have to pay some *frais de dossier*—admin charges—but when he looked them up on his computer, it turned out they'd be about as much as a decent bottle of champagne. Tough, I thought, I'll celebrate with one bottle instead of two. The bank manager checked on the *promesse de vente* that the deadline for refusal wasn't past and told me he'd inform the seller's solicitor that the deal was off.

We smiled and shook hands, and I was out of there ten minutes later, a free man.

The problem was, how to deal with Jean-Marie. Go marching in there with a triumphant grin on my face? No, he'd put me down as a *hystérique*.

Ask why he'd tried to betray me, his loyal English protégé?

No, he'd put me down as a naïve dickhead.

Mention apropos of nothing that I'd decided not to buy the house his friend Lassay had found for me?

No, Lassay would tell him all about our conversation, so he'd know I was being coy.

Jean-Marie didn't broach the subject when he returned from his mysterious travels, so I did what any self-respecting Parisian would have done after a narrow escape from the clutches of a lying, treacherous con artist.

I shrugged and said nothing. *C'est la vie*. Parisian life and all its hypocrisies went politely, discreetly on.

If anything, our relations got slightly better—he was less overpoweringly chummy when I saw him and seemed more respectful toward the man who'd outmaneuvered him.

Seemed being the operative word.

Marie and I didn't buy each other Valentine's cards, but then, as she said, we weren't in love, we were lovers. We were each other's *cinq à sept*, she said—that is, the person you meet to make love with between 5:00 in the afternoon and 7:00, before you go home to your spouse. Although these days, with flexible working hours, you can do it more or less when you want. It was, Marie informed me, just one of France's unique sexual traditions.

For instance, they call an overnight bag a *baise-en-ville*—"screw in town"—meaning that it contains just enough luggage to take when you want to go to Paris for a night of illicit sex.

And on itemized phone bills, only the first few digits of the numbers that you have called are listed—this is to protect married people who have been careless enough to phone their lover from home. True.

Then there was the porn.

Of course, I'd hired the odd film in my time, and during my lonelier moments I'd surfed for free home movies on the Web. But everything was so much less furtive in France. Porn mags were advertised openly in newsagents' windows. Obscenely graphic comic books were on sale in every bookshop. And hard-core, penetrative, ejaculatory porn was on mainstream TV, on one of the six basic terrestrial channels, pretty well every week. Marie had a whole collection of videos that she'd recorded off the TV. These included the "news" program just before the movie, which was usually about who was making which new film or which new porn starlet had made her screen debut. There were profiles of creepy-looking directors (we fast-forwarded them), plus clips of half a dozen films in production and interviews with the stars as they masturbated to keep things going between scenes.

Keeping things going—that's basically how Marie used porn. With the condom effect, after a couple of outings (or innings) my spirit was willing but my flesh was weak. Well, not weak, exactly, just less motivated. So Marie would slot in a video and we'd watch together.

If the droop in my motivation happened at a time when there was a porn movie on TV, we'd watch it live. And one Saturday at midnight, we switched on to find a group interview with all the usual actors and the word *Liberté!* flashing on the screen. The actors were all naked, and their spokesman hardly seemed at all distracted by the fact that he was getting a blow job as he read from his autocue. About a dozen French porn stars were lounging on an immense four-poster bed. The girls were showing us their most intimate piercings, and the guys who weren't speaking had the tools of their trade draped casually across their thighs or pointing up toward their belly buttons. The spokesman's voice droned on monotonously (he was much more gifted at public copulation than public speaking), and it emerged that the actors were going on strike for two weeks because French TV's governing body had announced that it might ban porn from mainstream channels.

"Eez terrible," Marie announced, unplugging my penis from her body. She had been sitting on my lap, casually massaging me with her ample rear end.

The spokesman declared that this ban on televised porn would mean the end of France's *liberté d'expression*. The woman whose face was attached to his lower body nodded in agreement. For obvious reasons, she wasn't free to express herself verbally.

The declaration ended, the screen went blank, and Marie turned off the TV. She announced gravely that out of solidarity with the actors, she wouldn't watch any of the videos she'd recorded from that channel during the whole duration of the strike.

To be honest, I was relieved.

These movies were very unsexy, I thought. The problem was that, like all areas of French society, porn was a cliquey affair, so you just got the same people mechanically shagging each other all the time. You saw enough of their faces during the long, boring "acting" bits to recognize them. (Being French, they had to talk endlessly before they actually got down to action.) So after a while, it was like having to watch your cousins getting it on together, which is not considered very erotic where I come from. All in all, I would have preferred it if the actors had kept their clothes on and made public information films about queuing and being polite to customers. That would have been very new and sexy.

Anyway, Marie didn't need the help of porn stars to keep a man interested. One Friday, after a short bout of *cinq à sept* at my apartment, she took me to a Martinican restaurant in the Marais. Her family was from the French West Indies, and this place, she said, did real home cooking like her mum made.

The place was highly kitsch, with a garish mural of fishing boats apparently flying across a sloping sea. There was jangly Creole music playing, a sort of bouncy, hyperfast reggae that got between your shoulders and made them jiggle about, even if you were a no-rhythm English white boy like me.

The waiter, a young black guy, came over and made various

obscene innuendos about my going out with an Antillaise—not at all in a threatening way. It seemed to be his banter, his way of earning tips. I should eat the boudin—small spicy blood sausages—if I wanted to satisfy my woman, he said. And if we ordered an apéritif cocktail to go with the boudin, my manhood would stand as straight and tall as the glass it came in. (I just hoped my manhood wouldn't have a paper umbrella sticking out the top.)

We gorged ourselves on boudins, *gratin de christophine* (a kind of baked marrowlike vegetable), *accras* (spicy codfish cakes), red beans, rice, pork curry, fried fish, and coconut ice cream, and I was just about ready to go home for some horizontal digestion when Marie announced that I was taking her dancing.

She carried me across the Marais to the Third Arrondissement's small Chinese Quarter. For just a few streets, you felt as if you'd entered some kind of medieval Shanghai. Among the ancient Parisian buildings, there were Chinese restaurants where the menus were only in Chinese, food shops selling almost nothing I recognized as food except for the green bottles of Tsingtao beer, and handbag wholesalers piled high with huge packing cases fresh off the airplane. Even at 10:00 p.m., some of the wholesalers were in there counting and unpacking stock.

In the center of all this, behind a fading façade of enamel tiles, was an Afro-Caribbean disco. Inside it was tropically hot, cramped, and writhing. The music was similar to the stuff I'd heard at the restaurant. A fast, light, shuffling beat, with shrill guitars playing darting melodies. Couples were dancing, all in pairs. It was like the jiving I'd seen in the bar with Alexa, but these partners never let a chink of light get between them. Slickly dressed black guys were thrusting their enviably tight butts at women who seemed to take no offense at all. Well, the thrusting was strictly in time with the beat, after all. The women were split about fifty-fifty, blacks and whites. The men were almost all Africans.

There were a few white guys, and all of them were dancing with totally babe-alicious black women. The cynic in me said that there was probably a BMW convertible in the equation somewhere.

Marie and I gave in our coats, and then she tugged me toward the dance floor.

"I don't know how to dance this," I pleaded.

"Is simple, you imagine you are aving sex wiz ze music," she said, and carried on tugging.

She was right. Instead of trying to leap about to the rhythm, you just eased your weight from one foot to the other—one-two, one-two—and shoved your pelvis at your partner. The better dancers among us were doing more complex moves, but Marie's sex technique worked perfectly well.

What a great club, I thought. And what a good choice to have put on my tightest boxers—this was a club where a boy needed support and control from his underwear.

The trouble was, my spicy meal was getting shaken up into a raging tropical storm inside said boxers. After two or three numbers, it became urgent that we sit out the next dance.

Marie got us a table and some drinks, and I dashed off to ease the mounting pressure on my waistband.

When I got back five minutes later, the drinks were there but Marie had disappeared.

Was Céleste her surname? I wondered.

No, there she was, being dry-humped by a tall, lithe black bloke sporting a silver shirt and some more of those enviable buttocks.

I looked around to see if there were any women who might like a pair of British buttocks thrust at them.

No, there was not one woman sitting alone. And along the bar there was a row of guys waiting to pounce on any poor lady who might be abandoned, even for a few seconds, by her weak-bladdered partner. This, it seemed, was my mistake. In this club, you stand by your woman. Presumably if you need to visit the men's room, you carry her over your shoulder.

I could see Marie looking across at me, smiling, enjoying her dance, shrugging slightly (if eyebrows can shrug) about having been plucked away from me.

I mimed my despair about the lack of female dancing partners, and she seemed to nod toward the far corner of the club.

I peered into the smoky gloom. Over in the corner, there were a few couples having a drink or a smooch and, yes, a woman on her own—a black girl with long blond hair extensions bunched up on top of her head. She was staring blankly at the dance floor as she sucked a lurid cocktail through a stripy straw. There was no other glass on her table.

I did my best at this long range to examine her for hints as to why she might be alone.

She was heavily made up, with jet black lipstick and purple-shaded eyes. Her cleavage looked too bulbous to be entirely natural, and it was stuffed precariously into a low-cut T-shirt that was straining at the seams. A hooker, maybe? But then, I didn't want to sleep with her, and she was my only chance of a dance. I wove my way between the tables toward her.

"Voulez-vous danser avec moi?" I asked.

She let the straw drop from her mouth, looked me up and down, and nodded coolly.

"Okay."

When she got up, I saw that she was wearing a stretch miniskirt that was having the same problems containing her bottom half as the T-shirt was with the two masses of flesh up top. If the skirt had been any shorter, I was sure I'd have been able to read the words *for* and *hire* tattooed on each buttock.

Oh well, I thought, too late now.

She held out her hand and I escorted her as she wriggled her way theatrically to the dance floor. All the drinking couples looked up to watch her pass. It wasn't such a rare event for a white boy to ask a black prostitute to dance, was it?

She clung to me and we rubbed groins in time to the music. Marie was still getting hers rubbed by her smooth partner. I caught her eye and she smiled across at me, apparently amazed by my success at finding a new dancing partner.

She wasn't the only one. A couple of the other black guys dancing nodded to me and smiled, as if they were praising me, a bit patronizingly, for joining in the exchanging game. It crossed my mind that maybe this was one of those swingers' clubs that Paris is so famous for. If so, I was leaving after the next dance. As a rule, I prefer to choose whom I shag.

At the end of the number, Marie broke out of her clinch and came over. "Come, we av dreenk now."

Rather rude to my partner, I thought.

"Dans une minute, je danse une danse encore," I said sternly.

And in fact I felt as if I was getting the hang of the dancing style better with the prostitute. She seemed to have higher expectations and guided me to more intricate steps.

Plus she was a very deft groin rubber.

"No, we av dreenk now," Marie said. She smiled apologetically and wrenched me out of her rival's arms.

"Au revoir," I said. My partner simply tilted her head resignedly and smiled good-bye.

"You aven't seen?" Marie asked as I watched my hooker waddle her way back to her seat.

"Seen what?"

"You aven't feel?"

"Feel what?"

In reply, Marie reached down and rubbed my groin, which was still, let's say, enjoying the memory of its recent close contact with a miniskirt.

"Of course I felt that," I said. "But I didn't notice you trying to get out the way of that guy's thrusting pelvis."

She laughed. "You feel, but you don know."

"Know what?"

Marie stared over at the girl. "Ee as willy."

"No." I watched the girl's slender legs, her slim, wiggling backside. I recalled the smoothness of her cheeks (the ones on her face, I mean). "A man? No way."

"But you av feel is willy, non?"

I thought back to the dance. I pictured the smiles on Marie's face, on the other dancers' faces. They hadn't been approving my etiquette or admiring my footwork, they'd been watching the way I was getting a crotch massage from a transvestite. It now occurred to me that my partner had had rather a prominent crotch for a girl. But then I was still a novice at this genital-contact dancing.

"You were the one who pointed her out to me," I accused.

"As joke, stoopeed, serious Eengleeshman."

"Okay," I conceded, "from now on, the only person who's going to massage my trousers is you, Marie, okay?"

She agreed and didn't limit herself to the dance floor, either. Between dances, she kept up a constant, teasing assault with her hands. Especially when some African women got up to do the *hélicoptère*, a traditional dance in which women bend forward and quiver their backsides to give their man a stand-up lap dance.

Marie saw that I found the tradition quaintly interesting and encouraged my interest with her fingers.

By the time we got back to my apartment, there was absolutely no way I was going to sleep straight away.

An hour of exertion later, I finally let myself drift toward sleep as Marie ran a fingernail over my stomach.

"You see, even Eengleeshmen can learn amour," she said. "And février is entire month of amour."

Lucky for me it's not a leap year, I thought, and floated away to dreams of becoming a nun.

MARS

The Joy of Suppositories

THE FRENCH MAY have a reputation for being two-faced, but in some ways they're more straight-talking than us "Anglo-Saxons." The way they name some things, for instance.

A *soutien-gorge* is a bra, but literally it means "chest supporter," which sounds like a surgical appliance to stop old ladies' boobs from chafing their knees. A firefighter is the much less dashing *pompier*—basically a pump attendant. And the month of March is *mars*, like the planet. The god of war. This year, the name turned out to be especially accurate.

As the month of war began, I decided that it was time to name names. It was now almost six months since I'd started work in Paris. I had sample menus, prototype uniforms, job ads. By rights, the tearooms should have been ready to launch.

But all we had was chat.

This hadn't bothered me too much while I was distracted by my *maison*, but now when I went into work I began to sense a faint whiff of gangrene hanging over the project.

It was symptomatic of this that I didn't manage to assemble everyone in the same room until the end of the first week in March.

"Okay, look at this checklist," I told them, passing around progress charts that illustrated in five colors the yawning gaps in our strategy.

Marc, Bernard, Nicole, and Stéphanie moved aside their coffee cups and studied the grid of ticked and empty boxes.

Jean-Marie held up his sheet like a steering wheel and leaned back in his chair. He hadn't touched his coffee, I noticed. He'd just got back after a working lunch at the Ministry of Agriculture. Our machine coffee probably wasn't up to ministerial standards.

Marc looked up. He seemed to be worried. So he should be, I thought. The blank boxes outnumbered the ticks by at least two to one.

"Where you print dis?" he asked me.

"Print it? If you're worried about security, there's no problem. These are the only copies."

"Uh-huh. Look at dis." He pointed to the shameful progress of our staff recruitment plan.

"Yes?"

"It's vairy der-dee."

"Der-dee?"

"Yeah. Dis red, it is mo lahk brown dan red."

"Maybe everyone printed out Valentine's Day hearts and used up all the red."

"No. Dese new prinners are no damn good." He broke off and ranted at Jean-Marie in French about returning a batch of printers to the suppliers. A pile of American *merde*, he called them, joining in with the prevalent anti-U.S. sentiment in the country, even though his time in the States was probably the most prominent thing on his CV.

This was all very interesting from a sociological and printer technology point of view, but it wasn't exactly why I'd called the meeting.

"Is that all you've got to say? The colors aren't bright enough?"

Jean-Marie seemed to agree with Marc. He was grimacing at his chart as if all the colors were shades of puce.

A strange wheezing noise started to come out of Bernard.

"Zees," he hissed as if he was testing out the whistling capacity of a new set of false teeth. He held up his sheet and pointed to the top, where there was a cluster of ticks showing the few things we'd actually achieved.

"Yes?"

"What eez zees?"

"What do you mean?"

"What eez zees?" He mimed the writing of a tick in midair.

"A tick, of course."

"Teek?"

"Teek?" Now Stéphanie tried out the word for size.

"In England, they use ticks for positive things," Nicole explained. "In *mathématiques*, when the solution is good, the teacher give you a tick. When bad, a cross."

Bernard and Stéphanie found this fascinating and went off on a tangent of questions about what we did on forms if we had to fill in boxes—ticks or crosses? Marc asked them if they hadn't noticed that on some Web sites, when they confirmed something, a tick appeared in a box.

"Ah, yes. Vairy antress-ting," Bernard concluded.

By this time I was reaching for my imaginary Uzi and drawing tick-shaped patterns of bullet holes across their skulls.

"Jean-Marie?" I pleaded. He was still sitting there, looking vaguely pained by our conversation.

He pondered a moment before reacting, then began to wave my chart in the air as if he expected it to rattle.

"This is, as Bernard says, very interesting," he declared. "But, you know, when there is war on the horizon, it is best to—how you say?—drop your head?"

"Drop your head?"

"Yes, you know. Push your head down."

"What do you mean?"

He looked even more pained than before. "I mean, France and Britain have bad relations. If we have a war, who knows if 'nice cup of English tea' will sound so nice to the French public?" He did a tired shrug of surrender.

"Hang on, Jean-Marie, what are you saying here?"

Everyone in the room waited for him to formulate his answer. It came slowly.

"I am saying," he finally said, "that it is better for us if Mister Blair, Mister Bush, and Mister Chirac are friends. We cannot advance until we know the answer. We must wait to see. You go on vacation, Paul. Go to England for a week or two."

I couldn't believe this. I was being deported.

"You mean you're putting the whole project on hold in case there's a war? Isn't that a bit shortsighted?"

He ignored these questions, so I asked some more.

"What will you do if there is a war? Scrap the whole project? Do you know how long the first Gulf War lasted? Barely long enough for one pot of tea to brew."

In reply, he simply grimaced.

"And even if there is a war, do you really think Parisians will care? It'll be spring soon—they'll be much more interested in making sure they've got the right brand of sunglasses perched on top of their heads."

Marc, Bernard, and Stéphanie understood just enough of this to let out a faint "oh" of protest. Jean-Marie ignored them, too.

"If you go to England," he said, "can you FedEx me some indigestion tablets? I have a crise de foie."

Crise de foie—liver crisis—is what they call feeling sick after you've had too much to eat or drink. You've been so gluttonous that your liver is having a nervous breakdown.

"FedEx you . . . ?"

"Yes, in France, the indigestion tablets are only in pharmacies, and the pharmacists have announced a strike from this evening. I will not have enough. I must have too many official meals at the moment." He rubbed his stomach. "In England, lots of medication you can buy in the supermarket," he told the others.

The rest of my working day ticked away listening to a discussion in French of the merits of a deregulated pharmaceutical retail market. It was enough to give anyone indigestion.

Of course, I immediately sent out e-mails to Messrs. Blair, Bush, and Hussein, informing them that a new Gulf War could have catastrophic consequences on the unemployment figures among male British food company workers in central Paris.

I didn't get a single reply, though, so I went back home for my enforced holiday. And was shocked to discover how French I'd become.

For a start, like my old American chum, Jake, I forgot the simplest English words. Words, it seems, are like felt pens. If you don't use them for a while, they dry up.

I nipped into my parents' local branch of Marks & Spencer, and they'd changed the whole place around since my last visit at Christmas. So I went up to a young salesgirl and asked her:

"Where are the . . . ?"

Blank. The first word that popped into the pre-speech compartment of my brain was "slip." This (pronounced "sleep") is not a petticoat. It is the French word for what I wanted, and I'd been hearing it a fair amount from Marie, as in "take off your sleep, Pol."

The next word I thought of was *culotte*, which is for women.

Also used a lot by Marie, as in "Did you know, Pol, that you are talking to a woman with no culotte?"

By this time, the M&S sales assistant was sure I'd gone into a catatonic trance and was frowning up at me as if she thought I might suddenly collapse on top of her.

"Knickers," I wanted to say, but that wasn't it, either. What was the damn word?

"Underpants!" I shouted joyfully, and the poor girl jumped back a yard.

"First floor, on the left," she replied nervously, and went off to alert security that there was a male underwear fetishist with a long-delay stammer heading up the escalator.

Even when I could remember words, my parents said they detected a slight French accent.

My old schoolmates put it more bluntly. "You sound like a Frog," they said.

Down at my old local, where I hadn't been since moving up to London a couple of years earlier, sounding French was not exactly a good idea. With the war looming and France's opposition causing outrage in the tabloids, there were people there who would have taken an ax to the furniture if they'd suspected the polish on it was French.

My old friends were much more politically correct, but I still tried my utmost to sound like a local.

Unfortunately, I was lost. I didn't know who managed the town's football team these days (a treasonable crime punished by having to buy everyone a round of drinks).

When they switched to more international topics, I was okay until they got into serious analysis of the motives for the imminent sequel to the Gulf War. Since when had every Englishman become an amateur UN weapons inspector? And where had they all done their crash courses in advanced diplomacy? Discussing the political games being played on all sides was as exhausting to me as a week-long seminar on the rules of cricket would be to a drunk French pig farmer.

The Parisians, I realized, might be proud of their antiwar stance, but they didn't analyze it much. Saying "It's all about oil" was a kind of fashion statement, like wearing a thong that showed over the top of your jeans. And I'd become like them (except for the thong, of course). I didn't want war, but I didn't want to spend my whole life talking about not wanting it. I wanted to dismiss talk of war with one hip statement and get back to serious subjects like sex, holiday plans, and where to get good seafood.

Ah, yes, food. That was the worst problem. When my mum put her usual salad bowl on the table—uncut lettuce leaves, whole tomatoes, cucumber slices, sticks of celery—I felt an irresistible urge to ignore the mayonnaise and salad cream bottles and make myself some vinaigrette. There was only malt vinegar in the kitchen, though, and some cooking oil of unidentified vegetable origin. I did my best with the ingredients at hand, returned to the table with my bowl of dressing, and began tearing up some lettuce leaves with my fingers. It didn't occur to me that I was doing anything unusual until my dad asked, "Don't they have knives and forks in *Paree*, then?"

"Yes, but . . ." I didn't finish my explanation. Not because I'd forgotten the words, but because I realized how stupid it was going to sound to say, "One doesn't cut lettuce with a knife."

I cut the rest of my leaves with a knife and took a long look at the celery. I'd never seen it eaten in France—they eat only the strong-tasting root, diced up coleslaw style. Celery sticks belong to the class of vegetables, like swede and parsnip, that the French think only just good enough to feed to horses or cattle. Crunching into the hard, stringy flesh, I now agreed with them. Where was the taste? My palette seemed to have been spoiled. One hint of blandness in my food and I started to look around for the nearest hungry horse to feed.

Another difficulty was that I had become allergic to the idea of eating bread bought from a supermarket. How, I wondered, had I and this whole nation survived for so many years without a bakery on every street corner? It now seemed like a basic infringement of human rights.

I was a foreigner.

So I filled my bag with indigestion tablets and English underpants and headed back to a city where I could get better food and more relaxing conversation. As I passed below the English Channel, I wondered how long it'd be before the French decided to brick up the tunnel as a snub to their warlike neighbors from hell.

As I had virtually nothing to do at work, I kept up a regular stream of chitchat with my English mates via e-mail. Chris, my friend who'd been made redundant by a French bank, felt obliged to send me every anti-French joke doing the rounds on the Internet. In just two or three days I accumulated about a hundred jokes, photos, cartoons, and songs. These ranged from the mildly satirical observation that Chirac's attitude might be influenced by the way his name ended in "-irac" to some highly undiplomatic visual suggestions of where the French president might like to insert the Eiffel Tower.

Needless to say, I was careful not to leave any of these lying about on the printer.

I kept an eye out for Jean-Marie but never saw him. The only inkling I got of his existence was that the indigestion tablets I'd left on his desk had disappeared.

Our *comités* weren't happening anymore, and everyone except Nicole and Christine was treating me as if I was a cross-Channel ferry that was about to capsize under them.

Whenever Bernard saw me, he shook my hand and smiled mysteriously at me. As walruses aren't known for being able to smile mysteriously, he just looked as if he was trying to fart. Stéphanie told me (in French) that she was sure France's experienced diplomats would gain the upper hand at the UN over the "unsubtle Anglo-Saxon barbarians."

"Probably yes," I replied (in French). "The diplomats of the Anglo-Saxons talk only Abba language and have wings on the head." She looked bemused. My French still wasn't good enough to convey irony. Marc never broached the subject of war when the others weren't there—I guessed from this that he secretly supported the United States but didn't dare say so. He knew that it was not exactly a fashionable opinion.

Marianne the receptionist didn't mention war, either, but she didn't need to. She glowered at me every time I entered or left the building and obviously thought that I personally wanted to go and bomb Iraq. Or maybe now that I was out of favor with Jean-Marie, she was simply letting her natural unfriendliness show through. She informed me through gritted gray teeth that I shouldn't have taken a holiday without filling in a holiday form and that she wasn't altogether sure I was entitled to a holiday anyway, having been with the company for less than a year.

"Okay," I told her. "I will return the holiday to you." Bugger diplomacy, I decided. This was war.

Christine was her usual friendly, beautiful self but was spending most of her days on the phone to her fiancé or her mum, the former to reassure him, on the hour every hour, that she still adored her *chaton d'amour* (love kitten), the latter to argue about arrangements for the wedding, which was, as far as I could gather, now only a year away. It was being planned more thoroughly than our whole chain of tearooms.

Nicole was the only one of my colleagues I still had meaningful conversations with. I knew that this was partly because she wanted to keep her English up to scratch, but that was okay with me. We started going out to lunch together a lot. The weather was getting better, and it was sometimes good enough to sit outside. Some of the brasseries near the office had overhead heaters between their terrace tables, so if the sun was shining, it almost felt like midsummer. You just had to be careful standing up in case you inserted your head, Chinese hat style, into the gas flames.

It was Nicole who kept me up-to-date on the way worsening Anglo-French relations were affecting my project. With every bitchy skirmish between governments, my tearooms became less and less likely to come to fruition, like a hillside of vines gradually getting its buds knocked off by successive rainstorms. The French media repeated every anti-Chirac headline in the excitable British press, and you'd have thought we Anglos would not have been flavor *du mois* with Parisians in general. But outside of the office, the subject rarely came up.

When I bought my baguette, my atrocious accent flying like a massive Union Jack above my head, the *boulangère*'s only comment was, "Seventy cents, please."

And whenever I walked past a McDonald's or a KFC, the place was always full. Did the clients really think that Happy Meal was a traditionally French concept?

If the mood was slightly somber in Paris, it had little to do with international politics. It was because of the pharmacists' strike.

As my trusty guidebook told me: "In Paris, there is one pharmacy approximately every ten metres, with its green neon cross flashing out a call to the French to come in and overmedicate themselves. And, to paraphrase the old song, you never see a pharmacist on his bike. The licences to set up a pharmacy cost a mint and are bought and sold as voraciously as Monet paintings."

Now, the pharmacy shopfronts were locked up behind iron grids. And below each forlornly unlit green cross, there stood a cluster of sneezing, moaning pharmacy addicts praying for a miracle.

I didn't know it, but I was about to join them. The first blow to my health came, ironically, when a team of doctors flew back into Paris. One of them was Marie's boyfriend.

"Boyfriend?" I asked incredulously when she announced over the phone that we wouldn't be spending the hours of darkness naked together for a change. "You have a boyfriend?"

"Yes. He was not in Paree."

This woman, who for the past month had been wholeheartedly engaging in every sexual act known to humankind with me, felt some kind of allegiance for another man?

"What is he? A monk? A eunuch?" Only this could explain her unquenchable libido, surely?

"No, ee eez doctor." She explained that her boyfriend was a member of Médecins sans Frontières, the French medical charity. He'd been based in Baghdad and had just been warned that British and American bombs might not be able to distinguish between French doctors and Iraqi troops. They took the hint and got out of the country.

All sorts of questions about the doctor's sexual performance, Marie's ability to switch her affections on and off, and my role as some kind of full-size dildo popped into my mind, but it didn't seem worth asking them.

"You av leave some condom at my apartment. You want I send them to you?" she asked.

"No, keep them. You might need them. You never know when your boyfriend will go out and leave you alone for the afternoon."

"Uh?"

"Keep them. I don't need them anymore."

"Why don you tele-fon Florence? She lahk you," Marie

suggested. Florence was her half Indian friend I'd met in the bar. "Ah av tell her you are okay for French woman now."

"What does *that* mean? English women do like sex, you know. Maybe it's just you personally that has to get herself shagged four times a night, every night."

Marie laughed. "You are angry. Call Florence, she is calming you."

"You mean her boyfriend's away for the week and she needs servicing?"

I rang off and breathed a few curses about screwed-up French womanhood. The only thing that could make things worse would be if Élodie came rushing home from the United States in protest at her host country's enmity toward France. But then, knowing Élodie, she would live anywhere as long as there were plentiful supplies of drugs and male models.

One result of getting dumped by Marie was that I was calm and relaxed the day war finally broke out. I'd slept a full eight hours. I had had moments of semiwakefulness, but as I turned over in bed, I was so relieved to find that I hadn't been woken by a hand (or, worse, mouth) tickling my nether regions that I fell instantly back into deep, dreamless slumber.

It took a few minutes of journalists' excited babbling, and several bombardment sound effects, to pierce my consciousness as I lay in bed that morning, relishing the fact that at least one place in the world—my mattress—was a combat-free zone.

Sex, I decided, is wonderful, but it's like champagne. If you're forced to have four glasses at every meal, you start to fantasize about a glass of water.

So it wasn't until I was actually standing under the shower, letting the blistering hot water massage some life back into my stiff muscles (which were stupidly complaining about the lack of a nighttime workout), that I took in the news.

War?

I turned off the water and stood there dripping, the cold air gradually seeping into the cubicle and making me shiver.

War.

We all knew it had been coming (expect, perhaps, the people who'd been obliterated in the first night's air raids), but it was still a shock.

And it spelled a kind of death sentence for me, too. Not as bad, I had to admit, as getting a bunker-buster bomb on your head or receiving a grenade in your tank, but a blow nonetheless.

I took my time getting into work. I gave Marianne my brightest "Bonjour." She replied with a grunt, which I thought was promising. If she'd already prepared my redundancy notice, I'd have got a charming gray smile.

I went up to Christine's office and asked her straight out.

"Alors?"

"Alors quoi?" She pulled a paper tissue from the large flowery pack on her desk and blew her nose. "Oh, la guerre? Oui, les pauvres enfants." She shook her head and broke off our conversation to call her mum and ask if she had any spare cough medicine and make sure that hostilities in the Middle East would not disrupt supplies of silk for wedding dresses.

I threw my bag onto my desk and called Nicole.

"Alors?" I asked her.

"Qui est-ce?" Of course, she didn't recognize my French voice. People's voices change a lot when they speak in a different language.

"Paul."

"Ah, Paul, hello. It is offal this oo-ah, no?"

"Yes, you're right. War is offal. What er . . . ?" It sounded preposterous, but there was no other way of putting it. "What impact do you think the war will have on our tearooms?"

"Ah, yes." She thought for a moment. "I don't know. You must talk with Jean-Marie."

"But he's not here. He's never here."

"Yes. Then I suppose you continue as normal."

I pondered the idea of continuing to do nothing except e-mail friends, read anti-French jokes, and drink coffee. It didn't sound too unpleasant a prospect, but it wasn't what I'd had in mind as a career.

Jean-Marie didn't turn up that day or the next. Or the next. It was like the phony war in 1939, when France carried on living almost normally for months. And then the enemy came and stomped all over them.

It was difficult to judge what the others thought about the tearooms. Mainly because it's difficult to judge what someone thinks if you never see them.

That's not quite true. I did *see* the other members of my "team." I bumped into Bernard by the coffee machine, reading the instructions on a tube of muscle relaxant cream that he'd just borrowed from a colleague. Stéphanie popped up to inquire how London was looking (she still had fond memories of her trip with Jean-Marie) and to ask if by any chance I didn't have any painkillers. Marc came round trying to swap his nicotine patches for some fungicidal cream. I didn't dare ask what it was for. If my colleagues were anything to go by, the pharmacists' strike was bringing out half-forgotten ailments and slowly edging the whole nation toward its collective deathbed.

Finally, Jean-Marie rolled in one afternoon, looking breezy, as if he'd bought shares in Kalashnikov just before the war broke out. He saw me through my open office door and hardly broke his stride. He knocked, unnecessarily, and came in. I clicked away the anti-French cartoon I was looking at and stood up to take it like a man.

He shook my hand and said a bright "Hello."

"How are you feeling?" I asked. He didn't get it, so I rubbed my stomach. I hadn't seen him since my enforced holiday.

"Ah yes, very good, thank you. You do not have more indigestion tablets, by any chance?"

"No, sorry."

"It's okay. I am very grateful." I wondered if his gratitude to the British would extend to letting me keep my project alive.

"So, what are your conclusions about the war, then?"

"The war, yes . . . Let me put down my affairs and we will talk." He held up his case. "Come to my office in five minutes."

It didn't sound good.

Five and a half minutes later—never be exactly on time for a French meeting—I knocked at his office door and found him pouring out coffees. Christine was there, too.

"Sit down, Paul," he said, and pushed a white cup and saucer toward me.

I sat down and ignored the cup. I smiled as if to say "Get on with it, then."

He gave a long speech about the war, politics, fluctuating prices on the world market, employers' national insurance contributions, the state of his upper bowel (well, he may not have mentioned that, but I'd stopped listening by then, waiting for the punch line).

"So," he concluded, "what I suggest is that you continue until the end of your contract, or at least until the end of the war, as our English teacher." He smiled as if he was a magician who'd just produced a live iguana from his coffee cup.

"Pardon?"

"It will be excellent for us. We already send some people to English lessons. Now they can come to you. You will maintain your salary, of course."

Of course, I thought, got to keep paying him for Élodie's apartment.

The fact that teaching English wasn't in my job description didn't even occur to me. The only objection that sprang into my mind was a picture of me having to be nice to Marianne as she maimed irregular verbs at me. Or, worse, having to make *conversation* with her.

"No," I said. "No."

"Take some time. Think," Jean-Marie said. But the more I thought about it, the more Marianne's gray teeth came into focus.

I walked the scenic route home from work. Scenic routes in Paris are perfectly suited to existential pondering.

From the Champs-Élysées to the Marais, you can walk a route that is almost entirely car-free and takes you past some of the city's most beautiful vistas. You can stroll along musing romantically about whether or not you're just about to meet the love of your life or which bridge you're going to throw yourself off.

I went down to the river at Alma Bridge, where the colonial soldier was still keeping his baggy pants dry, then along the banks of the Seine toward Invalides Bridge. Just down from street level, along the old cobbled riverbank, there are still rusting iron rings from the days when working boats would be tied up along the whole waterway. Now, once I'd passed the *bateaux mouches*, most of the boats moored by the river were converted barges whose only cargo was garden furniture and large potted plants.

The sun was at my back and glinting into my eyes off the gold leaf on Alexandre III Bridge. I could never work out why the gold never got stolen. It was real gold leaf, apparently, and looked as if it'd been troweled onto Neptune's crown in the middle of the bridge, a mere scalpel thrust away from theft. Perhaps, I thought, I ought to go and buy a scalpel. When the pharmacies reopened, of course.

As you walked toward the softly rushing current of the river, you could easily imagine that a boat would pull up and the most beautiful, intelligent, apolitical, and sexually well-adjusted girl in the world would invite you for an evening cruise.

As it was, I saw only a homeless man setting up his cardboard shelter in the damp shadows under a bridge.

At Concorde, I crossed into the Tuileries and walked through the tree-lined gardens toward the glass pyramid in the middle of the Louvre.

Here, I stopped for a drink. The café overlooking the pyramid (or pyramids) had opened its terrace, and I treated myself to a highly alcoholic cocktail. The tourists at the other tables had their noses in their guidebooks. There is a class of tourists who never seem to see the things they're visiting, I thought. They prefer to look at directions to the next place they're not going to look at. A hot-air balloon piloted by naked can-can dancers could have flown past and no one would have seen it except me.

But this, I realized, was the rejected male talking. Soon I was going to turn into one of those people who sit in Parisian cafés and type their rantings into a laptop computer, hoping all the while that someone will come up and ask, "What are you writing?" when in fact everyone steers clear because they're scared you'll want to explain what you're writing.

I walked past the pyramid between the "arms" of the Louvre, through the empty, windy Cour Carrée, and out onto the street. After a little jiggle past the Samaritaine department store and across the river, I was right down on the riverbank again, walking toward the islands where Astérix's cousins built the first city of Paris. There wasn't a modern building in sight to drag you out of the Middle Ages.

I found a bench and sat until it got dark, looking upriver toward Notre Dame.

What the hell was I going to do during the war? It sounded a mite melodramatic, but it was a real question. My job had effectively disappeared. Even if the war ended quickly, there was no realistic way Jean-Marie was going to get the tearoom project back on track. It would be too far behind schedule. I had nothing to keep me in Paris. No woman, a few friends who were more occasional drinking pals than soul mates, and an apartment for which I was paying the man I least wanted to pay in the whole of humanity right now.

I was, frankly, in the *merde*.

It was probably that hour sitting by the river that caused my cold. Well, when I say cold, it was more a cross between malaria and tuberculosis. With some of the most painful symptoms of pneumonia thrown in. Overnight I developed a raging temperature and lungs that seemed to have turned into phlegm factories.

If I'd been in the United Kingdom, I would have done my patriotic duty and avoided wasting the doctor's time with my trivial sufferings. (What hardworking GP wants to hear about a mild case of malarial TB?) I'd have gone to a pharmacy and bought myself something hot and lemony. But the pharmacists were still on strike, of course, so I had to go to a doctor.

In Paris, this does not involve looking for your local health center. Doctors operate out of normal apartments and advertise their services on little brass nameplates outside the building, giving their name, specialty, and phone number. As soon as you notice these, you realize they're everywhere. Within coughing distance of my apartment I saw nameplates for pediatricians, osteopaths, dermatologists, dentists, gynecologists, psychiatrists, orthodontists, optometrists, and even radiologists. And those were just the names I understood. Strange to think that in a normal apartment building you could live next to someone who was doing X-rays or staring between women's legs all day long. You'd have to share your lift and staircase with sick or mad people. The communal rubbish bins down in the hall could be full of old teeth and amputated warts. It didn't seem healthy.

Most of the plaques said that you had to fix up a *rendez-vous*, but I finally found a *médecin généraliste* who gave his consultation hours, and those hours were now. It was just after 10:00 a.m., and he went on till 12:00, then started again at 2:00.

He was called Jean-Philippe Diofoirus, and he operated out of a century-old building on the rue de Rivoli.

I pushed open the heavy, varnished street door, crossed the scruffy entrance hall, and climbed the carpeted stairs to the third floor, coughing and wheezing all the way. There was a lift, but it looked so small and rickety that I was scared of getting stuck in there and running out of paper tissues before the repair man set me free.

There was another brass plaque on the apartment door and a sign telling me to ring and enter. I did so and found myself in the empty entrance hall of a white-walled apartment. There was no sign of a receptionist. A wooden-floored corridor led off to my left, and a white door in front of me announced itself as the *salle d'attente*. I took a step toward the waiting room and the floor creaked loudly. This was the only noise I could hear other than the hum of the traffic outside. I half expected to find a waiting room full of skeletons, patients who'd turned up and sat in the empty apartment until they died.

But no, when I opened the door to the waiting room, four or five living people turned to examine me for contagious symptoms. They were all sitting in armchairs arranged around the walls to face the dark gray marble fireplace with its gold-framed mantelpiece mirror. I was in a fairly normal-looking Parisian sitting room. I could have been arriving at a particularly dull party.

One or two of the people murmured "Bonjour" as I walked in, so I did the same. There were two old ladies sitting silently by the wall nearest the fireplace, a teenage girl changing the CD in her Walkman, and a mother with an overdressed baby in its buggy. The baby was bright red in the face, looking as if it was about to explode. Whether this was because it was constipated, feverish, or full of explosives I didn't want to know.

The waiting, I found, was just as boring as in a British doctor's waiting room, except that the magazines were better. Here in France you got fairly recent copies of *Elle*, with their highly readable photo reports on maintaining the perfect buttock shape and how to firm up your breasts through self-massage. The girls shaping their buttocks and massaging their breasts really didn't need to worry, but I wasn't going to tell them to stop.

Once I'd settled in, I noticed that I could hear the faint murmur of the doctor's voice through the wall behind me. He was talking a hell of a lot, trying to persuade his patient to get out and let the next patient in, I hoped.

For the first half hour I was content to sit and suffer in silence, apart from the occasional sneeze and groan of agony.

But by this time only the teenage girl had gone in, and I could hear her pouring out all her troubles to the doctor.

At this rate, I was going to be stranded here through the doctor's lunch hour. Or hours. And before that, I was going to be splattered in bits of exploding baby. Just take the poor thing out of its Antarctic sleeping bag, I kept willing its mother, but she was as engrossed by *Elle* as I had been. Probably reading the cookery pages, I decided—baby marinated in its own juice.

I wondered if the French nonqueuing system worked here as it does in most other areas of life. Perhaps, I thought, when the girl comes out, I should barge authoritatively into the surgery as if it was my birthright, the way people do when they get on a bus in front of you.

But when the doctor emerged, he shook hands with the teenage girl and popped his head into the waiting room to call, "Madame Bouvier."

So there was a line, I concluded, and he knew some people's names. Not because they'd made an appointment, I hoped.

Madame Bouvier was the mother and had apparently come just to check whether or not the baby was cooked, because she was in and out in ten minutes. The old dears went in together, still silent, as if trying to remember what was wrong with them.

I put down my magazine and concentrated on the doctor's voice, listening for farewell sounds. By now I was at the head of a line of three people, and one of them, a late-middle-aged man with a flat cap, darting eyes, and good-quality but slightly frayed clothes, looked like an arch line jumper. He was sitting forward on his seat, hands on his knees, ready to spring into action. Or maybe just suffering from acute piles. When he'd come into the waiting room, he'd called out, "Messieurs, dames" (a way of saying hello to a room full of people), as if he were announcing his presence rather than wishing us good day. And he didn't even glance at the magazines. The sort, I suspected, who would have no scruples about pushing in front of a dying Englishman on the grounds that his piles are more important than my near fatal respiratory disease.

The doctor walked the old ladies to the door and turned toward the waiting room. Monsieur Line Jumpeur called out, "Bonjour, Docteur," and the doctor nodded hello. This was it, I thought, I was being consigned to the lunch hour. I took a deep breath and lunged upward out of my chair, startling the doctor into saying a curious "Monsieur?"

This was another time when I should have prepared a short speech. How, I wondered, did I say, "You don't know me, but I need you to save my life"?

I finally settled on "Bonjour," and he smiled and ushered me toward his office, clearly not too put out by seeing strange people in his waiting room.

"I am cold," I explained in French. "No," I corrected myself. In fact, I had done my best to memorize some key vocabulary, like cough (*tousser*), lungs on fire (*poumons en feu*), and atchoo (*atchoum*).

The doctor turned to a brand-new flat-screen Macintosh and interrupted me to ask for my name, address, date of birth, social security number, and so forth. I'd forgotten: In France, admin comes before health.

I'd learned from experience to carry all my ID with me at all times, so it took only ten minutes or so to start up a file on me, by which time I'd all but finished my supply of paper tissues. As he typed, I decided that he didn't look like a doctor at all. He was much less terrifying than an English doctor. With his jeans, tweed jacket, healthy outdoor look, and unkempt hair, he seemed approachable rather than weighed down beneath the collapsing structure of the British health system. He was a youth hostel manager.

I described, or displayed, my symptoms, he weighed me, listened to the paper-tearing sounds in my chest, stuck a tongue depressor down my mouth until I was nearly sick, and announced that he was going to take my temperature. He picked up a thermometer attached to what looked like a staple gun.

Now, I'd heard about where French doctors stick thermometers. Marie had told me a Marquis de Sade story in which some poor guy is raped using a pistol. It had failed to turn me on then, and now I was even less excited to see that de Sade's sick fantasies had infected the French medical profession.

"No, no," I said, pressing my buttocks deeper into the cushioned top of the examination table. "I am not hot."

"We must see if you have a fever," said the doctor, pointing his pistol up at the ceiling like some duelist eager to get the bloodshed over with.

"Is it fast?" I asked.

"Yes, I click it and it shows me the temperature." He smiled reassuringly. And the barrel of his thermometer pistol didn't look very long at all.

"Oh, okay, if it is fast." I shifted my weight to be able to pull down my underpants, but before I'd had a chance to tug on the elastic, he'd stuck the gun in my ear and clicked.

"Hm, 38.9. Hot."

I laughed with relief.

"No, you have a fever," he said, wondering why I looked so pleased to receive the bad news. The days of the rectal thermometer were long gone, it seemed.

The doctor returned to his computer to type out my prescription.

The prescription was something of a surprise. As I said, I didn't usually bother a doctor with a cold until I'd completely lost my voice and was unable to swallow without a general anesthetic. Even then, I'd expect the doctor to give me a prescription for nothing more than tea and aspirin.

This French doctor was slightly different. First he asked me what I already had at home.

"Nothing. Some aspirin," I replied.

He looked a little put out and reeled off a list of names of medicines that he thought I really ought to have in my medicine cabinet. I shook my head at each one.

"I see," he said, and made up for my years of self-neglect with a shopping list of antibiotics, painkillers, sprays, menthol rubs, and inhalants that would have cured a herd of bronchitic giraffes. "Will you take suppositories?"

"Suppositories? I don't know. They are big?" Though I wasn't sure what a "big" suppository was or if they even came in different sizes. Until then, I'd lived such a sheltered life that I'd never shoved *anything* inanimate into my own back passage.

The doctor held up his right index finger and measured off the top knuckle joint.

"I will try, maybe," I said. Try to put them in the bin at the first opportunity, I meant.

He added them to my prescription and printed it out for me.

Looking down the long list, I understood why there was a despairing mob outside every pharmacist's in town. If you multiplied my experience by the number of diseases known to medical science and the number of French people, and then factored in the relative seriousness of the ailments, you were looking at a nation hooked on medication.

"Where can I buy this?" I asked.

"You will have to go to the emergency pharmacy. There are one or two pharmacies open only for the distribution of emergency medication."

"I am emergency?" I asked hopefully.

"Yes, you have a prescription."

Gratitude surged through my veins like a dose of paracetamol. The doctor gave me a sheet of paper with three addresses on it.

"Go to one of these. They are the only places open. You will have to wait a long time. You may be cured before you receive the medication." He laughed at his sick joke, the healthy so-and-so. "You are working in Paris?"

"Yes," I lied.

"Do you want an arrêt maladie?"

This, he explained, was a sick note. I said yes, please. Any excuse to get away from the threat of teaching English.

I stood up to go, and suddenly it was the doctor who was looking ill.

"It is necessary to, er, pay," he said, blushing. He didn't use the word *payer*, preferring the more formal *régler*, meaning "settle a bill."

"Ah, yes." I sat down again. "How much?"

He flinched as if it was indecent to be so direct and leaned forward across his desk to unfold the treatment form he'd given me, where he'd written the fee for the consultation. It was about the same as five or six beers in a normal café.

"Most of it is, of course, reimbursed by the social security. Do you have a mutual?"

"A mutual what?"

"Company health insurance."

"Oh, probably, yes."

"Well then, they will pay the rest, and you will receive a one hundred percent reimbursement."

A slightly complicated but pretty good system, I thought. It was just a shame they didn't introduce the same scheme for beer.

I walked (or dragged my aching, shuddering body) across the Seine toward the nearest emergency pharmacy. This took me past the hospital called Hôtel Dieu, the "God Hotel." Not a promising name for a hospital. It sounded like a stopping-off place on your way to the afterlife. This was borne out by its location—it overlooks Notre Dame cathedral.

But outside the hospital was something much more promising. The notice boards by the main entrance suggested that you could phone and make appointments with every kind of specialist imaginable. To a Brit brought up on six-month waiting lists to see any hospital staff more specialized than toilet cleaners, this was like seeing a list of the home numbers of the world's top ten super-models. I got out my phone and keyed in the numbers of the lung specialist, the ear, nose, and throat specialist, and, just in case, the lab where I'd need to go for a brain scan. You can't be too careful.

I trudged on across the second branch of the Seine to a large pharmacy on the boulevard St. Germain, near the medical school. I could tell when I was getting close because even above the grind of the heavy traffic I could hear the wailing of the sick.

Well, that might be a slight exaggeration or an echo of the wail I felt like making when I saw the line. At least a hundred people, old and young, standing and on crutches, were queuing along the pavement toward the boulevard St. Michel—with invalids like me trotting along the pavement or hobbling across the road to join the line. I put on a burst of speed and took my place. As I got my breath back, I tried to work out how many hours I would be standing here. There were only about five hours till nightfall, I calculated, I really ought to have brought a mattress or a tent.

Like most French lines, this one was two or three people thick. You inched ahead in millimeters, if that's possible, keeping your nose and your toes just in front of the person who arrived after you but stood beside you. In a way, this did give the line a forward momentum, because as soon as you had a molecule of air between you and the person in front, you closed the gap.

The man behind me, a tall, athletic type in jeans and a sports anorak, started a conversation of sorts.

"You have a prescription?" he asked me with the suspicion of someone who can't see all the items in your basket in the five-items-and-under checkout line.

"Yes." I pulled it out of my pocket.

"Ah. What have you got?"

I snuffled. "A cold," I said, regretting instantly my attempt at bravery. I should have said "cholera" and cleared my way to the front of the line. "You?" I asked.

"Fonkle."

I waited, thinking that he had just cleared his nose before replying. But no more information came.

"Fonkle?" I repeated as best I could.

"Yes."

After much description, some eloquent hand movements, and an even more eloquent wince, I deduced that he had a boil, a *furoncle*, in his crotch.

"Ooh," I sympathized. "Is good that God invented boxer shorts, eh?"

Thus ended our conversation.

The next person to talk to me was a well-to-do middle-aged career woman who asked if, when I got to the front of the line, I wouldn't mind trying to get some medication for her.

I could phone her when I got within a few meters of the pharmacy, she said.

"You have no prescription?" I asked.

"Yes, but I can't wait."

"Why not? You are very urgent?"

"Why not? This queue it is so *long*," she said, looking ill at the mere notion of getting in line.

"Eh, you must wait, this is a queue," said the man beside/behind me.

"I will pay ten euros," the woman said.

"Show me your prescription," the man said, and dropped back half a millimeter to cut the deal.

As far as I could see, there were several such deals going on and just as many irate people raising their voices to heckle the culprits. To no avail. The paying pushers-in pushed in, the hecklers heckled, and the self-pitying line edged slowly forward, blaming God, the state, the weather, and everyone else for their misfortune. If you wanted to be very cruel indeed, you could have said it was a microcosm of French society.

It was around 2:00 p.m. when I finally got to the pharmacy.

Stooping down to a hatch in the iron shutters was a white-coated *pharmacienne*. She was a very posh and beautiful blond girl in pearls and a crisp blouse with the top two or three buttons open. A tonic to a suffering man. She was wearing a badge that told me she was on strike.

She was very friendly and not at all rushed, which may have partly explained the length of the line. She disappeared for several minutes to assemble my mountain of colored medicine boxes.

"All this I must take?" I said when she finally reappeared. I didn't know if I even had the strength to carry it home.

She explained that she had to give me two boxes of six tablets of antibiotics because the prescription was for eight tablets—I was going to throw away almost half the treatment. Not to worry, she said, it's all refunded by the social security.

"Or my mutual?" I asked, looking in-the-know.

"Yes."

Massive waste was, it seemed, budgeted into the system.

Did I know what to do with them all? she asked me, her finger hovering over the suppository box. I'd work it out, I assured her. I just wished I knew enough French to tell her that we Brits know our arse from our elbow *and* our mouth.

When I finally got home, it took me the rest of the afternoon to read the instructions on all the boxes. It was dark by the time I finished all my rubbing, snorting, gulping, and inhaling. I did, I must admit, also do a little thrusting. I tried a suppository for size, just for the hell of it. The instructions were translated into English and promised me that "the suppository's actions purify the tracheal conduit without aggressing the digestive system," but all I noticed was a rather unpleasant sensation, as if I was about to mess my pants, then a warm, melting feeling as the vapors traveled toward my lungs via the service escalator. And next morning, a greasy explosion when I went to the toilet. I could see that some people of an anal disposition could find it appealing, but it was nothing to write home about.

When I arrived back at work (or at the office, at least), Marianne, who was wearing a neck brace for some reason, smiled at me. So she'd heard. I plonked my sick note down on the reception desk and ignored her speech about being on human resources duty only between such-and-such a time.

"Bonne journée," I wished her, and headed to the elevator.

While I'd been away, I'd had time to read my work contract and consult the Internet about French employment law. It turned out that there were healthy compensation packages for having your fixed-term contract terminated before it was up and lots of rules about having to do only what your job description said.

There would be no English teaching for me. I was going to negotiate my way out of there with enough cash to be able to loaf around in Paris until I decided to do anything more than loaf.

I'd made an appointment to see Jean-Marie, and he was sitting in his office, with the door open, when I arrived. He was looking postively festive in a white silk sirt and red tie.

"Ah, Paul," he called out when he saw me. Suddenly he was grave. His captain-of-industry expression, I supposed.

I went into his office.

"You are cured, I hope," he said, still grave.

"Yes, thank you. You too?"

"Yes. Sit down."

"I'll just go and put my coat—" I gestured toward my office.

"No, no. Just sit down, please."

I sat, wondering why the hurry. Had Britain and America invaded France? I hadn't listened to the news that morning. Maybe I was to be sent to an internment camp?

"There is a problem," Jean-Marie said. He certainly looked as if he was rehearsing to make a presidential TV speech about the need for courage in the face of the Anglo-Saxon enemy.

Especially sitting as he was below his medal for bovine bravery.

"Yes, that is what we are here to talk about, Jean-Marie."

"But this is a new problem."

"Ah?"

"Yes, I am afraid we must fire you."

"Fire me? But you're the one who's stopping the project."

"We must fire you for serious fault."

"Serious fault?"

"Yes, *faute grave*, we say."

"What *faute grave*? I've just given my sick note to Marianne. I wasn't—"

"No, no, it is not your absence. It is this."

He pushed a sheaf of papers across his desk at me. I looked at the top sheet and understood.

"You've been snooping in my e-mail," I said. The papers were printouts of all the anti-French jokes I'd received and carefully not printed out.

"Snooping? No. Your mail messages are stocked in our company's computer system."

So it was Marc who'd been snooping.

"But you can't fire someone for receiving a few jokes."

"A few jokes?" He held his finger and thumb apart to show how thick the pile was.

"Just because someone makes jokes about France, you can fire me? But that's totalitarianism."

"Oh no." Jean-Marie laughed bitterly. "It is not because they are about France. Not at all. No, it is the *time*. The time you took to read them. Hours! The e-mail is not for private fun, it is for work."

This was total hypocrisy, of course. Everyone in the company, including Jean-Marie, wasted hours a day on coffee breaks, smoking breaks, long lunch breaks, calling the baby-sitter breaks, reserving train or plane tickets for upcoming weekend breaks, and, more recently, trading in secondhand aspirin breaks. But, as with all the best hypocrisy, the truth didn't matter. He'd got me. I knew it, he knew it. All that remained to be discussed was the price.

"I can contest this with the inspecteur du travail," I said.

"If you stay in Paris long enough to wait for the decision."

"Mine isn't the only interesting mailbox in the company."

"What do you mean?"

"I mean, I just happened to be in Stéphanie's office one day and she'd left her e-mail open."

"Ah." He gave this some thought. "I'm sure she has threw her old messages in the, how you say, corbeille?" His English slipped, but he kept his cool.

"Maybe she printed them out and left them lying around for people to find."

At this, Jean-Marie glanced across toward Christine's door.

Through the glass, we could see that she was on the phone.

He spoke softly. "Who might be interested in these messages?" Meaning, I suppose, his wife or the Ministry of Agriculture? Or other people. For all I knew, there may well have been even more going on between him and Stéphanie than sex and illegal beef imports. I did a Parisian shrug. Not for me to say, not my problem. As always, the shrug worked.

"Very well," Jean-Marie said. "I will forget these jokes. You have done your best for the company, so we will give you the entire, how you say, dédommagement?"

"Compensation."

"Compensation and terminate your contract prematurely for economic reasons. Okay?"

"And let me stay for free in Élodie's apartment."

"Ah, merde, là tu exagères!"

If he hadn't looked so murderously furious, it would have been funny. I'd tried to dip into his personal pocket and he'd reacted as if I'd stuck a suppository up his backside without asking permission. Suddenly he was as red as his tie, and his temples were almost visibly throbbing.

"I tell you what, Jean-Marie, you give me a little end-of-contract bonus and I'll pay it to you as rent."

He leaned forward across his desk at me, grumbling obscenities. *Petit merdeux* seemed to be the most frequent.

He told me, still in French, to "fuck the camp," as they say, out of *his* apartment by the end of the month.

"Why, or you'll report me to the housing department?"

This provoked more temple throbbing and a deep, inarticulate, animal growl.

I got out my phone, where I'd keyed in the numbers of all those specialists. It looked as if Jean-Marie was going to be in urgent need of a cardiologist.

AVRIL

Liberté, Égalité, Get Out of My Way

ON APRIL THE first, you understand why the French admire the British sense of humor: We have one.

No, that's unfair to some very funny French guys, including one comedian called Coluche who drove his motorbike into an articulated truck. Not as a joke. It killed him, and I now wished it hadn't. I could understand just about enough French to follow some of his old sketches on video, and I thought, This is what France needs now—someone who really takes the piss out of politicians. Not just the ruling party, not with clever irony, but a real below-the-belt debunking of the whole cushy lot of them. He actually stood for president in 1981, as *le candidat bleu-blanc-merde*, and rumor has it he withdrew because the secret services made it clear that he wouldn't survive very long if he stayed in the running. He would have thought of a good spoof for my first April Fool's Day in France. All the French do is stick fish on one another's backs. Not live fish—that might actually be funny. A large turbot flapping between someone's shoulder blades could be genuinely amusing.

As I sat in the window of my local gay café (in the mornings it was no different from any straight Parisian café except that the waiters bore traces of last night's makeup), I watched a group of schoolkids jostling one another and trying to pin crudely drawn paper fish on one another's anoraks.

"Why a fish?" I asked the waiter as he brought me the newspaper I'd asked for.

"Why not?" he replied, which was a fair point. After all, everything else in France is centralized—why not April Fool's jokes?

French newspapers do print spoof articles, but they're often fish based. So when I read on the front page of my newspaper that journalists were going on strike, I was almost sure it wasn't an April Fool's joke.

The journalists were downing tools because, they said, the campaign for the upcoming local elections was boring. I could relate to that. Now that the Iraq war was all but over and forgotten, it must have come as a shock to reporters to have to write about who was going to win power in Camembertville-sur-Merde, population three goats and a hairy old lady. But at least these local elections had more at stake than your usual round of arguments about which party will devote the most money to building playgrounds for goats. It was a year after the presidential elections when a far right Fascist candidate had nearly got elected. There was a real prospect of an embarrassingly high number of regions voting in Fascist local representatives.

The reporters didn't exactly phrase their protest as "The election campaign is too boring." The newspaper quoted a journalists' union official that they were striking "in protest at the various political parties' failing to address the important issues facing the country—the recession, welfare reform, unemployment, and the French role in international affairs post-Iraq."

But I'd heard for myself how mind-numbingly boring the campaign could get. It was a radio interview with a politician, and the gist of the interview, as far as I could gather, was "Thank you for coming onto the program, Mr. Politician" and "Those are fascinating policies," with a subtext of "Hey, millions of people are listening to us, let's talk as pompously as possible and they'll think we're intelligent."

In this last newspaper before the presses fell silent, I read a breakdown of the various parties' programs. It was true that they didn't address what I saw as important issues.

The Communists were promising retirement for all state employees at age thirty-five. The Socialists were proposing absolutely nothing because they couldn't elect a leader who would propose things. The center right parties (of which there were about ten) were all promising employers that they would no longer have to pay workers and would be exempt from prosecution for any industrial pollution that killed fewer than one hundred thousand people.

The Far Right was proposing, less realistically, to have immigrants barbecued in every *place du marché* on Friday nights. And in a similar vein, the rural party promised to change the law on endangered species so that hunters could now shoot dodos, unicorns, mermaids, and American tourists. It was, as Coluche would probably have put it, *liberté, égalité, merde*. And I half wished the reporters would stay on the job to write about it, because I had plenty of reading time now that I was banned from working.

I had quickly settled into a not unpleasant time-wasting routine. I really don't know why *far niente* is an Italian expression, because Paris is the perfect place for it. Breakfast at a café (stare longingly at passing women). Wander to an art exhibition (stare longingly at young female tourists and the art students with part-time jobs as security staff). Lunch at a café (see "breakfast" above), take in a movie (drool at the heroine), go to the pub with English mates (talk so loudly about women that you scare them all off).

The only thing that sometimes disturbed my routine was the

weather, which was playing frustrating games. A day might start off bright and warm, and you could see that the girls had light, revealing summer clothes under their coats. But then, come lunchtime, it would cloud over or rain, and the revealing clothes would stay unrevealed. I was cured of my cold, but I was still suffering. It was officially springtime in Paris, and I was finding that the relief at not being forced to have sex four times every night does not last very long.

I met up with my old friend Jake the American to discuss my predicament. He was still carrying on with his international sex project. And not only had we forgiven each other for the "fuck off out of the bookshop" incident, he was now positively grateful to me. At the next writers' group meeting, he'd been able to express so much politically correct outrage at my lack of respect for women's literature that one of the budding authoresses slept with him. Which gave him yet another poem (she was from New Zealand). Luckily, he didn't offer to read it to me.

Now we met up at the Luxembourg Gardens, a large public park in a rich area just south of the Latin Quarter. The park has a circular boating lake where on weekends kids can hire toy yachts. It also has one of the few public lawns where you are actually allowed to walk. This morning, a weekday, it was covered with a light sprinkling of toddlers and their attendant mothers and baby-sitters.

Jake and I were sitting outside the park's small café. This is housed in a small pavilion, with a terrace of light green metal chairs laid out under a stand of towering horse chestnuts. Today the leaves were young, almost yellow, and twisting in the breeze.

We were comfortably away from the traffic but in danger of being pooped on by pigeons. This wouldn't have mattered to Jake. He was almost superhumanly scruffy. His eyes were totally hidden by droopy, unwashed hair, and his old suit jacket now looked as if it had been chewed up by a French pig and excreted all over him. He probably wouldn't have got served at the café without my relatively chic presence.

We dispensed with the war ("It's always the civilians who suffer," "Why do so many people swallow the line that politicians feed them?" and so on) and then got down to the meat of the matter. I brought him up-to-date on my Jean-Marie and Marie situation and asked him, as a man who was apparently willing, no, *anxious*, to sleep with any testicle-free human being over the age of consent, what to do.

Jake laughed and swung his leg at a pair of pigeons with malformed feet who had hobbled over to see if they could beg a crumb of food. Or had wanted to try a bit of pig excreta. "Ah, you are in lack," he said.

Over the past few months, his English had disintegrated almost beyond recognition, but I now knew enough of the French expressions he was translating to understand him.

"Yeah," I agreed, trying to remember the last time I'd had any physical contact with a woman outside my dreams and the meaningless pecks on the cheek from colleagues saying good-bye.

"What have you done before, when you, like, found your girlfriend the photograph?"

"Photographer," I corrected him. Sometimes I couldn't help myself. "She was a part-time waitress."

"Voilà your solution."

"Yeah, but I seem to go to different bars now, where the waitresses all get chatted up nonstop and don't even *see* anyone who hasn't got the keys to a Mercedes sports car poking out of his trousers. Or to English pubs, where the barmaids all have French boyfriends."

"Yeah, it's problematic."

We sipped our coffees, watched the sunlight flickering down through the leaves, and wondered why the sweating two-mile-an-hour joggers didn't stay at home instead of scuffing their feet along the ground and kicking up dust for us to breathe.

"Besides, you're looking for something different, Jake. You just want to shag them, right? In a way, that makes things easier."

"Non, non, man. Sometimes I'm obliged to really boss, you know. Like, tell her I love her and such conneries. I can put *weeks* before I have a result."

"But I want more than that result, Jake."

"Oh, you want to install yourself in her apartment?"

"Yeah. No. I mean, I really want to *meet* somebody."

"Meet somebody? Oh, you must become an English teacher, man. You meet beautiful women and they're obliged to talk with you during, like, an hour."

"Teach English? No way." I shivered at my momentary vision of gray teeth.

"Allez, Paul. You know I have a course this morning with a real beautiful woman here there." He nodded through the trees toward the main street outside the park. "In an assurance society there. She's your type. Office worker. Chic. Trop belle pour moi, you know what I mean? And she is not at all an exception."

I shook my head and turned away to watch the old waiter, a gray-haired black-waistcoated guy of about sixty, as he served a coffee and a croissant to a middle-aged woman in an expensive cream-colored leather coat. He stayed to flirt, she laughed.

Why not get a waiting job? I thought. Anything except teach.

"In Paris you must go in the sense of the hair," Jake declared. This may well have been a deeply wise observation if I'd been able to understand it.

"Go with the flow," he explained. "Regard those people."

He pointed toward the boating lake. There were no model yachts on the water, but plenty of people were strolling or jogging in the sun.

"What about them?"

"See the way they walk?" Jake waved his right arm as if it was a car going round a roundabout French style, to the right. I saw what he meant. Almost everyone was acting exactly as if they were on a roundabout, coming out of one of the walkways or down the steps and heading right to go round the lake.

"It's the same thing in the metro stations," he said. "People comport themselves like in a car. You try to mount up the stairs on the left, they believe you're crazy. They all go with the flow, at the right. It's the same in politics. The politic leaders all come from the same *école*. They don't want to change France. They all want just one thing, for France to be capital of the planet. Et voilà."

"So what's this got to do with teaching English?"

"Ah, that is the biggest flow these days. Whatever the politicians say, all French want to learn English. Regard me. I do my best since a year to get fired. I go to the courses, okay, but, like, I insult stupid students, I dress any way."

"Why do you want to get fired?"

"The dole is, like, seventy percent of your last salaire, you know? But they never fire me. They need me. Because every person in France wants to learn English. It's for that that you should teach."

"But I don't have any teaching qualifications."

Jake's whoop of laughter made every pigeon between him and the Eiffel Tower take to the air in terror.

*   *   *

"What did you have for dinner last night, Sylvie?"

"I made some crap."

"You mean *crêpes*? Pancakes."

"Yes, pan-cack."

The hardest thing was to keep a straight face.

"Okay, Philippe, what would you say to the waiter if you had no cutlery?"

"Er, excuse me, I want a knife and a fuck."

It was cruel, and my French wasn't any better than their English, but sometimes you couldn't help but giggle.

"At five p.m., I was working."

"Good."

"At seven p.m., I was sitting on ze train."

"Okay."

"At nine, I was listening ze radio."

"Was that a.m. or p.m.?"

"No, FM."

And occasionally, especially during role plays, you just wondered, What the hell am I doing here?

"If you do not pay our invoice, sir, we will contact our lawg."

"Your log?"

"Yes, our lawg."

"Your lump of wood?"

"Oh? Okay, we will contact our lumpawoo."

"No, you mean *lawyer*."

"Sorry?"

"Look—I'll write it. L-a-w-y-e-r."

"Yes, *lawg*."

"Okay, you go ahead and contact your log."

*　　*　　*

But overall, Jake was right. For a few weeks, at least, English teaching was fun, a bit like visiting a load of houses that you don't particularly want to buy. You can be nosy. It gives you a really good close-up of other people's lives without any emotional commitment.

Jake's school was happy to take me on, happy in fact to give me classes the very day I knocked on their door, especially because I'd had a "real" job, unlike so many of the no-hopers who put on a tie and become English teachers in Paris.

The owner of the school was named Andrea. She was a tough fifty-year-old German, a slim, business-suited mass of opportunistic gristle. She spoke perfect English and even more perfect French. She had large diamond earrings and deep creases across her suntanned forehead, the combination of which suggested that the language-school industry was a place of both pleasure and pain.

The photocopy of my *carte de séjour* was still warm when Andrea handed me the address of the company where I was to teach that afternoon.

"But what do I teach them?" I asked.

"Just go and talk to them. Introduce yourself, ask what they do, tell them what you have been doing, and take note of their errors. When there are twenty minutes of lesson to go, start analyzing their errors. Or, if they talk until the end of the hour, say you will analyze the errors next time. It sounds very professional. And takes up more time. And don't forget to make them sign the presence form. That's how we know how much to bill them."

Andrea looked at me as if I ought to have left the office by now. Teacher training course over, it seemed.

I didn't have any beautiful women students. I had a tired working mum who needed English to work behind the counter in a bank on the Champs-Élysées but preferred to talk about what she cooked for dinner (hence the "crap"). Three engineers who were off to China to sell telecommunications masts and were terrified of catching SARS. I taught them not to say, "I don't hope to catch it." I failed abysmally to get them to pronounce "lawyer" properly, but they seemed satisfied anyway. And I went to a large hotel where the manager (Philippe, the "knife and fuck" man) wanted a transfer to the United States and needed to convince his head office that he could deal with his staff and customers in English. I pretended to be one of his waiters, a visitor from the head office, and, slightly worryingly, his American secretary, and that was it. Signature on the form, out of there.

If I was stuck for teaching material, I'd whip out the day's English paper and we'd talk about something in that. I tried to get them talking about the French journalists' strike, but a surprising amount of them hadn't even realized there was a strike or didn't care. They didn't read daily papers much except for the freebies given out at metro stations, which weren't on strike because they weren't recognized as journalism by the unions. And no one missed the TV news, half of which was usually given over to plugging the film that was due on afterward. As far as my students were concerned, the lack of official news was not news. By contrast, they loved reading stories about David Beckham's haircuts. Not that I wrote that down in the "subjects covered" section of the presence form. It was always "discussion of British culture inspired by study of contemporary design."

And that, give or take a few practice books and cassettes, was all there was to English teaching in Paris. You just had to accept being the world's lowest-paid chat-show host.

Jake was right. What made it so effortless was that these people all had an almost desperate desire to learn English. They now seemed to blame all the world's ills, from genocide in Africa to the price of coffee, on America, but this didn't stop them wanting to learn its language. Iraq war? What Iraq war? . . . Bad Franco-American and Anglo-French relations? Who cares? . . . Would they like to have lunch in a typically English tearoom? Yes, please, where is it? (Yes, Jean-Marie, where indeed?)

I kept my eyes on Jean-Marie, and my ears. Via the Internet and Nicole, I followed his political goings-on. I still saw Nicole for lunch once a week, though now I had to be very careful not to ask her to sign a presence form at the end of every meal.

She said Jean-Marie was spending more time than ever out in Trou. Stéphanie would go up there sometimes to take work to him. (Work *and* play, I thought.) According to what Stéphanie told Nicole, Jean-Marie was visiting all the farmers within his electoral boundary, as well as showing up on market days to shake hands and buy something from every stall. And when he was in Paris, Nicole said, Jean-Marie often received visits from national political figures, including—she whispered—a certain party leader who had once suggested that Auschwitz, if it had existed at all, was just some kind of precursor to the Club Med.

"No," I objected through a mouthful of undercooked tuna steak. "I think Jean-Marie would rent his dead great-grandmother out as a call girl if he thought there was money in it, but I don't believe he's a Nazi."

"No, not a Nazi. Not a *real* Nazi. You do not understand how . . . what is the word?" Nicole waved her fork in the air. "Respectable. It is to be Fascist in France. It is just a form of nostalgie."

"I didn't know you were political, Nicole," I said, feeling slightly disappointed. In my acute state of sexual cold turkey, I was even contemplating asking her if she wanted to learn some more intimate English vocabulary. "Ooh," maybe, or "aahh" and "Yes, keep doing that to me, Paul, you unstoppable love machine." But if she was political, no thanks. I'd been through all that with Alexa. I'd say one word off message and it'd be orgasmus interruptus.

"Not very political, no," she said. "But my family is from the southwest, near Carcassonne. Traditionally we are Communists."

"Oh yeah?" Suddenly she'd become sexier again. I always think of Communist women as leggy blond farm volunteers, giving their all for Uncle Joe in the haystack. Not that Nicole was a leggy blonde, even through my sex-starved eyes.

"But again. It is not the same as you think. My usband did not hunderstand this. My family do not want to kill capitalism. They are just members of the hagricultural co-operative. Which is Communist. It is tradition. My father ad been in the Communist Resistonce hagainst the Nazis. Ee elped the Hamericans."

She was getting even sexier. Daughter of a Resistance fighter? With me the fugitive English pilot, forced to hide under her bed. And then one night, when her dad is out blowing up a railway, she says, "There's no need to sleep under the bed tonight," and I teach her all those English oohs and aahs.

". . . and Jean-Marie as big, big political hambitions."

"Uh, what, pardon?" She'd brought me back from 1944 with a jolt.

"Jean-Marie. E does not want to be the major of a little town only."

"Mayor."

"Yes. Mayor. Thank you. This nuclear central . . ."

"Power station."

"This nuclear central power station, it is han important regional question. If e can av henough political power in this region, the power station will surely be constructed. Ee will be respected as a, ow you say? Un homme d'influence."

"A man of influence."

"Thank you. It will elp is political carrier. And, huh—" She gave a philosophical laugh. "Ee will certainly profit from it financially also."

"Will he now?" These elections were becoming less boring by the minute. I ordered myself a slab of chocolate orange fondant dessert to celebrate.

"Hey, Nicole, I didn't tell you. I've started teaching English."

"Ah, wiz a school?"

"Yes, giving proper lessons. I was wondering if you'd be interested in learning . . ."

One day in mid-April, when I had a free morning, I went out to read the paper at the gay café. Just before midday, I came back to make myself a quick sandwich with the fresh baguette I'd bought. But my front door seemed to be stuck.

I tried my key three times (the normal way, upside down, with yell of frustration and accompanying kick of the door), and it wouldn't work. "Oh, I get it. The council is playing a belated fish-free April Fool's joke, changing the numbers on all the HLM doors so we try to get in the wrong apartment," I said to myself, sounding more ridiculous with every word. After all, even some-one like me who hasn't been to Oxford or Cambridge remembers which floor they live on.

"Or maybe my key has melted in my pocket because of the animal heat emanating from my underpants."

This wasn't particularly likely, either, I decided. A more credible explanation for the problem was that, as I now noticed, the lock itself was of a different make from what it had been an hour before. Someone had changed my lock.

My phone rang. The call was from a number I didn't recognize.

"Bonjour, Monsieur Wess," a polite male voice said. It then explained, politely, that if I wished to get in the apartment and retrieve my belongings, I could return at four o'clock that afternoon and do so.

"Who are you?"

"You are not the legal occupant of the apartment, and you therefore have no legal right to occupy it," the voice said, which in my opinion kind of avoided the question.

"Are you from the HLM department?"

"Do you wish to return at four o'clock?" Again, not exactly a straight answer.

"Yes," I said, trying to set an example.

"Until four o'clock, then," the voice said. "Bonne journée."

I decided to rip out the vocal cords of every person who ever wished me *bonne journée* again. I also wondered what the hell was going on.

When in doubt, ask your concierge. These Portuguese women know everything that's happening everywhere. If Saddam Hussein had tried to hide in Paris, the bounty on his head would have been used to build a new garage on every house in Porto.

I went down to see Madame Da Costa in her *loge*, a tiny one-room apartment on the ground floor near the front door of the building. She lived in there along with her husband, who was about two feet taller than her, and the biggest TV I've ever seen. Their three teenage sons ate there but slept in another building somewhere. In the morning, I occasionally saw one of them rushing in from the street in his pajamas.

Madame Da Costa opened the net-curtained glass door of her *loge* and let out a faint whiff of cod. She was dressed in a long-sleeved black T-shirt and black leggings, and her hair was sticking out from her head in dark, unbrushed waves. She looked a bit like a chicken—all chest and crest. When she saw me, she immediately leapt back inside.

I was definitely a pariah in these parts, it seemed.

But no, she re-emerged, flustered, her hair held in place with a headband, and apologized for not distributing the post yet. She thrust a fistful of letters at me, the top one of which was addressed to a Herr Doktor Helmut Ringelnetz.

"Non, non," I said. "I mean, oui, thank you for the letters, but I come for a different reason. My—"

Dammit, how did you say my lock has been changed without my consent?

"My door does not want my key," I tried. I held up the key and mimed someone suddenly finding that it is, to all intents and purposes, no longer a key.

"Ah, oui!" Cogs were whirring in her mind, events clicking into place. "Two men come this morning, they make a lot of bof, boom, crack!" Now she was the one miming. "I go up, they are breaking the door. I ask who they are, they say, you shut mouth, we just change lock, then we go. And they do it and go. Poof! They were not for you?"

"No."

"No, you don't make noise. Not like the others." She looked up at me with her approving smile. It felt good to have a protector, even such a miniature, spherical one as Madame Da Costa.

"Were they from the HLM department?"

"No. One man was normal, private lock man. The other was big"—she puffed out her barrel chest, clenched her biceps—"very

chic. Like . . ." She looked for the right word. "Like bodyguard."
She nodded to herself. "Like bodyguard for the lock man.
Bizarre." She frowned.

"Très bizarre," I agreed, and told her about the phone call I'd
just received.

Ten minutes later, I had an old sweatshirt in Portuguese
national football colors (green, red, and sweat stain) wrapped
around my hands. My eyes were closed, and I was praying that
when I opened them again, my fingers would not have been turned
into raspberry coulis.

This was because I knew that Monsieur Da Costa was swinging
a sledgehammer at me, aiming for the huge chisel that I was
holding against the new lock.

One deafening, bone-juddering thump later, the door swung
gently open and we were inside snooping about.

Everything was just as I'd left it. Kitchen with three days'
washing up, my bedroom decorated with a patchwork of discarded
socks and underwear, Élodie's room locked in case I got lonely
and started snuffling around in her lingerie drawer.

Madame took it all in for gossip's sake and then announced that
we'd better get carrying.

"But I don't leave," I objected. "I change the door again, and
stay here."

"Non. You do not see big man. Bodyguard," she reminded me,
doing her chest-puffing thing again.

Monsieur, who hardly spoke any French, nodded in support of
his wife and said something to her in their usual guttural tones.

"He say they are angry at four o'clock. You must go."

"Go where?"

They had a quick conference, and Madame patted me on the
arm. "We find you apartment. Bodyguard don't find you."

Monsieur went to get some boxes for my books and CDs, and I began packing my suitcases. Madame stayed to watch.

"It is that girl, that Élodie," she said, spitting out the name and crossing herself against the she-devil who used to dirty her landings.

"No, she is in America. It is her father." This seemed the most likely explanation. There was something about the smoothness of the whole lock-changing and telephoning operation that had Jean-Marie's name stamped all over it. Someone had waited till I went out, sabotaged my door, then waited till I came back again so that they could phone me at the opportune moment. The planning was as tight as one of Jean-Marie's collars. The only thing I couldn't work out was why he'd bothered. Surely with the elections coming up he had more pressing things to think about.

"But it is not his apartment! I report him to the municipalité!" Madame Da Costa was outraged.

"No." I broke off from scooping up dirty socks and warned her against trying to take Jean-Marie on. "You will lose your job and he will not lose the apartment. *This* is my victory," I told her. "We break the door, I take my things. It is enough."

I didn't have many possessions, but by the time they were all stacked in the concierge's *loge*, there was almost no room left in there for oxygen.

I perched on a suitcase, a bin bag full of clothes on my lap, a mug of coffee in my hand, and mused on how low I'd sunk. From my peak as a country-house-owning, boss's-daughter-shagging marketing director to a homeless dropout with nothing to hug except a bag of my dirty boxer shorts. Not exactly one for the *Forbes* list of business success stories. Every bloody thing I'd attempted in Paris was a total screw-up, thanks mainly to Jean-Marie. Oh, and the war, of course. What did you do in the war,

Daddy? Got locked out of my apartment. April Fool was right. April twathead.

"Don't you have to work today?" I asked Madame, who was watching me anxiously, sharing my gloom.

"No, we work at night."

"Don't you want to sleep?"

"We finish four o'clock, sleep before the boys go to school. Sleep in the afternoon, maybe."

"Where is Monsieur?"

"He gets the car. He takes you to new apartment. With friends."

"Friends?"

When Monsieur returned, we quickly filled up a new-looking Renault estate, not that much different from Jean-Marie's bossmobile. The concierges and their families don't spend much on accommodation, but they know how to invest in French consumer goods.

He drove me two or three streets across the Marais and pulled up in the large, cobbled courtyard of a slightly down-at-the-heels medieval building. The entrance was a peeling old horse gate, and the *loge* was up a small stone staircase leading into one side of the arch. A frosted-glass door led into a chilly kitchen.

This was filled by an immense fridge and a long dining table with a small TV at one end. The TV had at some point in its life been splattered with white paint. Only the screen had been cleaned. The second room was a dark bedroom with double bunk beds along either wall. The curtain was closed, and the room smelled of body heat and male armpit.

Monsieur Da Costa motioned me to be quiet. I could see dark lumps in two of the beds. One of the lumps was snuffling softly, as if chewing a piece of gristle in his sleep.

We unloaded the car and quietly slid my things in among the suitcases and packing cases that were already taking up half of the bedroom floor. The place looked like a bolt hole for evicted men.

It took two trips with the car to fetch all my stuff, and then Monsieur said his farewells.

"You are good here. Here key. Au revoir."

I thanked him, shook his hand, and I was on my own in the kitchen with only four plastic folding chairs and a kitsch Virgin Mary wall clock for company.

What the hell should I do? I wondered. Wait until one of the sleeping beauties woke up and introduce myself as the surprise new lodger? Go back to Madame Da Costa and ask what the arrangements were in terms of rent and how long I could stay? Or head straight to the railway station and get the hell out of France?

I'm not a quitter, so I decided to head straight to the railway station and book myself a ticket for two weeks later. I figured it'd take me that long to fumigate my dirty washing and throw out or give away the stuff I didn't want to ship home.

But where was home? Not with my folks, I thought. Anything but that.

"You bastard, Jean-Marie," I moaned at the innocent Virgin. That would be his real victory, sending me scurrying back to Mummy.

I hoped that in the fortnight I had left, I would be able to send some farewell *merde* his way. It would be good to leave my mark on him.

I was between lessons that afternoon, sitting in a smoky, lonely corner of a café, when my phone rang. I recognized the lock breaker's number.

It was just after quarter past four. Of course, they'd turned up late. Make the Englishman wait.

"Oui?" I answered in the macho voice of someone who now has a friend with a sledgehammer.

"You broke the door?"

"Which door?"

"Your door."

"I don't have a door."

"You will have to pay for the lock."

"Which lock?" I thought it was a shame my students weren't listening to me. This was a good example of how to ask open questions. We could have carried on for hours. Which lock? Which apartment? Which shampoo? Which Belgian philosopher?

The caller, who was presumably the bodyguard guy, finally lost his cool and gave my old address.

"Ah, yes, I know that address. I suggest that you send the bill to the occupant, Monsieur Jean-Marie Martin. That's M-a-r—"

"Petit merdeux," the voice interrupted, recalling Jean-Marie's favorite description of me last time I saw him. They'd obviously been discussing me.

The voice was still growling on threateningly, so I hung up and made a note to myself to change my phone number. Only another fortnight and I'd be out of their reach for good.

My three new roommates were a friendly enough bunch. Two of them, Pedro and Luis, worked nights cleaning with Monsieur Da Costa. The other, Vasco, I finally worked out, after he seemed to explain to me that he was some kind of pole-vaulting percussionist, worked days for a scaffolding company. They were all unreconstructed workmen of the testicle-scratching, freestyle-burping variety, but they didn't look down on soft-handed types like myself. They were my age or a little bit older, roughing it for a few months at a time, sending all their money home to their families, and accepted me into the fellowship of exiles.

When I got back *chez nous* that first evening with a couple of bottles of wine, they were just cooking up what was probably lunch for two of them, dinner for the other. It was basically fish and chips. From what I saw subsequently, they ate this for almost every mealtime except their respective breakfasts. They offered me a share of that first lunch/dinner, and I had to bite back the urge to refuse. The frying pan was so fat encrusted, inside and out, that you couldn't tell what color it had been. The chip fryer, an enclosed bubblelike contraption that hid your chips from view while cooking them, was open and seemed to be full of the same engine oil that had been in it when it was sold ten years earlier.

The food itself tasted fine, especially washed down with my wine, and though we hardly shared any words of a common language except *ça va* and the names of a few footballers, we bonded over clinking glasses and an old episode of *Baywatch* on Portuguese cable. Pamela Anderson's lips were totally out of sync with her voice, but then as far as I knew, they had been out of sync on the original, too. I hadn't paid that much attention to the dialogue.

I slept opposite Vasco, on the bottom-left bunk, which I seemed to have inherited from a pot-bellied grizzly bear, to judge by the bulging dip in the springs. I realized that I hadn't slept in the same room as another guy, apart from the odd post-drink crash-out on a bedroom floor, since my school's last geography field trip, when we used to have nightly farting competitions in the boys' dorm. Vasco could have farted at international competition level, and I didn't want to give him any complexes, so I always did my best to force out a sympathetic good-night fart before dropping (or drooping) off to sleep.

The apartment was as cramped to live in as a long-distance train compartment. You were always stepping around somebody or their luggage. A couple of months earlier, it would have been deeply depressing. But now, just a few days before throwing in my cards with Paris, it felt no more inconvenient than a transit lounge stopover on a flight back from Asia. I just had to accept that there seemed to be little chance of me picking up any more Parisian babes before I left the city. Bringing one back to my shared bunkhouse would have cooled down the fieriest female erogenous zones.

In my last full week before leaving Paris, my boss, Andrea, sent me to teach a five-day course in a large computer hardware company. There were two of us teaching different groups. The young sales execs were being taught by a Floridian gal called Carla, whose main teaching qualifications were suntanned thighs and an utterly captivating technique for perching on the edge of a desk. Her presence forms were always overflowing with signatures and telephone numbers. She was no fool. She'd negotiated a raise from the pragmatic Andrea on the basis of those legs and spent half her time doing marketing for the school whenever Andrea thought that a short skirt was necessary to clinch a deal, which, this being Paris, it often was.

My group consisted of the ones who didn't care about getting into Carla's group or hadn't been pushy enough to get in there, plus a few who wanted to learn business English from a real English businessman (or ex-businessman, anyway). This would have meant more work for me, but I dug out some of my reports on tearooms and taught them the key vocabulary from those.

They all thought the tearooms were a great idea, of course, which would have been infuriating if I hadn't been so exhausted by having to concentrate for seven whole hours in a day. I was like the Portuguese guys, slaving for cash to take home. You really earned your money on these all-day courses. It was much tougher than working in an office. You can't e-mail your mates while standing in front of a class of ten students. Well, not discreetly, anyway.

Carla and I went to the canteen together, usually without our students. The students almost always used lunch with teachers as an excuse to practice excruciating small talk.

It was one lunchtime while Carla and I were at the canteen that our chat was timidly interrupted.

"Pol? C'est toi?"

I looked up to see a pleasant female face smiling at me. I knew the face but couldn't get the name quickly enough.

"Florence, Marie's friend," she told me in French. It was the half Indian girl Marie had tried to fix me up with and whom I'd never phoned. She looked good, but very different. In the bar her long black hair had been loose, and she'd been in tight, low-cut jeans. Now she wore a ponytail and was wearing a sober khaki shirt and denim skirt.

"Oh, yes, hi. Do you work here?" I asked.

"Oui." She looked across at Carla. I did the introductions. Florence and Carla gave each other that look that says, "Has she slept with him?" Not in a competitive way (unfortunately), just to try to get the situation straight in their heads.

"Won't you join us?" Carla suggested, and Florence sat next to her, opposite me, at our canteen table.

"We're both teaching English here for the week," I explained.

"We work for the same language school."

"Ah, you are an English teacher now? Why did you leave your other job?"

"Oh, it's a long story." Which I didn't particularly want to tell.

"So the Englishman and the American woman come to distribute propaganda for Monsieur Blair and Monsieur Bouche?"

Carla laughed. "Yeah, right. All these guys hate me because they see me as a symbol of the great American imperialist power." She gave a fierce imperialist growl that would have had all the men in the company signing up for ten years' worth of English lessons.

"And Paul looks like James Bond," Florence said.

"Well, I do feel as old as Sean Connery, if that's what you mean."

"Hey, you guys want some coffee?" Carla asked, gesturing over her shoulder toward the café-style bar in the corner of the canteen. There was always a throng of people waiting to get served there after lunch, but Carla usually managed to get herself invited to the front of the line.

"Yes, good idea. You coming with us?" I asked Florence.

"No, you two stay there, I'll bring them over," Carla said.

While Carla was fetching the coffees, Florence talked about her job at the computer company. She was working in the accounts office. It wasn't interesting, she said, but she didn't feel like looking for anything else at the moment. A very typical attitude among highly qualified French people, I'd found. If your company was doing okay, you had practically zero chance of getting fired, so you just hung in there, bored and static but safe, like someone stranded on a desert island with a plentiful supply of dehydrated chicken soup.

I began to wish that Carla would come back and save me from this sad story, versions of which I'd heard in so many of my English lessons.

As if reading my mind, Florence suddenly turned on a flirtatious smile. "Why didn't you call me?" she asked.

"Oh, you know . . ."

"You found someone else?" She looked over to Carla, who was at the bar chatting to, or being chatted up by, a gaggle of young men whose tongues were hanging down the front of their suits.

"Carla? Oh no, she's just a colleague. She's got a boyfriend."

"Someone else, then?"

"No, no. There's been no one else," I confessed, more glumly than I'd intended.

It was true. I hadn't even tried it on with Nicole. Instead of offering her private tuition in *l'anglais de l'amour*, I'd asked her if she wasn't interested in getting VianDiffusion to pay for English lessons with my school—Andrea had promised me a 10 percent commission on any business I brought in. Nicole took it as a clumsy hint that I wanted to be paid for talking to her in English and got a bit upset. I gathered from what she said that a suggestion on my part to switch our weekly conversations from the restaurant to her bedroom would have been less upsetting, but by this time it was too late. She was too sad and vulnerable to be used as a stopgap. I can be an annoyingly moral bastard sometimes, I told myself later, alone in bed with a magazine. That was when I still had a room of my own.

Something in what I'd said, or the way I was looking, made Florence laugh. It was a loud, happy laugh.

"What's so funny?"

She had beautiful teeth, I noticed, no fillings.

"Nothing," she said, still laughing.

"Hey, have you noticed anything?" I asked her.

She looked around at the other tables, which were emptying as people returned to work. She turned to see if Carla was coming back, which she wasn't.

"No?"

"You're speaking in French and I'm speaking in English. Isn't that weird?"

"I had noticed." She smiled.

"I've never done that with anyone before. Either I speak in English and have to put up with someone's awful accent."

"Like Marie?"

"Yes, like Marie." We laughed together. "Or I try to speak in French and can't say half of what I want to say."

"And what do you want to say?" Florence asked. A typical woman's question, I thought to myself, especially when accompanied by that teasing look in the eyes. Dark, attractive eyes, too, it occurred to me. Suddenly I wasn't so keen for Carla to come back after all.

"This is going to sound incredibly clichéd," I said.

"Yes?"

"But you are so *silky*."

"Why is that clichéd?"

"Oh, you know, like, Oriental silk."

"Ah, yes. That is clichéd." Florence laughed and kissed my hand, which was draped down over her naked shoulder and onto her equally naked left breast. "But it is not silk. It is the result of the thousands of liters of cream and lotion that I use every week on my body."

"Hmm. It's true, you do smell lotiony." Her back smelled of coconut. I had been washed ashore on the desert island, I thought, but without the boring chicken soup.

She turned to face me in her large bed.

"I don't usually bring men back here on the first day," she said. "You do realize that?"

I nodded and looked around at where she'd brought me. I hadn't had much time to admire it before we'd leapt into bed. The room would have been as overdone as an ethnic decorator's showroom if it weren't for the fact that Florence herself was the real thing. The bright red wall hangings and the Kashmir curtains had been sent over by relatives in Pondicherry, an old French dependency in south India.

"Well, I suppose usually you at least get the men to buy you dinner beforehand." We'd met up straight after work and come back to her apartment in the Twentieth, near the Père-Lachaise cemetery. We were in bed by 6:30.

She tried to hit me in protest at this slur, but I grabbed her and pulled her close to prevent her from getting in any punches. Which was, I suppose, the idea.

"When's *your* boyfriend coming back from Iraq?" I asked, only half-jokingly.

"Imbecile. I have no boyfriend. And me, I'm not just a toy, am I? Just someone to fuck because you haven't got anyone else?"

"You should have asked me that before you took your clothes off."

This provoked more outraged struggling, more hugging, and then a frantic search on the floor for another condom from the packet we'd bought in her local pharmacy on the way over.

It was dark when I opened my eyes to find her staring at me from a few inches away on the other pillow. I stared back, meeting her eyes for a long time, which I usually feel uncomfortable about.

This prompted me to make a wild suggestion.

"Tell you what, Florence. This weekend, let's go and get an AIDS test."

She lifted herself off the pillow and leanted across to kiss me.

After all, these days it's about the most romantic thing a guy can say to a girl.

Our tests were negative, though the nervous agony of tearing open the results probably gave us some terminal heart condition. We had to go and make love just to calm down.

Well, calm down was not exactly the best description. It turned out that in her spare time, Florence gave classes in something called *Pilates*—a cross between yoga and stretching, she said. She applied all her techniques in the bedroom, too, so after a couple of hours in bed with Florence, you ended up with aches in places you didn't know could ache. And several steps closer to Nirvana.

I tore up my train ticket (well, cashed it in, anyway) and moved my stuff into her apartment. Pedro, Luis, and Vasco said brief, unceremonious good-byes, and we wished one another luck (I think). That little *loge* really was a kind of oasis for nomads struggling through the Parisian desert.

In comparison, Florence's place was almost obscenely roomy. It was a three-room duplex on the top two floors of a modern building that looked out over the cemetery. There was a balcony running along the upper floor. On a fine day, you could get out of bed and sit there naked, waggling the soles of your feet (or anything else you wanted to waggle) down across the rooftops of Paris.

A cynic would have said that I was just taking advantage of this amazing new sex-and-accommodation deal. I would have replied by asking Monsieur Da Costa to hit the cynic with a sledgeham-mer. And then, as I left the pulped cynic to die, I'd have wished him "Bonne journée."

One Saturday, the journalists ended their strike, even though the election campaign had droned on as boringly as ever. As with so many of these French strikes, absolutely nothing seemed to have been achieved. Stopping work really was a kind of folk art form, strike for strike's sake.

That morning, Florence and I were sitting on a bench in the cemetery, which was not as gloomy as it sounds. Père-Lachaise is light and airy, like a miniature city. There's a grid system of wide, roadlike *allées* dividing up neighborhoods of graves. And many of the tombs look like model houses. It is, though, a quiet and green city, with stands of mature trees and no traffic jams. A pleasant place to laze away the first really summery morning of spring.

We had a couple of take-out beakers of coffee and a bag of croissants on the bench between us. I was reading an English music mag, and for the first time in weeks, Florence had bought a French newspaper. (Front-page headline: JOURNALISTS' STRIKE OVER. Slightly obvious, I thought.)

There were quite a few people in the cemetery, both flower-bearing mourners and tourists looking for Oscar Wilde, Chopin, and Jim Morrison.

"Hey, isn't that your old boss?" Florence asked.

I looked up at the approaching group of cemetery-goers. They were young, hair in their face, baggy jeans, small rucksacks slapping at their backsides, the two genders distinguishable only because the girls were showing more navel. They were squinting from their map of the cemetery to the signpost giving the name of the *allée*.

"Not unless he's had his belly button pierced."

"No, *here*." She thrust her paper at me.

There, on an inside page, was a photo of Jean-Marie with a delegation of grim-faced farmers. The caption said the farmers had come to Paris to fill the Trocadero fountains, just across the river from the Eiffel Tower, with rotting strawberries. Not as a modern art statement. These were Spanish strawberries that they'd hijacked at various roadblocks around the country. The short article explained that the farmers were protesting about cheap Spanish strawberries flooding the market and killing French production. It didn't mention that mid-April is too early for French strawberries, but that didn't seem to trouble the farmers or Jean-Marie.

There he was, the farmers' champion, promising to do his utmost, at some unspecific time in the future, when he would hold some unspecified position of influence, to ban all imports of foreign food, especially the produce of the Spanish profiteers and the "Anglo-Saxon invaders."

He was looking the consummate French politician—impeccably chic suit, stiff shirt and tie, insufferably pompous smile. *Liberté, égalité, vanité.* The farmers stood around him, caught literally red-handed, as if they'd just murdered all his political opponents, leaving the politician himself squeaky clean.

One of the gang of French Jim Morrison clones came over to our bench.

"Où est . . .?" he began.

"Là-bas, à droite," Florence told him.

"Merci, madame," he replied politely, and the gang trooped off. One of them began singing, "Radders on ze stom . . ."

"He's an idiot," I said. "Jean-Marie, I mean. How can he say he'll ban foreign food imports? Is France going to start growing coconuts?"

"France does grow coconuts," Florence said.

"What, in giant, nuclear-powered underground greenhouses?"

"No. France includes some Caribbean islands and Pacific islands."

"Colonies?"

"No, some are part of France, they are départements just like

Dordogne. So France grows coconuts, bananas, mangoes. And to be fair to him, even though I agree he is an idiot, he says that France *and* its overseas territories *and* its traditional friends in West Africa can be self-sufficient in food. We are not like England, you know. France does not accept that it has lost its empire. We say we are against globalization, but really we have never stopped globalizing."

"Oh." So the guy actually had some kind of cogent plan. I had to admit that he was good. His antics with British beef proved that he didn't honestly give a bull's testicle about French farmers, and the sheer enormity of his hypocrisy had a symmetrical beauty about it.

But surely there had to be a chink in Jean-Marie's election campaign?

"What about caviar? That comes from Iran or Russia, doesn't it?"

"I think there are sturgeon farms in France now," Florence said. "His plan will never happen, of course, but it is interesting. It shows that France chose all her colonies for their food. In fact, the only thing I can think of that he couldn't get according to his plan, apart from very specific products like Russian vodka or Canadian maple syrup, is tea."

"Tea. Of course. Logical."

"Yes, tea comes mainly from old English colonies, doesn't it? Some is produced in Vietnam, which is one of our ex-colonies, but not enough."

"So Élodie was right. Tea would be a drug."

"Élodie?"

"My boss's daughter." Florence looked curious, but there was no way she was getting any more details about Élodie. "I mean, tea would be a banned drink under President Jean-Marie. More illegal than grass. People would make tea leaf badges and England would become a kind of Amsterdam where French junkies could go and get high on Lapsang souchong."

"Perhaps, but I will have my secret supply."

"How's that?"

"My uncle in India. He is in import-export. He can send me tea."

MAI

1968 and All That

I N   M A Y   1 9 6 8, the students ripped up the cobblestones from the streets of Paris and bombarded the police barricades until Charles de Gaulle's ultraconservative government fell. French people will tell you that *mai soixante-huit* changed France profoundly. Personally, I couldn't see any evidence of this. It was like Jake said—they still go with the same old flow. The students who were throwing cobblestones are now ultraconservative bosses, the political establishment is still the political establishment, and there's even a Gaullist president in power. The only real change seems to be that most of the cobblestones are now tarmacked over.

But May is an important month in the French calendar. Because if the French year begins in September, it ends in May.

We had bank holidays on May 1 (the ironically named *fête du travail*, as if during a *fête du vin* you did everything but drink wine), May 8 (for VE Day 1945), and May 29 (Ascension Day). They all fell on a Thursday, so each time people had what is called a *pont*, a bridge, when they took the extra Friday off to make a four-day weekend. Coupled with the French thirty-five-hour week, it meant that Florence and I had a hell of a lot of lie-ins in May.

There wasn't much time for work in June, either. As well as

having a bank holiday Monday, lots of people had to use up their year's holiday allowance by the end of the month, so they took a week or so off before their main summer vacation.

In any case, it was nearly July, so there wasn't much point doing any work until *la rentrée* in September.

Basically, in France if you haven't done what you planned to do by April 30, you're in deep *merde*.

As if all this weren't enough, in the May I'm talking about, the teachers went on strike just after May Day. They got nearly four months' holiday a year, but they didn't get the *ponts* and felt underprivileged. So Florence's office was full of young kids photocopying their faces and punching staples through their fingers. Even less work got done than usual.

And on the basis that striking is a kind of French folk song, everyone else decided to sing along—the post office workers, shop workers, truck drivers, actors, oyster openers, cheese ripeners, waiters' waistcoat makers, baguette lengtheners, sausage shrivel-ers, and every sector of French industry you could name. The police stayed at work long enough to tear-gas a few demonstrators, then they came out as well.

Not a good climate in which to start a new venture, you might think. But this is what I did.

I chucked in my teaching job early on in May. Most of my regular students had canceled their classes because of their eternal weekends anyway. So I said good-bye to my German boss, Andrea (who asked if I had any friends/children/pets who might want to become English teachers), and went to see my old bedmate Marie. This was the week before the bank workers went on strike.

Marie's boyfriend was away, but Florence assured me that I was in no danger. Just to be safe, I arranged to meet in Marie's office, which had glass walls with a view right out into the street. If anything untoward did happen, it was going to be in full view of the passing crowds.

I flatter myself, though. From what Florence told me, Marie really had seen me as some kind of sexual literacy project. Englishmen are *coincé* (uptight, or literally "stuck"), as I'd proved by running away after our first encounter, and she wanted to unstick me. Now that I was standing on my own two feet, Marie was happy for me, like a French worker who hears that his son has gone on strike for the first time.

I'd seen Marie in her workclothes before, or seen her taking them off anyway, but it felt strange sitting opposite her in her office, client to financial adviser. And even stranger when my financial adviser clinched the deal by kissing me full on the mouth. Even French banks don't usually extend to that service.

She gave me a twelve-month loan, with zero collateral.

"What if I can't pay it back?"

She shrugged. "Don't ask stoopeed question. You will pay. You are nice English boy. And you are my fren."

In Paris, where there's a friend there's a way. She told me that the money would be available as soon as the strike was over.

The reason I needed the loan was, of course, to start up a tearoom. With Florence's direct access to cheap tea, it had suddenly become obvious. Why give up on a viable project just because the almost totally ineffectual team that I'd wanted to get rid of is got rid of?

Florence and I had sat down together and run through the economics. With her knowledge of accounts, she'd whipped up a convincing business plan in no time. She reckoned she'd be able to give up her boring job and join me at the tearoom within a year. The ultimate accolade—a French person with a job for life was going to give it up. The idea had to be a winner.

My one potential obstacle was Jean-Marie. I was going to be using his research, his tests. Would he try to stop me by enforcing some clause about not competing with your ex-employer? Or to be strictly legalistic, *present* employer? Officially I was still working for him.

It was clear to me now that he'd only dropped the tearoom idea to further his political career. He'd got some kind of promise from the right wing and farmers' parties that he could go far if he played his cards right, so he'd cleaned up his act and axed his "Anglo-Saxon" food project.

Unluckily for him, however, if I revealed everything I knew (and could prove via e-mails) about the beef imports, I could put him out of action as a businessman and scupper his political ambitions.

There was no point telling anyone about his desktop affair with Stéphanie, because accusations of adultery would only increase his score at the polls. President Mitterrand, for example, gained maximum posthumous respect after his illegitimate daughter attended his funeral. A French politician without a mistress is like a sheriff without a gun—people think he has no firepower.

Similarly, there was little point alleging that Mayor Jean-Marie was going to benefit financially from the construction of a nuclear power station in his region. That would be like "revealing" that a prostitute profits from sex. Everyone expected it.

But I knew that if I threw the English beef at him, it would stick.

The elections were to be held on the third Sunday in May, so I had just a few more days to apply some pressure while he was feeling vulnerable.

I phoned his office a week before the election and persuaded Christine to put me through. She said she'd probably get yelled at for doing so but took the risk "because I was always such a gentleman with her." So not sleeping with a girl can have its upside after all.

"Yes?" was all Jean-Marie growled at me.

"I need to talk to you."

"I do not need to talk to you."

"Perhaps not, but I need to talk to you."

Luckily he didn't say "I do not need to talk to you" again or we could have carried on till one of us died of starvation.

"Talk," he said, and rustled some papers as if to say he wasn't necessarily going to listen.

I didn't want to resort to overt threats of blackmail over the phone. Well, actually I did, but I thought Jean-Marie would put me down as a crude amateur and tell me to get lost. So, without mentioning English beef, I just made it clear that I was determined to meet him on Monday or, at the very latest, Tuesday morning.

We agreed to meet at his Neuilly apartment at 7:00 p.m. on Wednesday.

"I have a dinner that evening," he told me, stressing that this was in no way an invitation for a cozy night in.

"So do I," I told him. At a cheap south Indian place with Florence and Marie, to celebrate our new start. Unless Jean-Marie had had me thrown off his balcony by then.

On that Wednesday, the general strike hit its peak, and the city attained a level of dirty, angry, traffic-jammed, blacked-out, fresh-baguetteless chaos that was, everyone said, worse than May 1968.

At which time, having broken their previous record for disruption, the strikers all went back to work so they could use up the rest of their annual holiday allowance.

Jean-Marie's wife answered the door. She looked as perfectly maintained as ever. Roots dyed, check. Tan freshly topped up, check. This season's Dior bracelet, check. Breasts perched at exactly eighty degrees south, check check.

She shook my hand and led me into the lounge without bothering to make small talk or even give me a smile of recognition. Unless she'd been hitting the Botox, I was persona non exista in the household these days.

The lounge was as breathtaking as ever, with its amazing vista over the Bois de Boulogne (how many top-floor apartments in a capital city have a view of only trees?). But the room had changed in one telling way since my last visit. Over the fireplace, on the marble mantelpiece, there was now a dramatic clay bust of Marianne. Not Jean-Marie's receptionist. No one would want her staring at them from their mantelpiece, poor girl, even if she was covered in clay. This was Marianne the revolutionary heroine, the French equivalent of Uncle Sam. This being France, instead of a bearded old uncle who looks as if he should be advertising fried chicken, they have a seminaked woman.

To my untrained eye, Jean-Marie's bust was beautifully sculpted. The name "Marianne" had been written by hand into the clay in a curly old script. You could even see the finger marks of the sculptor where he had perfected the swell of that patriotic cleavage. This was a one-of-a-kind antique work of art. Jean-Marie was investing heavily in his new political career.

If I'd been any kind of serious blackmailer, I'd have lifted it off the mantelpiece, threatening to drop it and symbolically shatter his future if my demands were not met. But I contented myself with admiring it in close-up and risking the tiniest fingertip touch of one of the remarkably hard nipples.

"You are not the first," Jean-Marie said, almost causing me to swipe his statue off its shelf. He'd appeared in the room behind me, in royal blue shirtsleeves, his collar still tieless for the moment. "If you look, there is a minor, how you say, dark place, where people have touched her breasts. They prefer the right one, I think." He chuckled to himself at his piece of political satire. He seemed positively jolly compared with how he'd been on the phone. It crossed my mind that he might have asked his lock-breaking bodyguard chum to prepare an amusingly violent death for me after our chat.

He stood his ground, waiting for me to cross the room toward him, and shook my hand tersely. It was in marked contrast with the first time I came here, when I almost felt as if he was going to whip out the adoption papers and declare that I was now his sole son and heir.

We sat on opposite golden-armed antique chairs in the center of the room, and he took some chunky cuff links out of his trouser pocket. He began to fold back his cuffs as we spoke. He was playing Monsieur Indifferent.

"I presume you have someone else living in the apartment now?" I asked to break the ice.

He shrugged. That particular ice floe remained intact.

"Just out of interest, Jean-Marie, why did you bother? I was paying the rent."

He took a deep breath, trying to work up the inclination to tell me. "Sometimes, a friend has need of an apartment," he said.

"I see." So it was all part of the politics, I guessed. Scratching someone's back. Maybe it was for the bodyguard himself. The Front National guys need to have muscle around them because France's large Arab population doesn't look kindly upon racist politicians.

"Tell me, why do I have the pleasure of your visit?" he asked.

"I need a favor."

"Oh!" He laughed incredulously at my effrontery, just as my team had done when I'd dared to cast aspersions on the quality of French teabags.

"Two favors," I said.

"Ah?" He stopped laughing and became fascinated by his cuff link again. "What are they?"

"I'm going to open an English tearoom."

"Ho! And who gave you this idea, uh?" He shook his head as if he was disappointed but not surprised by this betrayal. "And why am I interested?"

I thought I caught a flash of anxiety in his eyes.

"I don't want money, I have money," I said.

"Yes. My money. I have paid you for one year to do nothing." Somehow he combined looking outraged at my ingratitude and relieved that I hadn't come with a begging bowl.

"It was your choice that it came to nothing, Jean-Marie. You stopped the project."

"The war stopped the project." He put on a mournful expression, no doubt practicing for future political photo opportunities.

"Whatever. In any case, I'm borrowing enough money to start up a tearoom. What I don't have yet is premises. So I want to rent one of the places you bought. At a market rate, of course."

"They are occupied by the shoe sellers." He finished the first cuff and turned his attention to the second.

"The one I want is empty at the moment," as he must have known. "I want a one-year lease with an option to buy the property after the year is up. Again, at a market rate."

I could see the pocket calculator in Jean-Marie's brain doing the sums. The result sent a brief smile flickering across his mouth. He thought I was selling myself short.

"You would pay me? Buy from me?" he asked jovially. This

time there was no anxiety in his eyes. Quite the opposite. "After what has happened between us?" He finished with his cuffs and sat back in his armchair, enjoying the conversation now.

"Yes, you bought the best premises for an English tearoom, and this one's empty. It's a logical solution."

"No one will know that I give my property for an English tearoom?"

"I won't tell anyone."

"It would not be in your interest, no." He examined me closely for any signs of trickery, then shrugged. "If it is empty, maybe you could hire it."

"Okay, thank you."

"I said maybe."

"Okay. Now the second favor."

"Ah?"

"I want the name."

"The name?"

"My Tea Is Rich. You were right, Jean-Marie. Every French person I've asked thinks it's a great name."

Jean-Marie roared with laughter, so loudly that his wife popped her head around the door to make sure I wasn't inflicting some kind of tickling torture on him.

"You want to buy this name you hate? My name?"

"I know, I know," I said, trying to cut through the infuriating note of self-satisfaction in his voice. "For months I did nothing but antagonize the other team members by trying to oppose the name, but I was wrong. I didn't realize that you all think 'my tailor is rich' is the funniest sentence in the English language, and now I'd like to use it."

"What will you give me for it?"

"Nothing."

The last traces of laughter disappeared. "Out of the question."

"Legally, I don't really need to pay anything. Bernard never got around to registering it."

"What? No . . ."

"Yes. I warned you about him. John Lennon really did have Bernard in mind when he wrote 'I Am the Walrus.' "

"Uh?"

"Sorry, private joke."

"Yes, your English humor." He laughed bitterly. "You know, I will never admit it"—he leaned forward conspiratorially, as if his statue wasn't to be trusted with secrets—"but sometimes I wish we could do things the Anglo-Saxon way. Someone is no good, you fire him." He snapped his fingers. "It is so simple, so wonderful."

I brought him out of his reverie. "You mean like you fired me?"

He just grunted, as if I'd tried to tell an old joke.

"Or, let's say, some French product is expensive, so you secretly buy a cheaper English equivalent?"

He shot me a warning glance, reminding me telepathically that he had people working for him who were scary enough to silence a Portuguese concierge.

"I only mention these things now, in confidence," I added, "because I'd like to be sure that you will grant my favors. I need your agreement."

Jean-Marie just sat staring at me, the king weighing up the pros and cons of either laughing at the jester or having his head cut off.

"I need to be sure that you'll let me have the premises and that you won't oppose me when I register the name, and then I can finalize my deal with the bank."

Jean-Marie didn't move a muscle for a full ten seconds, then suddenly put up his hands as if in defeat.

"Do we agree, then?" I asked. I held out a hand to shake on the deal.

He lowered his arms and tentatively held out one of his large, brown hands, with its bulletlike gold stud at the cuff. I took the hand and squeezed. It was limp.

"Okay," I said, "I'll fax the details to your office tomorrow morning at nine, then send a courier over at eleven to pick up the signed rental agreement."

Jean-Marie's grip on my hand tightened, and he pulled me closer. Were we going to seal the deal with a kiss, Marie style? I wondered.

But he came just near enough for me to see the veins in his eyes and get a close-up of his hair, the way it was greased tightly back in dark, dyed strands, a lot like the hair on his sculpture. Not quite as clay colored, though. More oil spill colored.

"Nous sommes quittes, alors?" he hissed. I caught a faint tang of alcohol on his breath.

I pulled my face away. "I don't think France and Britain are ever really quits," I said. "But we usually manage to maintain cordial working relations."

"Ho," he scoffed, still holding on to my hand.

Sitting there on our matching thrones, physically connected, I suddenly felt as if we were part of a chain. The chain of French businesspeople and politicians who are constantly scratching one another's backs, as opposed to stabbing them, which would be counterproductive. Jean-Marie was going to win his election, and I had proof of his total hypocrisy but was going to keep quiet if he did me a favor or two. I suppose I'd entered into some kind of web of corruption. But it felt completely natural. It was just the way France works.

"We're friendly enemies," I said. "It's the way things have been between the Brits and the French since Napoleon, isn't it?"

"Since you burned Jeanne d'Arc, oui," he grunted.

He let go of my hand. I got up.

"Bonne soirée," I wished him. "Oh, and merde."

I left him to get ready for his dinner.

I wasn't being insulting, by the way. When saying good luck before any kind of challenge, like an exam, a theater performance, or (I supposed) an election, the French wish each other *merde*.

Merde happens, you see, and it can even bring you luck. As long as someone else treads in it.

FIN

A NOTE ON THE AUTHOR

Stephen Clarke is a British writer working for a French press group in Paris. He has previously written comedy for BBC Radio. He is currently working on the next volume of Paul West's adventures.

The text of this book is set in Fournier. Fournier is derived from the *romain du roi*, which was created toward the end of the seventeenth century for the exclusive use of the Imprimerie Royale from designs made by a committee of the Académie des Sciences. The original Fournier types were cut by the famous Paris founder Pierre Simon Fournier in about 1742. This Monotype version dates from 1924. Fournier is a light, clear face whose distinctive features are capital letters that are quite squat in relation to the lowercase ascenders, and decorative italics, which show the influence of the calligraphy of Fournier's time.